SOUTH AFRICA

Political boundaries   Principal railways

Native reserves, including land
scheduled for purchase

0   50   100   150 Miles

CAPRIVI

PROTECTORATE

Bulawayo

Beitbridge

PORTUGUESE EAST AFRICA

Limpopo R.

Crocodile

Mafeking

TRANSVAAL

Pretoria

JOHANNESBURG

Mbabane

Lourenço Marques

SWAZI-
LAND

Vaal R.

ORANGE FREE

Kimberley

STATE

Bloemfontein

Maseru

BASUTO-
LAND

Pietermaritzburg

Tugela R.

Durban

INDIAN

Orange R.

PROVINCE

Great Kei R.

East London

OCEAN

Great Fish R.

Port Elizabeth

R. W. FORD

THE PEOPLES AND POLICIES
OF SOUTH AFRICA

THE PEOPLES AND POLICIES OF
SOUTH AFRICA

LEO MARQUARD

SECOND EDITION

CAPE TOWN
OXFORD UNIVERSITY PRESS
LONDON NEW YORK

1960

Oxford University Press, Amen House, London, E.C.4

GLASGOW   NEW YORK   TORONTO   MELBOURNE   WELLINGTON
BOMBAY   CALCUTTA   MADRAS   KARACHI
CAPE TOWN   IBADAN   NAIROBI   ACCRA   KUALA LUMPUR

First published August 1952
Second impression December 1952
Second edition 1960

PRINTED IN THE UNION OF SOUTH AFRICA BY
THE RUSTICA PRESS, PTY., LTD., WYNBERG, CAPE

TO THE MEMORY OF FOUR GALLANT
SOUTH AFRICANS WHO FOUGHT AND
DIED FOR THEIR COUNTRY:
JOHN, CHRIS, IAN, AND GERHARD

PREFACE

During the eight years since the first edition of this book was published, South Africa has undergone a great many changes. I could not have undertaken the complete revision that these changes entailed were it not for the assistance of Mr. Clive van Ryneveld, M.P. At a time when he was immersed in parliamentary duties and involved in a serious party-political crisis, he found time to make the detailed and careful notes that enabled me to do the necessary rewriting. I am deeply grateful to him for this.

My thanks are also due to various readers who took the trouble to point out errors and to criticize statements in the first edition. The errors have, I hope, been removed, and the criticisms have all been carefully weighed.

Finally, I owe, as always, more than I can express to my wife's constant encouragement and faithful criticism.

L. M.

Claremont, Cape
March 1960

NOTE

It seems advisable to remark briefly on the use of terms in this book. No account of South Africa is at present possible without distinguishing between the various population groups. It is, of course, not scientifically accurate to speak about the 'European race' or the 'non-European races'. Nevertheless, these terms are convenient and are commonly understood, in South Africa and elsewhere. An alternative is to use 'white' and 'non-white', which have become officially favoured on the ground that American citizens arriving at the Jan Smuts international airport do not regard themselves as 'European'. Nor, for that matter, do the majority of 'white' South Africans. Both these alternatives are used in this book when it is necessary to distinguish broadly between South Africans who are classified as 'white' and those who are Coloured, Asian, or African.

There is a further difficulty. How does one describe a South African who is brown-skinned and whose mother tongue is one of the Bantu languages? He used to be called a 'kaffir', and the word is still in common use though only the crudest of politicians uses it in public. Since 1910, legislation refers to 'natives', and it gradually became the custom to use an initial capital and write 'Native'. Roughly between 1910 and 1940, the word 'Bantu' came to be used by those white people who felt that 'Native' was derogatory and not sufficiently distinctive; and in 1958 'Bantu' was given legislative sanction when the Department of Native Affairs became the Department of Bantu Administration and Development.

In the meantime, the word 'African' had come to be used by a number of white people and by the Africans themselves whose leaders had never really accepted any other designation; as early as 1912 the African National Congress was established, and since the growth of African nationalism everywhere in Africa, the use of the term has become widespread. There are linguistic, ethnographic, and political arguments for and against the use of Bantu and of African, and much energy is expended on proving that one or other term is 'correct'. It is reasonably clear, however, that the leaders of roughly two-thirds of the population of South Africa wish to call themselves Africans, and no amount of legislation will change that. In this book, therefore, the word African is used except where reference is made to official and other documents or where its use would be confusing.

CONTENTS

1

Historical Background

IN THE MID-SEVENTEENTH CENTURY THE ELEMENTS OF WHAT IS today a complicated human society were beginning to assemble in South Africa. England was then colonizing North America; Holland was a thriving commercial and trading state; France and Holland and England were competing for the trade of the East. In southern Africa, Hottentots and Bushmen roamed at will, hunting game and fighting each other; and African tribes from central and eastern Africa were migrating southwards and settling in parts of what are today the Transvaal, the Orange Free State, Natal, the Cape Province, South-West Africa, Basutoland, Swaziland, and Bechuanaland. Then, in 1652, European civilization came to southern Africa when a trading station was established at the Cape. Cape Town was the half-way house between East and West. And, in due course, North and South —Europe and Africa—met in the interior.

Within fifty years of the establishment of the trading station at the Cape we may discern, dimly, the origins of most of the socio-political problems that have continued to harass South Africa down to the present time. Slaves had been imported from east and west Africa and from Madagascar, and it was partly from them that there were ultimately descended the Cape Coloured people who now number over 1,405,000 of the total 14,673,000 population. Despite the Company's instructions that the Cape was to be regarded purely as a 'refreshment station' where ships could obtain fresh food, the European population increased, and received further additions by immigration, and by 1700 the trekking of cattle farmers into the interior had begun. Three generations later this trekking was to bring them into contact with the African tribes, and that contact resulted in wars and in conquests, and today, in consequence, 9,751,000 Africans form part of the population of South Africa. It is frequently, though erroneously, stated that white men were in South Africa before the Africans. Men from Europe began to settle in what is now the Western Province of the Cape in 1652 and found only Hottentots and Bushmen; but there is clear evidence from early Portuguese travellers and from modern archaeological and anthropological investigations that Africans were living in what is now the rest of the Union from at least 1500.

By 1700, therefore, the three main elements of South Africa's population were present, European, African, and Coloured. The smaller Asian population was to come much later; and the European

I

population was, in due course, to consist of two main groups, English and Afrikaans. But for good or for ill, Western Europe had entered Africa from the south and the process had begun by which, in the fullness of time, a political Union of South Africa was to be established. Within the Union there is a white population of 3,067,000 which is at least eight times as much as the white population of the rest of Africa south of the Sahara and constitutes the largest single concentration in Africa of people whose ancestors came from Europe. What happens in South Africa, as between white and non-white, is of importance to central and southern Africa and to those countries of Europe that have colonial commitments, past or present, in Africa. It is of importance, too, to Russia and the United States of America. It is of profound and disturbing importance to the Commonwealth. Finally, it is becoming increasingly clear that what happens in the rest of the world is making an impact on all the inhabitants of South Africa.

To understand what is happening in South Africa we must trace, however briefly, some of the main strands in her history. Unless we do so it will be difficult to grasp present-day policies or to arrive at a reasonable evaluation of the difficult situation that exists there and elsewhere in Africa. Without some knowledge of the history that has made a multi-racial society it is tempting to apply formulas that will be valid in Europe but that may well need to be modified when applied to Africa.

By the end of the fifteenth century Portuguese explorers had discovered the trade route to the East, and for 100 years Portugal was virtually undisputed master of this profitable route. Lisbon became the new Venice; and of all the merchants who dealt with Lisbon the Dutch were the most important. At the end of the sixteenth century Philip II of Spain gained control over Portugal. In an attempt to subdue the recalcitrant Protestant subjects in the Netherlands he closed the harbour of Lisbon to Dutch merchants, hoping thus to destroy their main source of national wealth. It is probable that the Dutch would in any case have developed a direct trade with the East, and this threat to their religious and national freedom was an additional spur to action. By 1602 they had established the famous Dutch East India Company, the instrument by which they overthrew the might of Spain and freed their consciences along with their commerce.

Like the East India Company in England, the Dutch East India Company was a powerful, monopolistic, chartered company that enjoyed political influence and patronage so long as it increased the shareholders' dividends. Some of its main characteristics were: limitation and destruction of crops in order not to flood the market; ruthless exploitation of its territories of Java, Sumatra, and Ceylon; fantastically high dividends; corruption and bad book-keeping. All these ultimately brought about its fall, but not before it had—without really intending to do so—established a permanent Dutch settlement at the Cape.

In April 1652 the Company sent one of its officials, Jan van Riebeeck, to the Cape to set up a refreshment station at which its ships could get fresh vegetables and meat. His instructions were to confine his attentions to establishing the refreshment station and not to become involved in trouble with whatever inhabitants there might be. (Throughout its century and a half of rule at the Cape the Company was consistently to regard it as nothing but a refreshment station, a necessary evil, as it were, and an item in the East India ledger.) Jan van Riebeeck found loosely organized Hottentot tribes who owned cattle and were nomads. For a time the Dutch bought cattle for copper wire and beads, the traditional currency between Europe and primitive peoples; but, soon, the questions of grazing-rights and of land obtruded themselves. The Hottentots resented the occupation of their pasture lands near Table Mountain and constantly stole from and attacked the Dutch. This provoked reprisals, and two short wars compelled the Hottentots to recognize Dutch occupation. By degrees they accepted the situation and began to hire themselves to the Dutch colonists as farm-labourers and domestic servants. Meanwhile, the Company had imported slaves, chiefly from the East Coast and from Madagascar. Miscegenation took place between slaves and Hottentots and Europeans, and gave rise to the Cape Coloured population.

Jan van Riebeeck soon found that the cheapest method of supplying passing ships with fresh produce was to introduce free colonists as farmers and to buy their produce at prices controlled by the Company. Thus is was that, in 1657, the first few non-official Europeans came to the Cape to settle, and soon regarded it as their home. They were styled free burghers, and their number increased steadily though slowly.

Jan van Riebeeck left the Cape in 1662 after ten years of hard and discouraging work. He is regarded today as the founder of European civilization in South Africa; but it is doubtful whether he himself ever got beyond regarding the Cape as a refreshment station. It was some twenty years later that a vigorous successor, Simon van der Stel, first saw the possibilities for settlement. Urged on by him, the Company made its only real effort to encourage immigration. Dutch and German immigrants were settled; a new village was established and called Stellenbosch; local government was instituted. Most important of all, about 200 French Huguenots arrived between 1688 and 1700 to enrich the social and economic life of the settlement and to become absorbed in the Dutch population. The Company also sent out orphan girls as wives for the colonists. And so the population grew. By 1708 there were about 1,700 Europeans, men, women, and children, and about the same number of slaves. But colonization was slow. There was nothing in the history of the Cape comparable to the migrations to the American continent. The Company was fundamentally opposed to increasing its commitments.

Small as the population was at the beginning of the eighteenth century, it was sufficiently numerous and influential to challenge successfully a clique of high officials who were attempting to corner the Cape market for their private benefit. And it was showing signs of developing characteristics of its own—characteristics that stemmed from the motherland in Europe, but were to be moulded by circumstances until, in later centuries, the name Afrikaner became a description of someone who was European by origin but was neither Dutch nor German nor French. One of these characteristics was a strong sense of individual freedom and a hearty dislike of control by government. This might have been expected from seventeenth-century Calvinists. But Calvinism in Europe, while stressing the importance of the individual, was disciplined by fear and persecution into a cohesive body. At the Cape there was no outward compulsion that forced the individual to merge his identity in a defensive body. On the contrary, social and economic circumstances were such that the European colonists had every incentive to become somewhat undisciplined individualists. Slave labour, plenty of land, and a reasonably fertile climate conspired to produce a leisurely people, accustomed to being obeyed by slaves and Hottentots but themselves not obeying the law, resenting interference, and regarding government at the distant castle in Cape Town as something that should protect but not tax. And by 'protect' they meant that the government should see to it that the farmer had sufficient labour and that prices for farm produce were always at a maximum. As every government in South Africa knows, the word 'protect' has not entirely lost this somewhat specialized meaning.

The increasing demands of the Cape market for meat greatly encouraged cattle-farming. Since the land round Cape Town and Stellenbosch was not suited to ranching on any large scale, the cattle farmers began to move east from the Cape, across the Hottentots-Holland Mountains, to establish large cattle farms. These farmers were the *trekboere* (trekking farmers). They did not own the huge ranches on which their cattle grazed, because the economical Company, unwilling to spend more money on administering its distant subjects, refused to survey and to grant freehold. The land was on loan, and this system encouraged farmers to over-graze and then to move on to new pastures, still more miles away from the government at Cape Town. Only after three or four generations of *trekboere* had followed this nomadic life did government, in the shape of local administration, catch up with them. By then the *trekboere* had come to regard any government at all as interference with a man's personal liberty. They had also acquired a rooted belief that the possession of plenty of land was the natural right of all free men.

These nomadic cattle farmers were of the same Calvinist stock as those who lived near Cape Town and Stellenbosch; but they had even less incentive to maintain a corporate discipline and cohesion. They lived a poor life, spiritually, culturally, and materially. They developed an individual independence of the pioneering kind. What they needed they made for themselves; and they asked for nothing better than to be left alone. Their religion was that of the Old rather than the New Testament, a harsh and forbidding religion. Although Cape Town was in contact, however spasmodic, with ideas that came from Europe, the cattle farmers neither knew nor cared about things beyond their own material wants and the safety of their families and their herds.

During the course of their trekking the cattle farmers found the Bushmen. Small of stature, living on wild herbs and game that they killed with poisoned arrows, having only a rudimentary social structure, the Bushmen were unable to adapt themselves, as the Hottentots had done, to the ways of the white man. They were accustomed to hunt where they pleased, and the idea of private ownership of land was utterly foreign to them. They not unnaturally regarded the European farmers as intruders and did their utmost to defend their ancient way of life. But it was a forlorn hope. The cattle farmers organized hunting parties which killed adult Bushmen and captured their children whom they used as herdsmen. In one such party 250 Bushmen were killed. What remained of the Bushmen families fled north-west to the semi-desert lands where their descendants are to be found today, living in a reserve under the protection of the Union Government and having their language and their primitive art studied by a more appreciative generation.

During the last quarter of the eighteenth century the Dutch trekking farmers came into contact with the African tribes who were more advanced in culture than the Bushmen and Hottentots and who numbered millions where the others had numbered thousands. The original home of the southern Bantu or African was probably near the equatorial highlands on the eastern side of Africa, where, possibly 2,000 years ago, Negroes from the Congo and from West Africa mixed with Hamitic stock to form the Bantu people. Migrations caused by pressure of population, tribal wars, and slave-raiding brought the Bantu southwards through the present Tanganyika, Nyasaland, and the Rhodesias. The migrations were probably spread over hundreds of years, and by the middle of the eighteenth century some of the tribes had reached the Great Fish River in what is now the Eastern Province of the Cape. Like the Europeans, these Africans owned cattle and tilled the soil. They had well-developed social and political institutions according to which the chief was the depositary of tribal law and custom but, in normal circumstances, he was no despot, being controlled by the tribal council and the tribe itself. The Africans were heathen; they had no written language; they were haunted by the fear of witchcraft and explained everything by reference to the supernatural. Their social system was based on cattle and the communal ownership of land, and they practised a subsistence economy.

The contact between these virile people and the hardy trek farmers had many important results. It led, eventually, to the conquest and Christianizing of the African. Its more immediate result was innumerable cattle raids which ended periodically in war. Raids and counter-raids went on until some minor incident would precipitate a war during which the African tribe involved would gain a preliminary victory and then be defeated but not conquered. In fact, typical frontier conditions prevailed for close on 100 years until the middle of the nineteenth century.

Another important result was that the old habit of trekking farther into unoccupied lands could no longer be indulged. There was, to their immediate front, no longer an apparently endless stretch of unoccupied land. The land was in fact occupied by large numbers of Africans who also required grazing-land for their herds of cattle. This was one of the principal reasons that eventually led the Dutch farmers to trek round north-west of the African tribes and on to the highlands of the interior, there to establish republics.

By the end of the eighteenth century, when events in Europe altered the current of South African history, the refreshment station had grown into a colony sparsely inhabited by about 30,000 people. There were four districts, the Cape, Stellenbosch, Swellendam, and Graaff-Reinet. In the Cape there were Company's officials and a non-official population that lived by keeping lodging-houses, by fishing, by brickmaking, or by market-gardening. The chief attraction of keeping a lodging-house was the possibilities it afforded for smuggling and for making money from visitors. The Company strictly controlled all forms of commerce; it allowed certain minor

1

participation in local government; it kept down expenses and as a consequence connived at bribery and corruption in its officials.

At Stellenbosch there were well-to-do farmers who cultivated vines and corn, kept a few sheep and cattle, and built the beautiful old Cape Dutch houses that adorn the Cape to this day. They lived the leisurely lives of slave-owners. On the whole they treated their slaves well, and manumission for those who became Christians and literate was relatively frequent. In the Swellendam and Graaff-Reinet districts lived the stock farmers, occupying 6,000 acres or more at a time, trekking on when the need arose, far removed from the influences of the Cape, not so much lawless as a law unto themselves, and asking for nothing more than plenty of land and no interference from government. When the government did interfere in 1795 they rebelled and formed two short-lived republics. Five years later the British Government had to suppress two more rebellions in the same area.

The non-European population at this time consisted of slaves and non-slaves, the former being more numerous in the west and the latter in the eastern districts where the farmers were seldom owners but depended on what Hottentot labour they could get rather than on slaves. The slaves were of diverse origin—West African, East African, Mozambique, and Malay—and all these non-Europeans were already tending to merge ethnically to form the Cape Coloured people. There were as yet no Africans within the borders of the colony; but, as we have seen, the great clash between Africa and Europe had already begun.

When the French revolutionary armies invaded Holland in 1795, Britain, by arrangement with the Dutch King, occupied the Cape for the first time. The Company was by now bankrupt; and when the Treaty of Amiens of 1802 provided that the Cape should be restored, it was to the Dutch Republican Government, and not to the Company, that it was handed back. For three years the Cape was ruled by a brilliant Dutch advocate, Jacob de Mist, according to enlightened governmental principles then current in France and Holland. When Napoleon renewed the war against Britain it became clear to the British Government that it would endanger her trade with the East if the Cape were to remain in the hands of an ally of France. She accordingly occupied the Cape for the second time in 1806, this time with no intention of returning it. In 1815 the Congress of Vienna ratified the cession.

The British Government took a more serious view of its governmental duties than the Dutch Company had done. Government was reorganized; the currency was stabilized; circuit courts were introduced, to the annoyance of frontiersmen who found the courts interfering in what they considered to be purely personal matters such as relations with their Hottentot servants; the slave trade was abolished, and the government tried to overcome the labour shortage by pass laws that restricted the free movement of Hottentots.

Unemployment in Britain after the Napoleonic Wars led to emigration, and 5,000 British settlers arrived in 1820 to settle in the eastern districts. Their advent had a profound effect on the history of the country. It brought to the colony, and to South Africa, a most valuable new element in the population—an element that, because it was English-speaking and had friends and relatives in Britain, compelled the British Government to pay greater attention to the Cape. They had left England at a time when administrative reforms that were to come after the death of Lord Castlereagh were being widely discussed, and it was largely owing to the presence of the settlers and to persistent agitation by individuals among them that a whole series of reforms was instituted at the Cape. The freedom of the Press was achieved in 1827. In the same year a Charter of Justice established the independence of the judiciary and instituted trial by jury. In 1834 slavery was abolished; a Legislative Council, with an official majority, was set up; the old local courts of *Landdrost* and *Heemraden* were abolished, paid magistrates were appointed, and popularly elected municipal councils were instituted. Freedom of internal trade and the right to export surplus produce were granted; new towns were established and roads and bridges were built.

The first thirty years of British rule at the Cape were years of considerable economic expansion and administrative reform. The British Government had, however, done many things which the Dutch inhabitants heartily disliked. The English language had been declared the only official language, and, though this policy was reversed some thirty years later, it left a deep mark on the minds of South Africans. To this day Afrikaans political speakers can be sure of a ready response when they refer to 'old Lord Charles Somerset' and his attempts to suppress the Dutch language. An even greater shock than the suppression of their language was the shock to fundamental beliefs and traditions, more especially of the frontier farmers, involved in British policy. Largely as a result of the persistent advocacy of Dr. Philip, of the London Missionary Society, the famous Fiftieth Ordinance was passed in 1828. This Ordinance repealed the previous pass laws and established the principle of equality in the eyes of the law for 'all free persons of colour'. In the twentieth century, white opinion in Africa can with difficulty bring itself even to contemplate the doctrine of racial equality; and it may be imagined with what loathing the frontiersmen of 1828 regarded it.

Further, there had been more Kaffir Wars, as the frontier wars between European and African are called, and the British Government, strongly under the influence of the Liberals and the philanthropic movement, and not wishing to extend its commitments, had refused to satisfy the land-hunger of the trek farmers by the annexation of African territory. From about 1834 a few frontier farmers, despairing of obtaining more land on the old cheap terms, began to trek west of the Bantu territories, across the Orange River, and on to the highveld of what is now the Orange Free State. They really went to spy out the land, and could report back that there was plenty of excellent grazing-land which seemed to have no one on it. In the same year, 1834, another Kaffir War broke out and farmhouses were destroyed, stock stolen, and people murdered before the Africans could be subdued. The Governor, Sir Benjamin D'Urban, sympathized with the farmers in their plight and annexed a portion of the defeated Africans' land to hand out as farms by way of compensation. But he modified his policy when he found that he could not keep Africans out of the area, and he reversed it after being severely criticized by the government in London. The frontiersmen then realized that nothing more was to be hoped for from a government that refused to help the white at the expense of the black, and so began the Great Trek which was intended to carry them beyond the reach of the British Government.

The Trekkers, in a public statement issued on the eve of departure of one particular group, complained of the suppression of their language and institutions; of the lack of protection on the frontier; of the unfair way in which the liberation of the slaves had been carried out; of the unjustifiable odium that had been cast upon them by missionaries and other prejudiced persons. They complained that they had no voice in the government that taxed them. Anna Steenkamp, one of the Trekker women, spoke in her diary of the unbiblical policy of equality between black and white, and the phrase conveys some of the genuine horror with which the Dutch emigrant farmers viewed a policy that placed white and black on an equal footing and interfered in the relations between master and servant.

During the decade from 1836 to 1846 something like 10,000 men, women, and children left their homes in the Cape Colony, expressing the hope that the British Government would leave them in peace. They trekked northwards with all their possessions packed on ox-wagons or slung beneath the wagons—beds, furniture, a harmonium where they had one, pots and pans, and, always, the family Bible. The women in their long dresses and bonnets travelled in the wagons with the children; the men, in their rough clothes and with a rifle slung over their shoulders, usually travelled on horseback. All—men, women, and children—took their turn at leading the oxen and at herding the cattle. They underwent considerable hardships and dangers in the course of their wanderings. Wagons had to be taken to pieces and carried over the difficult mountain passes; there was always danger from wild animals; and there was danger from attack by Africans. Usually they trekked in small parties of twenty or thirty families and arranged to meet when they had reached the promised land; but there were larger parties under elected leaders to which the smaller parties eventually attached themselves.

The Voortrekkers[1] envisaged an independent republican state in which there would be no equality between black and white. They intended, they said, to obtain land justly, by purchase, and to found their state upon principles of religion and justice. After a good deal of quarrelling among the leaders as to where they should settle, Piet Retief, the most intelligent of the leaders, trekked eastwards with his followers towards the present Natal. At that time what is now Natal was ruled by the Zulu under Dingaan. The Zulu had been an obscure tribe that had risen to pre-eminence under Dingaan's predecessor, Chaka, a man of outstanding ability although, like Dingaan, he was a cruel and bloodthirsty tyrant and slew indiscriminately all who offended him or against the laws of his tribe. Against both there is a heavy record of savage and indiscriminate slaughterings of their own subjects and of other African tribes, for which there is not the excuse that may be found for Dingaan's murder of Europeans, who in his eyes threatened the safety of his country.

Piet Retief, having reached Natal, went to meet Dingaan and negotiated for the transfer of land; but the Zulu chief played for time and asked the Trekkers, as an earnest of their good intentions, to recover some stolen cattle for him. This done, a treaty was drawn up by which the Trekkers were given a large portion of Natal. Dingaan probably, as with most treaties signed with African chiefs, intended this land for use and not for ownership. But, whatever his intentions, the ease with which the cattle had been recovered by the Europeans had frightened him, and he determined to kill the white wizards. At a royal feast he had Retief and seventy followers murdered, and sent his soldiers to murder all the white people they could find. Vengeance followed about a year later when, on 16 December 1838, the Zulu were decisively defeated at the Battle of Blood River and their country was annexed.

Having conquered Natal, with its harbour at Durban, the Trekkers

---

[1] *Voor* here means 'in front of', and Voortrekker means pioneer. The word is frequently abbreviated to Trekker.

found themselves at odds with the Cape Colony. Merchants at the Cape feared the possible rivalry of Durban, where ships from the United States and from Holland had already begun to put in to trade. Further, though the Zulu had been defeated, the country was by no means settled. Thousands of landless Zulu roamed the country, and cattle-thieving was rife. This led to reprisals and raids, and generally to a state of unrest among African tribes right up to the borders of the Cape Colony. The Governor of the Cape, therefore, persuaded the British Government to annex Natal in 1843, to the disgust of the Trekkers, many of whom trekked back over the Drakensberg Mountains to the highveld of the present Free State and Transvaal. British authority followed them once more. In 1848 the Free State was proclaimed the Orange River Sovereignty with a Resident Commissioner to represent the British Government.

British policy with regard to the Trekkers had been vacillating. Like the Dutch Reformed Church, the government had frowned on such a dispersal of its subjects as the Great Trek constituted. To follow up its obviously reluctant subjects with administrative and police machinery would mean an enormous expense, and unless that expense could be justified on some such obvious commercial and strategic grounds as would be provided by Durban harbour, it would not be worth it. The new country was sparsely populated by a race of farmers who were antagonistic to British rule and possessed little or no cash income that could be taxed to pay for expenses. At that time, moreover, the existence of minerals, which was later to prove so attractive, was unknown. There was, therefore, no great incentive to Britain to retain her hold over the country occupied by the dispersed Trekkers; and under the re-alignment of parties that followed the repeal of the Corn Laws in Britain, parliament began to regard colonies as unwanted burdens. Accordingly, by the Sand River Convention of 1852, Britain withdrew all claims to exercise authority beyond the Vaal River; and two years later, by the Bloemfontein Convention, she withdrew south of the Orange River. These actions left the two Boer republics, the Orange Free State and the South African Republic (the Transvaal), independent of British control.

The European inhabitants of the two new republics were, as nearly as possible, equal in wealth and condition. Wealth consisted of land and stock, and there was certainly enough land for all. The Boer ideal, that when he sat on his *stoep* he should not see the smoke from his nearest neighbours' chimneys, could be realized in those spacious days. Twenty or thirty modern farms in the Free State could have been lost in the farm of a century ago. It was only later in the century, when the population increased, when towns were established and minerals discovered, that differences in wealth and status began to appear. But at the time when the Boers were establishing their republics, economic and social equality of all European citizens was reflected in the constitutions they made.

The constitution of the Orange Free State is a good example of what one might call natural democracy. A group of people with practically no book learning, many of them semiliterate, with few examples (in the 1850's) of democratic constitutions to guide them, with a strong sense of individual liberty, and with a rough economic and social equality, set up an efficient democratic constitution that contained many of the principles of sound constitutional government. There was an elected *Volksraad* (Legislative Assembly) and an elected president; the judiciary was independent; control of the commandos remained with the elected *Volksraad*; the legislature was supreme and controlled the executive; freedom of the Press and of the individual was guaranteed in the constitution. The constitution of the Transvaal was a rambling document that stressed the popular will but left vague such constitutional questions as the relations between the executive, the legislature, and the judiciary. Moreover, the constitution was frequently changed by simple resolution of the *Volksraad*. Nevertheless, it was only when gold was discovered and a highly specialized industrial community was superimposed on the agricultural republic, that the constitution failed to work with reasonable smoothness.

Many of the Africans who were living in the Transvaal and Free State were deprived of their rights to occupy land. This was sometimes accompanied by violence and war; but, much more frequently, it was a silent process comparable to the enclosure movement in England. Much of the land occupied by Europeans was, indeed, vacant land. Frequently the occupation was made in genuine ignorance that anyone else had a right to it; farms were granted to individuals without the knowledge that any Africans were in occupation. Population, African and European, was sparse, and on farms of from 50,000 to 100,000 acres it was quite possible for people to be living on the same land without being aware of one another's existence. Further, possession meant different things to Europeans and to Africans. To the former it meant physical possession, the right to property; to the latter it meant use. In those parts of the republics where there was obvious occupation by Africans, the Boers recognized the authority of the chiefs and left the people in possession of their land under the name of Reserves.

The Great Trek changed the course of the history of southern Africa. It withdrew from the Cape Colony, at a critical period, about a quarter of its Dutch-speaking population, thus leaving British ideas and institutions fuller play in the Cape Colony. In a period of ten years it opened up vast tracts of land to European occupation and established three new political entities; it thus opened the way to eventual expansion northwards. It brought millions of Africans under the political control of Europeans. In doing so it deprived many of them of their rights to tribal occupation of land and reduced the areas to which they had previously had free access; it also, in time, brought peace and the rule of law where formerly there had been intertribal warfare and general insecurity.

The Boers established republics with democratic constitutions that were in some ways in advance of those enjoyed by their compatriots in the Cape Colony. But these constitutions were (naturally enough at the time) for Europeans only; when the Cape achieved responsible government it was for all colours. Thus, two radically different policies with regard to non-Europeans became established in South Africa, and the difference has not yet been composed. The republican tradition in South Africa became firmly established, closely associated with the Afrikaners and opposed to Britain. The Trek thus created a gulf between Britain and the Afrikaners that has not yet been spanned. British policy from the Great Trek until the Boer War bred a deep suspicion in the minds of Afrikaners. Even now the Afrikaner cannot quite shake off the illusion that he is being followed.[1]

Because of their experiences with African tribes, experiences of wars and misconceived treaties, the Boers developed a firm conviction that a policy of equal rights for black and white is contrary to the laws of God and the dictates of common sense. They did not know what investigations have since revealed: that an African chief did not possess tribal land and had no authority to alienate it. The British Government, too, throughout Africa, acquired territory by hundreds of treaties with African chiefs. Indeed, at one time the Foreign Office provided printed treaty forms for the use of officials and explorers. The Boers made a few such treaties. But few or many, British or Boer, all the treaties were in reality valueless. In the first place, the chief had no power to alienate land; in the second place, what he thought he was doing was to give the Europeans the usufruct (not the possession) of land. In their ignorance of tribal custom, the Europeans (of all nations) made what they thought were contracts by which the land became theirs. To this day Europeans (of all nations) argue that the land of their particular colony was acquired by genuine treaty. What had really happened was that two totally different conceptions of landownership conflicted, and neither side knew or recognized the conflict.

[1] For a discussion of the use of the term Afrikaner see chapter 3.

Perhaps the most important result of the Great Trek is to be found in the influence it has had on the social and political thought of the Afrikaners and in the way it has affected their cultural and emotional life. Before the Battle of Blood River, where the Zulu were defeated, the Trekkers held their customary church service, and the preacher, Cilliers, vowed that if victory was granted, the Afrikaners would every year hold a thanksgiving service on that day. The Day of the Covenant,[1] 16 December, is still a national holiday on which the Afrikaans churches have services in remembrance of the vow made by Cilliers. When the services are over political speeches are made recalling the past and exhorting Afrikaners not to forsake the ways of their forefathers. In recent years Voortrekker dress has been revived, and the folk-dancing, games, and music of those days are very popular at these gatherings. Afrikaners regard the Great Trek as the greatest spiritual, cultural, and political event that gave birth to the Afrikaner nation. Through the mists of time, as frequently happens, some of the economic facts of the Trek are overlaid, and the reasons that caused the Trek are idealized in the popular mind.

The tradition of the Great Trek has a strong link with the rise of Afrikaner nationalism and of the Nationalist Party. As the Great Trek itself split the European population of South Africa, so the memories and traditions of the Trek tend to divide Afrikaners and English-speaking South Africans today. Politicians are fond of saying this need not be so; but it is a fact. South Africa is full of memories that its citizens cannot yet share with equal pride; and the Great Trek is still one of them. The time may come when Afrikaners, English-speaking South Africans, and Africans will all be able to find cause for satisfaction in the spread of Western civilization in southern Africa that resulted from the Great Trek.

We left the Cape Colony at 1836. From then it shared in the steady constitutional development that Lord Durham's report on Canada had persuaded British opinion to accept as reasonable. In 1853 representative government was instituted, and, in 1872, full responsible government. As we saw, there was no colour bar in the constitution; but franchise qualifications, applicable to all, kept the number of non-European voters small and enabled the European colonists to accustom themselves to the idea of a common electoral roll. The Cape Colony thus had an opportunity of showing whether a multiracial society could co-operate in running parliamentary institutions. So satisfactory was this experience that, in 1910, when the Cape Colony entered into Union with the other South African colonies, Afrikaans-

[1] Until 1952, when it was changed by Act of Parliament, this was called Dingaan's Day.

and English-speaking citizens at the Cape were practically unanimous in believing that a common franchise, restricted by educational and property tests for all alike, not only worked well but was the only sane policy. So convinced were the Cape politicians that this was a sound policy that they were prepared to forgo union rather than abandon their common franchise. We shall see later what the sequel has been.

From 1848 the British Government at the Cape gradually abandoned the policy of trying to maintain a peaceful boundary between the Cape Colony and the African tribes. Step by step African territory between the Fish River and the Natal border was annexed, and European magistrates and police were sent in to rule. In most cases the land annexed was reserved for African occupation. Missionaries, schools, hospitals, and other civilizing agencies began their slow and uphill task among the Africans.

Although the British Government had, in the 1850's, refused to undertake further commitments, subsequent events and the logical demands on the strongest government in southern Africa brought Britain back into politics north of the Orange River. To begin with, there were many people in the Cape Colony, and even in the Free State and Transvaal, who regretted the balkanization of South Africa and who were anxious for some form of federation or union. Sir George Grey, popular in the Free State as well as in the Cape where he was Governor, took soundings in 1856 and found the Free State not unwilling to consider federation. At that stage, however, the British Government had too recently withdrawn from the Free State and was unwilling to reverse her policy. Thus the first attempt at union came to nothing. The second attempt was made by Lord Carnarvon, Secretary of State for Colonies.

In 1870 diamonds were discovered at Kimberley and a dispute arose as to who owned the area. It was claimed by Waterboer, chief of a mixed Hottentot and half-breed tribe called the Griquas, by the Transvaal, and, with more justice, by the Free State. The negotiations and the arbitration by which the award went to Waterboer, who was then induced to come in under the British wing, left the Transvaal and Free State resentful. Even so, the statesmanlike Brand, President of the Free State, was prepared to discuss the proposals for a federation put forward by Lord Carnarvon; but by this time the Cape had been granted responsible government and the Cape ministers considered that Carnarvon had gone over their heads. Carnarvon's attempt was, therefore, a failure.

A third attempt was made in 1877. The Transvaal was in very low water. Economically it was on the verge of bankruptcy; politically it was rent by internal and personal disputes; and it was having grave difficulty in keeping the peace with its African neighbours. Sir Theophilus Shepstone, acting on behalf of the Imperial Government, went to Pretoria with a bodyguard of twenty-four men and persuaded a majority of the *Volksraad* to accept British rule. On behalf of the British Government he promised that responsible government would be instituted as soon as possible. When, four years later, the promise had not been carried out, the Transvaalers rose and fought the Transvaal war of independence. They won a notable victory at the Battle of Majuba Hill, which drew an admiring poem by way of tribute from *Punch*, and Gladstone decided to make peace as quickly as possible. By the Pretoria Convention the Transvaal's independence was restored, but Britain retained the right to veto her foreign policy, a clause that was to cause endless trouble later. The final, and most disastrous, attempt at federation will be described presently.

The discovery of diamonds in 1870 wrenched South Africa from her agricultural rut and began the process which was to alter her history. The economic effects were immediate: agricultural prices soared and, for a time, Free State farmers were selling eggs at a pound a dozen. Money and people poured into the country; from the Cape people walked and rode to make their fortunes on the diggings; Africans came out of their reserves in thousands to earn money and, more desirable, guns. It became profitable to build a railway line from the Cape to Kimberley, and African labour was required to do the rough work. Gradually people like Cecil Rhodes, Barney Barnato, and the Beits got control of the mines by buying out the small operators. In this way they established the enormous fortunes that were subsequently used to develop the gold-mines of the Transvaal and to expand the British Empire farther north.

The discovery, in 1886, of gold on the Witwatersrand made Kimberley look like a minor boom in a small town. Within a brief few years of the discovery there were more foreigners (Uitlanders) in the Transvaal, all concentrated on the Rand, than there were Boers. The construction of railways from the Cape and from Lourenço Marques was rushed through to take the mining material and the heavy and light goods that the Rand required. The effects of the discovery of gold were felt throughout South Africa like a seismic disturbance, and in London, where the capital for its exploitation came from, people began to regard the Transvaal in a new light.

Even before the discovery of gold had made the Transvaal a country of world importance the scramble for Africa had begun. Germany, France, Britain, Belgium, and Portugal were competing for African territories, and the Berlin Conference of 1884 had arranged for the peaceful partition of Africa among the European powers. Spheres of influence were demarcated on the map, and often these boundary lines were lines of latitude or longitude and cut through existing tribes. Everywhere treaties were made with chiefs who had little, if any, understanding of what they were putting their mark to.

To preserve as wide a sphere of influence as possible, the restless Cecil Rhodes, from his base at the Cape, pushed northwards, west of the Transvaal, through Bechuanaland, and on to the Rhodesias. In 1886 part of Bechuanaland was annexed to the Cape Colony, and three years later Rhodes's agents persuaded Lobengula, chief of the Matebele, to grant mining concessions which were used by those who came to mine for gold as giving them the right to settle. A Matebele war and a Matebele rebellion had to be fought before the title to Rhodesia was gained by the Europeans. A barrier was thus created around the Transvaal which effectually prevented Germany from joining her eastern and western African territories.

From his capital in Pretoria, some thirty miles from the teeming Rand, President Paul Kruger watched all these goings-on with growing fear and suspicion. His republic was well off because he was able to tax the Randlords. But he had reason to fear that the combination of capital and Empire would prove too strong for the weak republic. The constitution of the Transvaal was designed to serve an agricultural community and it was unable to adjust itself to the new strains to which it was put. Wealth in such great quantity corrupted the public service which was not capable of effectively governing the turbulent and lawless Johannesburg.

It was against this background that Cecil Rhodes, then Prime Minister of Cape Colony, plotted the final attempt to bring the republics into line with the Cape. Rhodes and Jameson, almost certainly with the knowledge of Chamberlain, decided to annex the Transvaal by a sudden stroke. The Jameson Raid was ill-conceived and badly executed. The noisy Uitlanders in Johannesburg were undependable, and the success of the Raid would have to depend on a rising in Johannesburg. In fact, the rising was to have been the excuse to cover Rhodes. Jameson would go in to restore order. But the rising never took place and Jameson's force was captured with little trouble by the Transvaal burghers.

The Jameson Raid was a complete failure but it had far-reaching consequences. Rhodes had to resign from a position where he had had great influence with the Cape Afrikaners, and they and all other Afrikaners now repudiated him and regarded him as the archetype of finance-imperialism. Jameson had very wisely been handed over by Kruger to the British Government to deal with. He was tried and given a light sentence; actually he did not serve the whole of it. A parliamentary inquiry at Westminster seemed to have but one object, that of protecting the Secretary of State for Colonies, Joseph Chamberlain. The British public was in an imperialist and jingoistic mood and regarded Jameson and Rhodes, not as political adventurers who had endangered the good relations between Great Britain and the Transvaal, but as empire builders who had had bad luck. All these things had the effect of turning the Afrikaners, from the Cape to the Transvaal, against Britain and against any idea of peaceful federation. The Raid, and particularly the refusal of the British Government to repudiate it whole-heartedly and unequivocally, destroyed what slender hopes there had been of a peaceful settlement with the Transvaal.[1] In 1899 a conference was held at Bloemfontein between representatives of the Transvaal and of Great Britain; but it failed to arrive at an agreement over the crucial question of Uitlander rights. Kruger could not hand over the vote to the Uitlanders without endangering Boer political power. On the other hand, the Uitlanders were paying the taxes and demanded an effective share in calling the tune. It was a position from which, in the atmosphere engendered by the Raid, neither side could extricate itself. Britain sent troops to South Africa, and in October 1899 the Transvaal demanded their withdrawal in an ultimatum. When this was refused, war began and the Free State, bound by treaty, joined the Transvaal.

Afrikaners call the war 'Die Engelse oorlog' (the English war), or the second war of independence, the first being the Transvaal war of independence of 1880-1. In England it is called the Boer War. Some people in South Africa call it the Anglo-Boer War. These names are perhaps indicative of the different opinions that exist on the question of responsibility for the war. In this book the term Boer War is used, for the sake of brevity and with no intention of apportioning blame.

Without going into any details of the war, there are a few points that can be made. The Boer War is still fresh in the memories of many people. It took place sixty years ago, so that men who are now no more than 75 years old may have taken part, as youngsters of 15, in the actual fighting.[2] Women of that age can recall the concentration camps in which they were and in which, possibly, their brothers or sisters or mothers died. Children and grandchildren of these people have heard Boer War tales at first hand, tales of heroism and escape, of hunger and privation, of cruelty and of kindness, and the tales are

[1] See Jean van der Poel, *The Jameson Raid.*
[2] Within a week of the outbreak of war the Grey College School at Bloemfontein, at which many Transvaal and Free State boys studied, was practically emptied of its senior classes. The boys had gone to the war!

often told with a humour that shows an absence of rancour or bitterness. The first three prime ministers of the Union were Boer War generals—Botha, Hertzog, and Smuts; and Smuts died in 1950. It is therefore only in comparatively recent times that the men who led the Boers in their times of trouble had one by one departed and left the stage to younger men. No wonder, then, that the Boer War occupies a great place in the thinking and politics and culture of the Afrikaner people.

During the first three or four months of the Boer War the British forces were checked and defeated on three main fronts. Then they gathered force and pushed on, leaving the main Boer forces to waste their energies and limited manpower in besieging Kimberley, Mafeking, and Ladysmith, or, as General Smuts did, to make dramatic but fruitless raids into the Cape Colony. When the sieges had been relieved, the two capitals, Bloemfontein and Pretoria, were captured, but the Boers hung on tenaciously for two years, living on the country, for the most part fighting their battles with ammunition captured from the enemy, and hoping for international intervention. It was a war of attrition, and when Kitchener tried to make contact with his elusive opponents he found that practically every farmhouse in the Free State and Transvaal was a Boer base. Strategically, he was bound to destroy these bases, and he decided to burn farms. Once this decision was taken, women and children could not be left on the bare veld to starve. So they were brought into hastily improvised canvas concentration camps.[1]

The concentration camps were, for the most part, badly run and with rudimentary notions of hygiene. The result was that 26,000 women and children died of fever. There were not enough doctors or hospitals or supplies, and the British Tommies themselves were dying by the thousand of fever. All the camps were not equally bad. As so often happens, a great deal depended on the humanity and common sense of the individual camp commandant. After the wave of indignation that swept the Cape Colony and Liberal circles in Britain, improvements were made. Camp schools were established and Dutch Reformed Church ministers from the Cape were allowed to minister to the spiritual needs of the people. The women themselves showed immense courage and adjured their menfolk not to surrender or to give up the struggle on their account; and as a matter of fact, there is evidence that the Boers did continue to fight in the knowledge

---

[1] See Lionel Curtis, *With Milner in South Africa*, for lively and statesmanlike comments on the Boer War and for condemnation of the burning of farms. *Adventures of a Boer Family*, by Victor Pohl, is a charming account, given without rancour, of how the war affected a Boer family.

that the women and children (in spite of the heavy death-roll) were being looked after. General Botha expressed his thankfulness that so many Boer families were in British hands; and President Steyn used the improved conditions in the camps as an argument to encourage the burghers to fight on.[1] Nevertheless, the burning of farms and the concentration camps left a deep mark on the Afrikaner people.

By the beginning of 1902 it was evident that the Boers could not hold out much longer. In May the final negotiations for peace took place and the peace treaty was signed at Vereeniging on 31 May 1902. (On the same day, eight years later, the Union of South Africa came into being.) The terms of the treaty were generous. Britain promised to grant responsible government as soon as the country was settled; the equality of the Dutch language, as it then still was, with English was recognized; the question of the non-European franchise was to be left until after the grant of responsible government; and Britain agreed to help in the economic reconstruction of the country. These promises were faithfully kept. By 1906 and 1907 the Transvaal and the Free State were granted responsible government, and the country recovered remarkably quickly from the ravages of war. Milner, whose pre-war policy had naturally been unpopular with the Boers, was mainly responsible for the efficient way in which administration was reorganized even while the fighting was still going on.

The way was now open for another move to combine the four self-governing colonies in South Africa, and in 1908 a National Convention met at Durban to discuss closer union. Though all parties were agreed on most of the terms of a constitution, there were various obstacles to be overcome. Union, rather than federation, was decided on and parliament was to be sovereign. But, as a compromise to allay the fears of the two smaller colonies of Natal and the Free State, provincial councils were given powers that could not be altered by Parliament until ten years after union; among these powers was the control of primary and secondary education. The question of the franchise was the most difficult of all. The Cape, with its liberal tradition, wanted to retain the Cape franchise, which had no colour bar; the Transvaal and Free State refused to grant the vote to non-Europeans. Eventually it was decided to leave the franchise laws of the four states as they were and to satisfy the Cape delegates by entrenching the Cape franchise in a clause which provided that it could be altered only by a two-thirds majority of both Houses of Parliament sitting together.

When the National Convention had reached finality the draft Act was taken to Westminster where it was passed by the British Parliament

[1] See Walker, *History of South Africa*. p. 499.

as the South Africa Act, 1909. By May of 1910 Union was an accomplished fact.

Much of the history of the Union since 1910 will become apparent, incidentally, in subsequent chapters, and a few main facts only need be told here. Since its inception the Union has been involved in two world wars, both of which interrupted normal life and, at the same time, enormously accelerated development. In neither world war was the European population united.

When the First World War broke out in 1914 General Botha was Prime Minister. A portion of the Afrikaner people had already broken away from the leadership of Botha and Smuts and, under Hertzog, had formed the Nationalist Party whose slogan was 'South Africa First', in contrast to Botha's policy of 'conciliation'.[1] When parliament approved the government's policy of invading South-West Africa, then a German colony, the Nationalist Party condemned the action and found considerable support in the Free State and Transvaal. Many Boer War leaders—de la Rey, Beyers, de Wet, among others —organized protests against participation in 'England's wars'. Officers in the Defence Force and in the burgher commandos openly declared that they would not obey instructions to fight. Some resigned their commissions, but Maritz, officer in charge of the troops nearest to the South-West Africa border, was treasonably in touch with the German Command and in due course went over to the enemy. Rebellion then broke out in the Union. Lack of organization or of cohesion among the leaders, who were all experienced soldiers, is proof that the Rebellion was not premeditated. It was, rather, a spontaneous rising with a vague hope of regaining the independence lost twelve years earlier. Neither General de Wet nor General Beyers had any real plans, and General Hertzog, political leader of the Nationalist Party, condemned Rebellion. The magic of de Wet's name attracted some of his old burghers and many young bloods; but the Rebellion was not widely supported and there were probably not more than 12,000 rebels all told. On the other hand, Botha soon had 40,000 men in the field, most of them Afrikaners, and by December 1914 the Rebellion was over.[2] General de Wet was captured and sentenced to imprisonment, but was soon released on parole and allowed to live on his farm.

Botha now turned his attention to South-West Africa, which he

---

[1] See chapter 7.
[2] An illustration of how close to the Boer War all these men, on both sides, were, is the story of General Botha on the morning of the Battle of Mushroom Valley, where he defeated de Wet. He was waiting anxiously for the expected attack; and when he saw de Wet's commando in the distance he said to one of his officers: 'Here they come. Here come the English.'

took in 1915, and which has remained ever since to trouble South Africa's international relations. After German South-West came German East Africa. Troops were sent to join the rather mixed forces that were operating there, and General Smuts himself went to conduct an exhausting and fruitless campaign against von Lettow, a campaign about which the two opponents swapped yarns at a dinner party in London after the war.[1]

Thousands of South Africans volunteered and went to England to join various British regiments and the Royal Flying Corps, as it was then called. A South African Brigade was recruited and sent to France, where it distinguished itself at Delville Wood. The Cape Coloured Corps was sent overseas and 7,000 Africans went as a Labour Corps. Out of a total possible of 685,000 European men of fighting age 136,000 enrolled for service and 76,000 went overseas.[2]

Between the two world wars industrialization took place at a rapid rate, too rapid for South Africa to be able to adapt her social economy with comfort. The balance of European population shifted from country to town; the number of manufacturing establishments increased from 2,000 to 9,000 and their output quadrupled; exports and imports doubled; the railway network increased by 25 per cent, even though the main lines from the ports to the mines had all been laid before Union; banking, agricultural production, revenue and expenditure, the public debt, and public service establishment, all kept pace with this industrial expansion. Unfortunately, housing and town-planning lagged far behind.

In political life, too, changes had taken place. The Nationalist Party came to power, with the aid of the Labour Party, in 1924. When, at the Imperial Conferences of 1926 and 1930, Hertzog completed the work that Botha and Smuts had begun and secured beyond any doubt the independence of South Africa as a member of the British Commonwealth, he declared that he had now done for the Afrikaner people what he had set out to do in 1912, and that, as far as he was concerned, a republic was neither necessary nor desirable. The extreme Nationalist wing, under Malan, would not accept this doctrine, and Hertzog's position became increasingly difficult. On the other hand, there was no longer any reason why he and Smuts should not pull together, and they formed the United Party with Hertzog as leader, a wise piece of self-effacement on the part of Smuts. Malan remained in the new party for a brief spell and then left it to lead the so-called 'Purified'

---

[1] When the writer was introduced as 'a fellow-countryman of General Smuts' to von Lettow's youngest daughter, she remarked: 'General Smuts and my father were great friends.'
[2] See Walker, *A History of South Africa*, p. 565, note.

2

Nationalists; at the other extreme a small group of ultra-British people, who considered that Smuts had gone too far towards the Afrikaner side, left his party and formed the Dominion Party. That the union of the two big parties was popular was shown by the next general election when the United Party won an overwhelming victory.

For the next seven years there was continued debate as to whether the Union could, and would, remain neutral if Britain went to war. When the test came, in September 1939, Hertzog opposed South Africa's entry into the war and proposed a benevolent neutrality while Smuts favoured immediate participation and carried the day with a majority of thirteen votes. Hertzog then asked for a dissolution to test the feeling of the country, but the Governor-General, advised by what was now the strongest party under Smuts, refused. For a few weeks emotions ran high and the atmosphere seemed favourable for a repetition of the events of 1914. The Nationalists were jubilant that Hertzog should have shown himself to be, as they put it, a 'true Afrikaner' and had, in effect, rejoined the Purified Nationalist Party; but as we shall see in a subsequent chapter, reunion between the Hertzogites and the Malanites did not take place. There was no rebellion, partly because Smuts acted with great wisdom and circum-spection and did not provoke trouble; partly because rebellion is not a step lightly undertaken; and partly because, in 1939, many Nationalists, in company with a great many people in other countries, backed Hitler's highly organized Germany to win and nurtured the illusion that a republic might well be snatched from such a situation.

Once more, therefore, South Africa was engaged in a life-and-death struggle as a partner of Great Britain; and once more she was divided on that very issue. All the moral and political authority of a consider-able opposition was used to hamper the war effort. One, among many, of the serious results of this was that throughout the war there was never an effective alternative war government. Criticism of war policy was, therefore, never really responsible and the government was never able to take the opposition into its confidence, and was thus deprived of all effective criticism.

South Africa's contribution to the common war effort was on a much larger scale than in 1914-18. Where her airmen had, in the first war, joined the Royal Air Force, she now had a large and efficient air force of her own; and South Africa became a training ground for the R.A.F. Two full divisions at a time were put into the field and others existed in skeleton form. The so-called 'little ships' operated round the coasts and in the Mediterranean, where they gave gallant service on the famous 'Alex-Matruh-Tobruk' run. And the graves of South Africans that are scattered over the Middle East, the Balkans, Austria, Germany, France, Italy, Poland, and wherever else British troops fought or British airmen flew, testify to the number of South Africans that were to be found in British units. A South African division assisted in the conquest of Abyssinia and of North Africa, and a brigade was sent to take Madagascar. Most of one division was captured or killed at Tobruk,[1] and after North Africa came Italy where a South African division and many Air Force squadrons operated.

South African industry, too, was geared to the general war effort, making boots and bombs for her allies as well as for her own troops; and agricultural products and manufactured foods were used to supply the hundreds of thousands of Allied troops that steamed round the Cape to the East and to Egypt. The Cape route served its highly important strategic purpose, and there must be many a Briton, or American, or Australian, or New Zealander, or Indian, who recalls the hospitality he received at Cape Town and Durban. Women played an important part, both in the services and by releasing men from industry and the professions to fight. Finally, 45,000 Cape Coloured and 80,000 Africans served wherever South African forces were to be found. They served as transport drivers, stretcher-bearers, hospital orderlies, gunners, batmen, and as sailors in the 'little ships'; and they earned high praise and many medals for devotion to duty, for courage under fire, and for gallantry. Many of them were wounded and taken prisoner, and 2,500 gave their lives for their country.[2]

Smuts represented South Africa at the San Francisco Conference and was one of the few people there who had also been present at Versailles at the end of the First World War. Three years later his party was narrowly defeated by a combination of the Nationalist and Afrikaner parties in the general election of 1948. His defeat, and his death two years later, mark the end of one phase of more than fifty years of South African history and the beginning of another and even more turbulent period.

The coming to power of a coalition of the Nationalist and Afrikaner parties in 1948, strengthened by their merging under the title of

[1] The story of the fall of Tobruk has been told in *Crisis in the Desert*, one volume of the official war history of the Union.

[2] It is an interesting commentary on South African history to note that when, in 1955, the Grey College at Bloemfontein celebrated the centenary of its foundation by Sir George Grey—a British governor when Bloemfontein was the capital of the Orange Free State Republic—a memorial was unveiled to past pupils who had lost their lives in three wars—the Boer War, when they fought against Britain, and two world wars, when they fought with Britain against Germany.

Nationalist Party[1] in 1951, meant that for the first time since Union a purely Afrikaans-speaking party was in power. Afrikaners had had independent republics for fifty years before the end of the Boer War; and it took another fifty years before they regained at the polling-booth what the Boers had lost on the battlefield. They had lost two economically and politically weak republics and they had gained the Union of South Africa. This was a notable achievement of political power by the Nationalists, marred only by the knowledge that their party did not yet have the support of the majority of voters and that it was the vagaries of the electoral system that had given them victory; moreover, they knew that about one-quarter of Afrikaans-speaking South Africans had voted against their party. Nevertheless, Afrikaner nationalism was in effective political control of government; and two subsequent elections, in 1953 and 1958, were to increase their parliamentary majority.

The purpose of this book is not to present a history of South Africa but to examine present-day conditions and policies and to introduce only such historical background as seems necessary for that purpose. The period from 1948 to 1959 is full of incident and some of the stirring events are described in other chapters where they more rightly belong. This historical introduction may well be concluded by noting that the period is characterized, in the first place, by the determined efforts of Afrikaner nationalism to consolidate its power and the struggle of its opponents to try to bring about a broader South Africanism; and, in the second place, by the efforts of the majority of white South Africans to retain political control of South Africa and the growth of an extra-parliamentary non-white opposition (supported by a minority of whites) determined to have some share in political and economic power. Other chapters will show that most of what has happened in South Africa since 1948 fits into that pattern.

[1] The Afrikaans title is *Die Nasionale Party* and the translation habitually used by that party is 'The National Party'. This is inaccurate. When the word 'National' is used in conjunction with words such as 'Government' or 'Party' the connotation in English usage is that the party or government represents all population or political groups in the country. This is patently not the case with *Die Nasionale Party* and it is misleading to call it The National Party.

2

The People

THE EXPRESSION 'A HOUSE DIVIDED AGAINST ITSELF' IS MORE APPLICABLE to the Union of South Africa than it is to any other country. Disraeli's 'two nations' become, in South Africa, at least five; and these are rent by subdivision and internal dissension. The history of South Africa is the story of strife between the various groups composing the political union. There is no single instance where the population of South Africa has been united during a great crisis. Until 1910, when Union was established, the story is one of war between tribe and tribe, between black and white, and between English and Afrikaner. Political union brought the warring tribes (white and black) under one central government; but in all international crises since 1910 the country has been sorely divided against itself. There have, it is true, been notable examples of co-operation between groups or individuals of the different 'nations'; but there has been no national front, no co-operation on a national scale. Economically, everything that has been achieved in agriculture, in mining, in transport, and in industry is the result of European skill, capital, and organization combined with non-European labour. The different 'nations' have combined to that extent, but, politically and socially, the divisions remain as obstacles to the real union which is hopefully implied in the title of the Union of South Africa.

In a final chapter, the whole question of what prospects there may be for a resolution of these differences and for the development of a genuine union will be discussed. It is a question of importance to Africa and to the world, no less than to South Africa. But before we can consider the question we must know more of the different nations that constitute the population of South Africa. We must consider the separate factors that make up the final equation.

A variety of different headings may be used to describe the people of a country such as Britain. They may be described under 'rural' and 'urban', or under 'industrial' and 'agricultural', or according to geographical regions. Though the word is no longer fashionable, the population could be divided into upper, middle, and lower 'classes'. When you have described the people of Britain under these or any other convenient subheadings you have not denied the essential unity of the people as British. What social differences and distinctions there may be in the way of language, of customs, of amusements are picturesque survivals rather than essential differences.

26

In South Africa the situation is different. You may indeed describe the population according to regions, or classes, or occupations; but it would be unrealistic not to subdivide these divisions into European, African, Coloured, and Asian. In the sense that all who live in Durban enjoy the same climate, are subject to the same physical wants, and would show similar physical and psychological reactions to aerial bombing or to the plague—in that sense you may speak of the 'people of Durban'. But to regard this as an expression of common citizenship is misleading. There is, of course, the argument that one should not stress differences, but should rather seek the essential similarities of all human beings. The differences are superficial, unreal. It is the similarities that matter. Unfortunately, this argument would lead to a description of things as they should be, not as they in fact are.

THE AFRICAN

You meet the African everywhere in South Africa. There is no farm or factory or town where he is not to be found. Where building and road-making are in progress; where European-owned shops and offices are being run; where ships are being loaded and unloaded, there the African will be. The traveller by train will see Africans at every station and siding; the traveller by road will, from time to time, pass an African who is walking hundreds of miles to a town or city. And when the traveller stays at an hotel for the night he will probably find Africans waiting on him at table and waking him with an early-morning cup of tea.

The Africans of South Africa form part of a group of about 70,000,000 who live in the southern half of Africa and speak one of about 200 related Bantu languages or dialects. They and the inhabitants of the High Commission Territories of Basutoland, Swaziland, and Bechuanaland, are called the southern Bantu, as distinct from the western group who live in French Equatorial Africa, the Cameroons, Belgian Congo, and Angola, and from the eastern group who inhabit the regions round the great lakes of the Rift Valley.

It is as impossible to generalize fruitfully about 'the African' as it is to generalize about the 'mysterious East' or about 'the Englishman' or about the inhabitants of the United States of America. Africans are individuals, each with his or her own personality, likes and dislikes, moods and hopes and fears. In general they are, possibly, more conservative than Europeans, because they are more closely bound by convention and tribal tradition; but any theory or policy that acts on the false assumption that the Africans are a mass rather than a group of individuals would be wrong. As individuals they react to external circumstances, to social life, and to other individuals in the same way as do the rest of mankind.

With this warning in mind, it is, nevertheless, convenient to describe a few general characteristics of the African. Africans have dark skins, varying from black to light brown; it is only for convenience, and not as an accurate description that they are called 'black' and that Europeans are called 'white'. Although not Negroes, they have Negroid features, such as thick lips, flat noses, and short, black, curly, 'peppercorn' hair. This latter characteristic is general, while other features vary considerably from tribe to tribe and from person to person, depending partly on the amount of Hamitic blood that is present.

Africans who live in or near European towns wear European clothes, in all stages of respectability or raggedness. In African Reserves or in European villages near Reserves they still frequently, though not by any means invariably, wear a blanket as a general cloak over a pair of trousers or a short skirt. There is a prevalent idea among Europeans that Africans in blankets are more graceful and dignified than when in European dress. African women, certainly, are picturesque in their brightly coloured blankets, their beads, and their gay doek (scarf) wound round the head. But it may be doubted whether this European belief has any stronger foundation than a general dislike of 'sophistication' among Africans. In any case, European dress is gaining ground rapidly. The blanket is itself a European product and Africans are merely discarding one European product for another.

There are in the Union some hundreds of African tribes divided into four main language groups. The Xhosa, Zulu, and Swazi belong to the Nguni group; the northern and southern Sotho, the Tswana-speaking tribes of Bechuanaland, and various tribes of the western Transvaal belong to the Sotho group; the Venda and Tsonga are two smaller separate groups. About half a million Africans have not yet been officially classified.

Although the Xhosa and the Zulu have different languages, these are, without serious difficulty, mutually understandable; but it would require considerable conscious study and practice for members of one language group to understand those of another. When educated Africans from different parts of the country meet in conference they most often speak English; and they use English in their professional or political contacts with Europeans. At the domestic service and master-servant level the medium would be English or Afrikaans, depending on the home language of the employer; sometimes, as is the case on many farms, it may be a Bantu language, and sometimes it is a hybrid called 'kitchen kaffir'. A more or less regularized version of this, called 'Fanakolo', is used as the lingua franca on the gold-mines, where many languages from southern (not only South) Africa are represented. It serves a useful purpose, but is deplored by educated Africans.

There are parts where the use of a Bantu language by Europeans is fairly common. Traders in the Transkei and in Zululand, and people who grow up on farms and villages bordering Basutoland or a Reserve, learn the language of their vicinity through early contact with African servants. In Natal particularly there seems to be a tradition that farmers learn to speak Zulu. During the last war it was said that when the Natal Carbineers really became excited they burst into Zulu; and when their signallers were in touch with the enemy they used it as a code.

Prior to European penetration into southern Africa no Bantu language had a written alphabet. That there is today a growing literature in all the major languages is primarily due to the missionaries who reduced the languages to writing. It is due also to African and European scholars and authors, chiefly at the universities, who have produced grammars and dictionaries and have encouraged the publication of translated and of original work. Since the passing of the Bantu Education Act of 1953 the Department of Bantu Education has laid great stress on the use of the mother tongue in African schools and has set about creating Bantu terminologies in all subjects.

A large proportion of African children do not go to school and grow up illiterate unless they later acquire literacy in towns where their friends or interested Europeans organize adult literacy classes. It is difficult to guess at the extent of illiteracy or to estimate how many Africans are ignorant of both official languages of the Union. It was officially estimated that, in 1957, some 56 per cent of African children of school-going age were at school; and in 1959 Dr. Eiselen, Secretary for Bantu Administration and Development, said that the number of literate Africans had risen to 35 per cent of the African population.[1]

Literacy, whether in a Bantu or a European language, is about twice as high in urban as it is in rural areas. With the great mobility of African labour it is probable that about half the African adult population is able to understand either English or Afrikaans, or both, at a very elementary level. It is evident that the use of Afrikaans is increasing but there are strong economic reasons for learning English and Afrikaans. The Bantu languages are those of a tribal peasant culture, flexible and rich in homely idiom and vocabulary. But if Africans are to learn the industrial and scientific and commercial arts

[1] See article by Dr. Eiselen in *Optima*, March 1959.

of the European it seems probable that they will, for some considerable time to come, do so through the medium of English or Afrikaans.

The fact that two-thirds of the population of the Union have a Bantu language as their mother tongue is one of those things that make it unreal, for the present at any rate, to speak about 'the people of the Union' in the way one would about a country with a homogeneous population. It is also one of the things that makes administration difficult and complicates social and industrial life. Political and administrative power rests with the European group; it is the Europeans who are the employers and control the economy. Many European officials who have to deal almost exclusively with Africans are proficient in a Bantu language and in some government departments officials are paid a bonus if they are able to speak a Bantu language; but it would be a counsel of perfection to suggest that, since Europeans rule Africans, they should know the language of those they aspire to govern. That would be reasonable in an African colony where the only Europeans are officials and missionaries, who might well be required to know the language of the people. In South Africa, however, apart from a comparatively small body of officials, contact between Europeans and Africans is limited and intermittent, and there is neither the moral nor the economic urge to acquire a Bantu language. This state of affairs has many disadvantages and produces the kind of misunderstanding, hardship, and injustice that results from ignorance on both sides. Nor is it merely a matter of linguistics. Closely associated with speech are gestures, customs, and manners. A turn of speech demanded by good manners in one language may be akin to an insult in another. A courteous gesture by a European may well offend against an African custom. These things, however superficial they may be, illustrate the reality of the differences between Africans and the rest of the population of the Union.

Native Reserves

The Bureau of Statistics estimated that the total population of the Union on 30 June 1959 was 14,673,000, of whom 9,751,000 were Africans, grouped, as we have seen, not in one but in many tribes and with no one common Bantu language. According to the Native Affairs Department Report of 1957, about 3,651,000 Africans were living in tribal Reserves—that is, in land set aside by parliament where Africans only may occupy or own land. The situation of these Reserves is shown on the end-leaf map and it should be realized that they are, for the most part, the shrunken remnant of land once owned by the tribes but conquered by the white man during the nineteenth-century wars. The rest of the African population is to be found in the towns and on European-owned farms outside the Reserves, the vast majority of them in the employ of Europeans.

It would be a mistake, however, to regard the population of the Reserves and the African population outside the Reserves as in any way static. There may be Africans who have never left their Reserves, and there are many Africans living in towns who have never seen a Reserve. But one of the striking characteristics of the present-day African is that he is a great traveller. There is a constant coming and going between the Reserves and the European areas, and this is in spite of legal restrictions on freedom of movement. Among many tribes a young man is not regarded as properly grown up unless he has had a spell at the mines or in a European town, preferably in a large city. Nor is this merely a matter of social convention or of curiosity to 'see the world'. The economy of the Reserves is largely a simple agricultural subsistence economy that cannot supply the cash needs of today, so that the African must take work in European areas in order to earn money. On the other hand, the European cannot run his economy without African labour, and a constant flow takes place between the Reserves and the European areas.

There is a tendency for the reader unacquainted with South African conditions to think of the Reserves as places where Africans have plenty of room and can live the simple life, at their own unhurried pace, tilling the soil and watching their cattle grow fat; places where African culture and tradition can develop uncontaminated by European influences; and, above all, places to which any African can retire after having worked in European areas, a haven of rest for the aged and weary. The reality is different.

The Reserves are, in part, those areas in which African tribes were living when they were originally conquered by the Europeans. After each conquest boundaries were fixed by the conqueror, who thenceforth occupied some of the land previously owned by the tribe. In this way the amount of land available for tribal use shrank after each of the innumerable wars between European settlers and African tribes. But peace and European medicine tended to increase the African population, so that pressure on land became ever greater. It was a process by no means confined to South Africa. It has taken place wherever in Africa there was any considerable European settlement. What chiefly distinguishes South Africa from the Rhodesias and East Africa is that, in the Union, there are many more Europeans in proportion to the total population than there are elsewhere. As European populations increase in the other territories the same problem of overcrowded Reserves will arise.

By the time that Union was established it had long been traditional among Europeans in South Africa to regard territorial segregation of European and African as a 'natural' policy. That is to say, it was generally accepted that there should be areas where Africans might own land, individually or tribally, and other areas where they might live and work, but might not own land. In 1913 parliament regularized this territorial segregation by the Land Act which demarcated the then existing tribal lands and made provision for the purchase by government of additional land. The difficulty was to find the additional land. European public opinion was opposed to the purchase of more land for Africans, and various commissions attempted in vain to demarcate further areas. Eventually in 1936, parliament passed the Native Trust and Land Act which provided for the purchase by the Native Trust Fund of a maximum of 7,250,000 morgen[1] of land additional, and if possible adjacent, to the then existing Reserves. Since then slightly more than 4,750,000 morgen have been purchased under the Act, bringing the total area of the Reserves up to just over 17,500,000 morgen, or about 12·9 per cent of the area of the Union. When the full amount of land has been bought the Reserves will occupy about 65,000 square miles, 13·7 per cent of the total area of the Union. The remaining 86·3 per cent is for European occupation only.

The overwhelming majority of Africans in the Reserves depend on some form of agriculture for a living. As a living it is primitive and poor. About 94 per cent live on communally held land, the remaining 6 per cent on individual holdings, chiefly in the Transkei and the Ciskei. The chief usually allocates land for cultivation, and grazing-land is common. There is little fencing; the soil is scratched rather than ploughed; only poor seed can be afforded, and there is an almost complete absence of proper methods of preparing the soil.

There are other factors that account for the low productivity of the Reserves. A very considerable one is that at any one time as many as 50-60 per cent of adult males may be absent, working in European areas. In addition, overstocking is ruining the land and is extremely difficult to combat. Africans are traditionally a cattle people who regard quantity as more important than quality, and in pre-European days there was plenty of land for the cattle population. Africans have always regarded cattle in a socio-religious light: they are the visible signs of tribal and individual wealth and importance; they are slaughtered for ceremonial purposes, at deaths or weddings, or for fertility rites. Most important of all, they are used as *lobolo*—that is, as the customary gift to the bride's parents in the African marriage dowry system. There is thus a strong inclination to increase the cattle population and to resist all well-meant attempts by government to

[1] The morgen is a South African measure of area and is equal to 2⅛ acres.

improve strains. The result is overstocking, which has reduced some parts of the Reserves to semi-desert conditions.

Here and there in the Reserves there are small signs that government attempts to improve standards of agriculture are bearing fruit. Agricultural schools operate, and trained demonstrators fight an uphill battle against conservatism and superstition. Too often the agricultural school is an oasis of sound agricultural practice waging a desperate war against the encroaching desert of bad agriculture and overstocking. On the whole, then, the Reserves are poverty-stricken areas, incapable of standing up to the periodic droughts of South Africa, and unable to support the existing population. They are, in fact, vast rural slums whose chief export is their manpower, which goes to the mines and factories and farms to earn enough money to pay taxes and to support the families in the Reserves. This is ironic, since it has long been the custom in South Africa to regard low wages for Africans as justified on the grounds that the African has one foot in the Reserves and that his labour in European areas is really only a part-time occupation. That was, probably, the case in the late nineteenth century. It is not the case today.

In the Reserves, tribal loyalty is still strong. A man prides himself on being a Zulu, or a Fingo, or a Xhosa, and tends to look down on other tribes. Tribal fights still take place in the Reserves and on the mines, where tribes are usually separately housed. With tribal loyalty go the conceptions of chieftainship and tribal customs, such as initiation ceremonies and *lobolo*. These retain a powerful hold over African imagination even when contact with the disruptive forces of Western civilization has been closest; but there is little doubt that such contact has weakened tribalism generally and that loyalty to chiefs and observance of tribal customs are gradually giving way to loyalties and customs with a stronger survival value.

This decay of tribalism is regretted by many Europeans and Africans, and there are Europeans who hold that every effort should be made to restore tribalism and tribal life. Seeing the devastating effects on the fabric of African social life of the clash between European and African cultures, they regard a return to tribalism as the only safe cure. The normal discipline and sanctions of tribal life tend to disappear under the impact of European civilization; and for a great many Africans nothing has yet adequately taken the place of those sanctions. It is doubtful, however, whether a return to an archaic tribalism will cure this evil, for tribalism cannot successfully survive contact with Western civilization and industrialization. And if tribalism is doomed, much thought must be given to its replacement by the moral and ethical concepts of the West rather than to the vain attempt to revive it.

The idea of setting aside specific areas for European and for African occupation is common in southern Africa, and is found in the Rhodesias, in East Africa, in Swaziland, and in Bechuanaland, as well as in South Africa. It is a policy that is employed both nationally and locally; that is, there are national Reserves, and, in urban areas, there are normally African and European townships side by side. The historical reasons for national Reserves are probably different from those to which separate urban townships owe their existence. Social habits, different standards of living, and the general disinclination of both races to mix socially are enough to explain the separate townships, though they do not explain the vast differences in social amenities that exist in those townships.

National Reserves for African tribes are, historically, the product of administrative convenience and the liberalism usually associated with the missionaries. For many years after the first clashes between European settlers and African tribes the policy of the Europeans was to establish a clear boundary between their country and that of the tribe involved. Each war was succeeded by a boundary settlement. Towards the middle of the nineteenth century, however, European policy changed to one of annexation. It is true to say that, with a few minor exceptions, this change was not dictated by a desire to annex land for European occupation. The new policy was instituted in despair of being able to maintain the peace by any other means. Sir Harry Smith, Governor of the Cape, was the originator of this policy in South Africa. The British Colonial Office, strongly under the influence of missionary opinion, would not agree to annexation purely for European occupation. Hence, though European magistrates and police were sent into the annexed territories to rule, the land itself was reserved for African occupation. Traders and missionaries were allowed in and the European administration confined itself to maintaining the peace and to giving a general support to the missionaries in their civilizing efforts.

Had South Africa remained an agricultural community, largely and sparsely inhabited by African and European cattle farmers, this policy of reserves for black and white might have provided a reasonable solution to many interracial problems. The earliest missionaries, most notably Dr. Philip in the 1830's, saw clearly that the Africans could not compete against the superior weapons and organization of Western civilization. They advocated territorial segregation in the interests of the African. It was a valid policy at the time and in the circumstances, a policy dictated by humanitarian beliefs. So far from believing that the Africans and the Europeans were equal, the missionaries believed that the African was the weaker and had to be protected. In the sight of God, they were equal, but in all other respects Africans required protection.

When the times and the circumstances changed—that is, when the discovery of diamonds and gold shattered the subsistence economy of South Africa by setting her firmly on the path of industrialization— the policy of territorial segregation began to lose much of its original validity. So far from wanting Africans to stay in their Reserves, European governments in South Africa urged them to come into the European areas to work. In the Cape Colony Cecil Rhodes introduced a money tax on Africans in the Reserves to force them to seek cash wages.

When the gold-mines needed African labour they set up agencies in all African areas to recruit it. Two world wars hastened the industrial revolution. The growth of secondary industries increased the demand for labour and for agricultural produce; and the sub-division of the nineteenth-century large farms increased the demand for agricultural labour. The result is that, today, agriculture, mines, and industries are all clamouring for African labour. Elaborate machinery exists for recruiting that labour, and farmers complain that their labour is 'stolen' either by the more attractive terms offered by industry or by other farmers, from distant districts, who come by lorry at night to entice their African workers away. With all these demands for African labour, more than half the African population no longer have any but the most tenuous connexion with Reserves. They have become permanently alienated from their old tribal lands, and if they did want to return to their original Reserve there would be no room for them in those agriculturally overcrowded slums.

While, therefore, the original intention behind the establishment of the Reserves was sound enough, much of the reason for their existence had disappeared. The conditions that made the system workable have altered. Those conditions are: a comparatively small agricultural population, plenty of grazing-land, and a subsistence economy. Population of man and beast has increased while grazing-land has not increased proportionately; and industrialization and a money economy have supervened.

The conception of Native Reserves has a tenacious hold on South African thinking, both European and African. There is a persistent cry from the Africans for more land to be added to the Reserves. Europeans of all political parties are practically unanimous in accepting the Reserves as part of the natural order of things. For decades there has been talk of 'rehabilitating the Reserves'. To restore the produc-tivity of the Reserves and to maintain a reasonable level of agriculture would require an enormous expenditure. The Tomlinson Commission[1] reported in 1954 that land in the Reserves was deteriorating at an alarming rate and that it would cost £35,000,000 to stabilize the Reserves, that is, to prevent further deterioration; after stabilization would come rehabilitation. The Commission added that large areas would become irredeemable if not stabilized within ten years. While governments, past and present, have spent money on soil conservation in the Reserves, nothing like the amounts required have been available, and by 1957 only about one-seventh of the land in the Reserves had been stabilized.

It is against this background that policies affecting the Reserves must be examined. The Nationalist Party, constituting the present government, regards the Reserves as the 'national home' of the African within which he can develop self-government and may occupy any position or practise any profession of which he is capable; outside the Reserves Africans will be temporary workers, migrants, and will have no political rights. Such, in broad outline, is the policy of the Nationalist Party, and the most important question in South Africa is whether such a policy can succeed.

The Tomlinson Commission Report may be regarded as the blue-print of this policy. After a thorough investigation the Commission made recommendations which, if implemented, would by the end of the twentieth century enable the Reserves to carry a population of 14,000,000 Africans out of a total estimated population of 21,000,000. The Commission drew a rough plan showing seven proposed African territories, and it is important to realize that this plan included the High Commission Territories which are at present administered by the United Kingdom. The recommendations aimed at producing economically viable areas in which agriculture and industry would be properly integrated. The Report postulated extensive soil-conservation schemes, the establishment of industries within the Reserves, and the expenditure over a period of ten years of more than £100,000,000. Finally, the Commission maintained that a modern industrial economy was not compatible with tribalism and rule by chiefs, that a revision of land tenure to provide for private ownership of land was essential, and that 'white' capital and enterprise were necessary for the fulfilment of the proposals.

The Tomlinson Report created an immense stir in South Africa. Statements were issued, pamphlets were printed, and conferences

[1] The full name of this important commission is the Commission for the Socio-Economic Development of the Bantu Areas within the Union of South Africa, under the chairmanship of Professor F. R. Tomlinson. The Commission was appointed in 1951 and reported in 1954. The full report is voluminous and a summary only was published.

were summoned. The largest conference, representing practically every aspect of Afrikaner thought, was enthusiastically in favour of the implementation of the Report. Here, it was felt, was the answer to those who had maintained that apartheid was purely negative and designed to prevent the African from progressing. Here was a positive plan, recommended by experts who favoured apartheid. True, it would cost a good deal of money, but the white population must be called upon to make the necessary sacrifices so that a just settlement of the vexed racial problem could be achieved.

There were other voices. Industrialists and farmers were fearful of their labour supply and their markets. Might not industries inside the Reserves, where labour was cheap, prove unbeatable competitors? Economists pointed out that, as a glance at the end-leaf map will show, the Reserves are fragmented, that their water supply is inadequate, their equipment of mechanical transport meagre, and their distance from the required raw materials for industry, considerable. In fact, all they have is a labour supply, and to make good the deficiencies would require much more than the £100,000,000 suggested, capital which could in any case be more fruitfully employed elsewhere.

The greatest blow to the enthusiasm generated by the Tomlinson recommendations came from an unexpected source. Dr. H. F. Verwoerd, then Minister of Native Affairs, issued a White Paper which revealed considerable disagreement with the main postulates of the Report. The amount of money the taxpayer would be called upon to supply, he said, had been exaggerated and it was possible to carry out all the recommendations on about one-quarter of that amount. Moreover, 'white' capital would not be allowed inside the Reserves but only on the peripheries, and the industries set up there would draw their labour from within the Reserves. Further, though the Commission might regard tribalism as incompatible with a modern economy, it was the government's firm intention to revive and strengthen tribalism, to bolster the power of the chiefs, and not to allow private ownership of land in the Reserves. Finally, in order to consolidate the Reserves, the Commission recommended the purchase of land additional to the 7¼ million morgen still to be bought under the 1936 Act; but the White Paper rejected this recommendation.

The White Paper knocked away the props that had supported the Tomlinson recommendations, though this fact was either unnoticed or ignored by many of those who wished to continue regarding the Reserves as a national home for Africans. At the beginning of 1959 Dr. Verwoerd, by then Prime Minister, made an important speech in parliament which gave fresh impetus to the policy of the Nationalist

Party. In this speech, which the Nationalist Press acclaimed as a 'new vision' of positive apartheid, the Prime Minister envisaged eight separate Bantu states, which he compared to colonies, and thought that they would progressively be given self-government, even leading to ultimate independence, with the possibility of an eventual commonwealth of white and black states. To this end his government proposed to press on with the policy of creating Bantu authorities that could assume increasing powers, of buying land to the limit of the 1936 Act, and of encouraging African enterprise. In this speech, as in the White Paper, the Prime Minister failed to come to grips with economic realities, and he and his new Minister of Bantu Administration and Development, Mr. M. D. de Wet Nel, have since then stressed the importance of reviving that tribalism which the Tomlinson Report held to be incompatible with a modern economy.

The practical administration of the Reserves will be described in chapter 5. Meanwhile it may be noted that whatever the theories may be, the fact is that the Reserves no longer are what they were originally intended to be. They have become, in actual practice, reservoirs of labour for the rest of the Union. Their existence enables people to argue that 'the Natives have their own lands where they can develop at their own pace', and to regard it as reasonable that, in European areas, they need have no political representation or civil rights. For years the existence of the Reserves has made it possible for governments and local authorities to think of urban housing for Africans as something temporary in which it would be unwise to invest too much capital or which is fully provided for by the creation of bachelor barracks. Finally, the existence of the Reserves has enabled governments to throw most of the financial burden of developing a backward area on the Africans themselves. But African poverty is such that African taxation cannot keep pace with deterioration in the Reserves.

Nor can the old argument that the Reserves afford a refuge for the African and a protection against competition with the better-equipped European hold water against the economic facts. Africans are an integral part of South Africa. Whether they live in a Reserve or in a European area their livelihood depends on the economy of South Africa, not on the economy of the Reserves. The economy of the Reserves, in short, cannot be isolated, as the conception of tribal lands cannot be reconciled with a modern industrial economy; and tribalism received its death-blow with industrialization. If the Reserves were to perform their earlier function of cushioning the impact of Western civilization on a primitive subsistence economy, there would be some excuse for them. As it is, they fail to protect the African, they ensure

3

that large areas of potentially valuable land shall be badly farmed, and they act as a will-'o-the-wisp to all shades of political thinking. On the other hand, the African has proved to be a good industrial worker, while he has not, except under European management, proved to be anything but an indifferent farmer. So far from needing protection, therefore, his value to his country and to himself is far greater as an industrial worker than it is as a so-called independent agriculturist.

A progressive and rationally conducted abolition of Reserves—a process of de-reservation—would do much to improve the economy of the country; it would clear the political air of much cloudy thinking; and it would benefit the African. Such a process of national slum clearance would cost a great deal of money; but it would be money better spent than that spent on purchasing more land to be wastefully farmed. A policy of this kind would, of course, have to be applied consciously and slowly, with safeguards against exploitation and against land speculation; it would have to include a national housing policy; it would have to overcome, with proper safeguards, the opposition of European trade unions and of Africans themselves; and it would have to include the gradual extension of political and civil rights to Africans.

To state these conditions may seem to condemn the suggestion outright as unrealistic and impracticable. Nevertheless, the conclusion from the facts seems inescapable that some such policy will prove to be the only real alternative to racial strife that will reduce the country to the state where neither white nor black will be able to maintain a reasonable standard of living.

Urban Areas

Between 1911 and 1957 the African population in European urban areas increased from 500,000 to more than 2,622,000, that is about 27 per cent of the total African population. A feature of this change is that the urban female population has increased much more rapidly than the male. In 1911 African females formed 19·2 per cent of the total African urban population; in 1950 they formed about 36 per cent.[1] This is probably a measure of the increasing stabilization of the African urban population. In 1911 African labour in the towns was predominantly migrant and temporary; today it is, increasingly, becoming a permanent feature of urban life.

The influx from rural to urban areas is, of course, not a phenomenon confined either to Africans or to South Africa. It is one of the major social characteristics of industrialization and of the twentieth century. In 1911 a minority of Europeans in South Africa lived in towns;

[1] See *Handbook on Race Relations in South Africa*, p. 240.

today a majority are urban dwellers. Since 1921 there has been a
steady flow of all races in South Africa from the country to the towns.
Orlando, an African township near to Johannesburg, did not exist in
1921. By 1936 it had a population of 10,000, and in 1946 this had
increased to 58,000.[1]

Urban population in South Africa is concentrated in the large
industrial, commercial, and mining centres. Of 834 towns and villages
officially listed, only 127 have populations of more than 5,000 of all
races, and only 59 have populations exceeding 10,000. According to
the latest official figures the total urban population is 5,397,000, and
of these 2,717,000 (or more than half) are concentrated in the major
centres of Cape Town, Durban, and the Witwatersrand. The
Witwatersrand alone has 1,665,000, or nearly one-third of the total
urban population, and included in the Witwatersrand figure are
949,000 Africans, or more than 40 per cent of the total urban African
population. It is in these towns that the increase of African population
has been the most startling and has caused the greatest concern to local
authorities and to the central government.

Africans living in or near European towns are employed in a variety
of ways. Close on 480,000 are miners; 360,000 are in manufacturing
industries; 390,000 (male and female) are in personal service; 110,000
in transport and communications; 20,000 in the public service; and
smaller numbers in the professions, and in the sport and entertainment
industries.

The rapid growth of the African urban population has created the
same kind of housing and administrative problems that faced the
industrial towns of Britain in the nineteenth and twentieth centuries.
And the result of the inability of local authorities to provide a solution
for the housing problems has been, as in Britain, the growth of slums.
In pre-industrial days in South Africa there were always a small
number of Africans in urban areas, apart from the gold-mines,
employed chiefly as domestic servants. When they were not provided
with quarters by their employers they constructed small houses for
themselves in locations near to the towns. This residential segregation
is part of the traditional policy in South Africa; and, when the first
influx into towns began, the principle was embodied in legislation by
parliament, which tried to control the situation.

The most important of these Acts of Parliament is the Natives
(Urban Areas) Act of 1923 as amended from time to time and consolidated in 1945. It empowers local authorities to establish locations and
to make regulations governing them and controlling the entry into
and residence in such locations; it places the responsibility for housing

[1] *Population Census*, 1946, Vol. I, U.G.51/1949.

on local authorities; and it compels local authorities to appoint managers of locations, to set up Native advisory boards, and to keep a separate Native revenue account.

By 1939 the problem of urban housing for Africans had reached critical dimensions. About half the urban population lived in controlled locations while some of the other half found accommodation with their domestic employers or in mining or industrial compounds. The remainder squatted, illegally, on or near municipal land where they erected 'pondokkies' of packing-cases, sheets of galvanized iron, petrol-tins, sacking, and any other material they could find. Neither these shanty towns nor many of the controlled locations had any of the amenities of civilized living, such as water-borne sewage, electric light, or running water laid on to the houses. With few exceptions the houses themselves were poorly constructed, lacked proper ventilation and heating, and were always hopelessly overcrowded.

During the 1939-45 war urbanization of all races increased rapidly and building practically ceased. Africans flocking to the towns first of all overcrowded the already occupied accommodation and then squatted on vacant land where shanty towns sprang up overnight. Municipal or government efforts to prevent this, or to exercise some form of control, merely exacerbated the feelings of the Africans who considered that the Europeans did nothing to assist them to establish homes from which they could go to work—for the Europeans— and did everything to harry and discourage them once they had constructed their pitiful shanties. In many of the established locations, as well as in the shanty towns, social and health facilities were almost entirely lacking; 60 per cent of the children at a conservative estimate were debarred from school because there were no facilities for them. Both parents had to earn, and the total result was the growth of an illiterate, untrained, and lawless class that preyed on Africans and Europeans alike. In the largest cities of the Union administration had virtually broken down in so far as the African population was concerned; to say the least, it had failed to keep pace with the demands made on it.

Though, as will be seen presently, great improvements have been made, some of the conditions just described still exist. In such anti-social conditions African family life, the discipline of tribal traditions, the customary good manners and natural dignity of the African must deteriorate. In their place are a host of municipal regulations restricting the manufacture of kaffir beer, controlling freedom of movement, prohibiting one thing after the other. In the interests of law and order the police must carry out these regulations; and the easiest and safest way to do that is by mass raids, when a body of armed police moves into an area. It is also, to the inhabitants, the most alarming and exasperating way.

An astonishing feature of this situation is that comparatively few Africans become real criminals. It is equally astonishing that Africans are able to maintain certain standards of conduct and behaviour in the midst of such poverty and administrative chaos. It seems improbable that the proverbial African patience and tolerance can much longer stand the strain put on them by such conditions. About 370,000 Africans are convicted each year for contravention of supervision and control regulations, and of recent years there have been an increasing number of sporadic outbursts of violence that take the form of stoning police cars when locations are raided and of the destruction of buses and the burning of schools. Increasingly, too, angry women take part in these demonstrations. The authorities are aware of mounting discontent and in 1959 the government bought a number of Saracens for police use in riots.[1]

It is worth while looking in some detail at the failure of the local authorities of the large urban areas to keep pace with the housing needs of the Africans. The story illustrates very clearly some of the factors that operate in a multiracial society that has become industrialized. Probably the main reason why the problem of urban housing for Africans was allowed to reach the dimensions of a national crisis was the absence of a definite Native policy. Just as, on a national scale, the idea of Reserves continues to exercise a baleful influence on political thinking, so the idea that Africans working in urban areas are migrants fogs economic thinking. Acting on this assumption, municipal authorities were, at first, reluctant to spend money on what they regarded as temporary housing. When, at last, public opinion began to realize that locations were likely to be permanent, housing had already lagged far behind actual needs. In an attempt to meet the situation, the government instituted sub-economic loans, and by 1939 more than £5,000,000 had been borrowed by local authorities for African housing; and a few municipalities, such as Johannesburg, floated additional loans on their own credit. By 1947, however, the situation was out of hand. In that year the Department of Native Affairs estimated that 154,000 houses were needed for urban and peri-urban Africans; but, since few local authorities had any accurate idea of how many Africans were living in their area, this number was a serious under-estimate. Moreover, building costs had risen steeply during the war, and in the post-war years local authorities and central

[1] Harry Bloom's well-known novel, *Episode*, illustrates how inflammable a racial situation can become when large numbers of Africans are congregated in slum-like and overcrowded urban locations and are harried by control regulations.

government haggled about the amount of loss each could be expected
to bear on sub-economic housing. Meanwhile, in spite of preventative
regulations, Africans were still moving into the towns and cities in
large numbers to meet the needs of an expanding industry.

Another reason for the failure to deal with this problem is to be
found in the wage structure in South Africa and in colour-bar habits
and regulations. Africans are, by social custom, by trade union action,
and by law, debarred from entering most skilled occupations. In the
building trade unskilled wages of Africans are about one-sixth of the
European skilled wages. (In the Cape Province the proportion of
unskilled to skilled wages is higher; also, a large proportion of skilled
work is performed by Coloured—as distinct from African—labour.)
Most local authorities used white skilled labour on their housing
schemes. They were not compelled to do so by law but were afraid
of the white trade unions; Europeans have votes, Africans do not.
The resulting costs of African houses were too high to bear an economic
rent for, in effect, houses were (and in some cases still are) built by
skilled workers earning six times as much as the Africans for whom
the houses were intended. No local authority can follow such a policy
for long, and the available money does not go far. The obvious
remedy is to train African building workers, a policy which European
workers have strenuously opposed for fear that the African will work
at a lower wage and undercut the European.

The Nationalist Party came to power in 1948 and inherited the
chaotic conditions described above, and it is greatly to their credit that,
once they had found their feet, they tackled the problems of urban
housing with energy and practical skill. There is a certain irony,
inseparable from South African affairs, in the fact that the government
that has been instrumental in building more permanent houses for
urban Africans than any previous government, was drawn from a
political party whose programme expressed most strongly the prevalent
South African assumptions that urban Africans are migrants and that
Africans should not be allowed to compete with white skilled labour.
Faced with the horrible reality of shanty towns, squatters' camps, and
overcrowded locations, the government jettisoned some of its theories
and, in 1959, the Minister of Bantu Administration and Development
was able to announce that in the previous eight years 500,000 Africans
had been housed in 100,000 family units and that building was
proceeding at a good pace.

Commencing in 1950, the government introduced a series of
legislative and administrative measures to enable it to carry out a more
effective housing policy. Under the so-called site-and-service scheme,
large new African townships were planned; and when water, light,

and sewerage had been laid on, sites were rented to Africans who could either build their own houses or have them built cheaply with borrowed money made available from government sources. Since the new townships were sited at some distance from the white city where most Africans worked, additional and subsidized transport was provided, the subsidy coming from a newly imposed tax on employers of African labour in the large cities. This tax, known as the Native Services Levy, consists of half a crown a month for every African employed in commerce and industry.

The new sites were intelligently planned and made provision for schools, churches, public buildings, a market place, a shopping centre, and playing-fields. In its desire to revive tribalism, the government insisted that the new townships should be ethnically zoned and that Zulu, Xhosa, Sotho, and so on should each live in their own areas. The arguments are that this will facilitate mother-tongue education; that it will give newcomers a more familiar and surer base, much needed in the bewildering city life; that it will enable tribal chiefs to maintain contact with their subjects; and that it will eventually make it possible to apply tribal law in urban areas. There is, of course, some substance in these arguments; but there are strong counter-arguments. If tribalism finds it difficult to accommodate itself to a modern economy in the Reserves, it will find it impossible to do so in the cities; many Africans (and the number is increasing) have become permanent urban dwellers and have lost all effective contact, or desire for contact, with the Reserves; much intertribal marriage takes place in the cities and the offspring of such marriages would find it difficult to say to which tribe they belonged; city life promotes an intertribal or non-tribal society, and to keep such a society apart by artificial zoning is likely to lead to tribal clashes such as occurred in African townships in Johannesburg in 1957 when forty Africans were killed and scores were injured.

In its housing policy the government cut across another cherished South African tradition by training and employing teams of African building workers to erect houses and schools at a cost far below what would have been possible with white workers. It also had to cajole, threaten, and dragoon reluctant local authorities not only to accept their responsibilities but to do so on terms which they disliked. Ministers have frequently complained that opposition to government policy was obstructionism based on party-political rather than on rational grounds. It is true that, with the exception of Pretoria, Bloemfontein, and one or two Reef towns, the big urban centres have city councils in which the majority are opposed to the Nationalist Party. But opposition to government policy was not entirely due to that. There are more solid grounds on which that policy might be considered objectionable. The insistence on ethnic grouping, against the advice and wishes of the city councils, is one. Again, in the desire to separate black and white by the greatest possible distance, the new townships were sited so far from the centres they served that the added costs in time and money were a heavy burden, despite subsidized transport, on workers and industry and commerce. Moreover, where a new township adjoined a main road, the government insisted that a 500-yard strip of so-called green belt should be left vacant, thus adding to the cost of land which the local authority had to buy.

There are two even more serious objections. In the first place, Africans cannot obtain freehold in the new urban locations. It is as if the government, having realistically recognized the *fact* that the urban African population is either permanent or becoming so, decided to pay lip-service to the apartheid *theory* that urban Africans are migrants. It is difficult to understand, except on ideological grounds, why the government missed this golden opportunity of promoting a more stabilized urban community and of gaining the good will of thousands of Africans by granting freehold rights. In doing so, it would only have been making a virtue of necessity.

In the second place, there was everything to be said for the new townships so long as they were intended to meet the genuine needs of shanty town and squatter populations. But in Johannesburg they were also used to accommodate Africans living in areas where they had long-established rights, including freehold, but which were now zoned as white areas under the Group Areas Act. To many people this action seemed uncomfortably like the story of Naboth's vineyard.

Despite the government's notable achievements in the housing of urban Africans, the end of slums and shanty towns is not yet in sight. The Tomlinson Commission estimated that, in 1951, there was a shortage of 167,000 family dwellings and that, during the next ten years, an additional 185,000 would be required. Of this total of some 353,000 houses, possibly 130,000 have been built; and even if the present rate were increased it would take another twenty years to catch up with the backlog. It may therefore safely be assumed that at least half the African urban population in South Africa still lives in slums where the survival of human values is a cause for wonder.

In those urban locations where the devastating effects of housing shortage are not so great, there is growing up a new African society, distinct from tribal life and imperfectly modelled on European social life, but full of an unstable vigour that is neither tribal nor European.[1]

---

[1] Anthony Sampson, in his book *Drum*, gives a lively account of this new urban society about which white South Africans know very little.

All the large Christian communities have branch churches in the locations: and the Africans have churches of their own that are, however vaguely, based on the European models. Cinemas, schools, sports clubs, shops and cafés, burial societies, debating clubs—all these familiar features of European urban life are establishing themselves in the African townships. Even social distinctions based on possessions and occupation are becoming marked in African urban society. Superficially the location may look like a poorer replica of the European town; but there are important differences. With small exceptions, Africans may not own land in European areas, so they can never look forward, as the European does, to complete home ownership. Again, since most local authorities strive to make the locations financially self-sufficient and not a burden on the European rates, social services are either non-existent or poor; frequently they are the result of the efforts of philanthropically minded Europeans. Finally, Africans are subject to a number of restrictive regulations that do not apply to Europeans. For example, an African who wishes to be outside the boundary of the location after a specific time at night must have a permit; the absence of such a permit may lead to summary arrest.

African communities living in urban areas have their own social problems. Tribal life is based on kinship; urban life, modelled on Western ideas, is based on the family. Problems of social relationships, of parental authority, of morals, that do not arise in tribal life, have all made their appearance under urban conditions. In tribal life your neighbour is your kinsman; in an urban township he is almost certainly not. The marriage of your children follows, in tribal custom, a well-marked routine; these traditional forms break down under the strains of urban life. The status of men, women, and children is clearly established in tribal life; each has his or her appointed place and tasks. In urban conditions these relationships are modified by external conditions and by terms of employment. Europeans are apt to think simply of 'the African' in the mass, not realizing that these urban townships are living communities of individuals whose social customs have been profoundly shaken by their new environment and who are having to adjust themselves both to European habits and to the new African society in which they find themselves. And their tribal customs have no rules to guide them in this new and uncharted situation.

Africans on European farms

There are about 2,120,000 Africans living on European farms, slightly less than half of them being female. There are African farm labourers in all districts of the Union, but the number in relation to the European farming population varies from province to province. In Natal there are about 16 Africans, of both sexes and all ages, to 1 European; in the Transvaal the ratio is 6 to 1, in the Free State 7 to 1, and in the Cape Province about 2 to 1. In the Cape there are 403,000 Africans on European farms and 312,000 Coloured workers, so that the ratio of Coloured and African to European is about 3·5 to 1. These are averages, and the ratios will vary from district to district, depending on the kind of farming—whether it is sheep-farming, or grain-farming, or more intensive cultivation. There is such a variety of farming in South Africa that we cannot generalize about numbers, conditions of service, housing, or wages, and the following description is intended merely as a reasonably accurate general picture.

There are two main systems, with plenty of local varieties, by which African farm labour is employed. The one is for a regular monthly wage plus payment in kind; the other is a system of labour-tenancy in which there is no cash wage: the African works a fixed number of days in the year in return for the right to live on the farm, to graze cattle, and to cultivate land. On most Cape and Free State farms, and in parts of the Transvaal and Natal, the first system is in vogue. It is notoriously difficult to give anything but a misleading picture of farm-labour wages in cash and in kind. It might be thought that cash wages, at any rate, would be easy enough to discover; but conditions vary so greatly that it is impossible to talk about an average cash wage. When it comes to wages in kind, the difficulties of giving a general picture are wellnigh insuperable. Wages in kind may consist of rations (usually maize, skimmed milk, and occasionally meat), grazing-land, arable land, living-space. It is clear that the value of these, either to the farmer or to the labourer, will depend on climate, fertility of soil, the price of land, the kind of stock grazed, and many other factors of that kind. The Minister of Native Affairs said, in the House of Assembly on 24 July 1958, that the head of a family on a farm earned on an average £6 10s. 0d. a month in cash and kind and that his wife and children might earn another £2 5s. 0d. This statement is really of little value unless it is known what district the Minister had in mind. Of more value are the figures given by Miss Margaret Roberts from the survey she carried out in the Albany and Bathurst districts of the Eastern Province.[1] She found that the average on 71 farms, in cash and kind, for a family of 6·5 persons, was £107 per annum.

While these figures are given to show the order of magnitude of farm wages, the reader is warned again that they have no general validity. All that may safely be said is that African farm wages are lower than urban wages and that, by any standards, they are inadequate.

[1] *Labour in the Farm Economy*, South African Institute of Race Relations, 1959.

This is amply borne out by the lengths to which farmers and the authorities go to make good the perennial shortage of African farm labour that exists in certain districts. One of the steps taken by government is the system of farm gaols by which a group of farmers build a gaol according to official specifications and hand it over to the Department of Prisons. In return, the farmers are entitled to hire prison labour at 9d. a day. The prison authorities claim that the system prevents overcrowding in city gaols and provides healthful outdoor employment for prisoners under strict official supervision.

A system, used chiefly in the Transvaal, that is open to abuse and to severe criticism is that by which farmers may recruit prison labour, as it were, at source. A farmer may interview an African prisoner serving a light sentence and, with the prisoner's consent, employ him at current wages for the remainder of his sentence. Conditions are laid down for the protection of the prisoner but there is no real check on the possible use of force to obtain the prisoner's consent. Moreover, by a departmental extension of the system it had become customary for the police to give an arrested African the choice of being tried or of going to work on a farm. In other words, the mere fact of arrest could be taken as proof of guilt. When it is remembered that there are a large number of statutory offences for which an African may at any time be arrested it will be realized how wide open to abuses such a system is. That it was in fact grossly abused came to light in the first half of 1959, largely through the efforts of a Johannesburg solicitor and the Black Sash.[1] It was then revealed that innocent Africans were being arrested in Johannesburg and, with no trial, sent to work on maize and potato farms in the Bethal and other districts, in some cases under appalling living conditions and subject to masters and African overseers who used physical violence to enforce discipline. It was also found that a few unscrupulous employers used illegal means, including force, to retain men after their sentences had expired. It was only by applying for writs of *habeas corpus* that relatives of those who had been spirited away were able to bring the matter to court and to secure a release. Under the public uproar that followed these disclosures this system of what was virtually kidnapping was stopped.

In parts of the Transvaal and Natal labour-tenancy is still common. The African contracts to work without any cash wage for either 90 or 180 days, either continuously or for two days a week. In exchange, he and his family live on the farm and may graze cattle and plough land, the quantities varying with different conditions, but being, in any case, much more than where a cash wage is paid. The African is, in fact, selling part of his labour for the right to occupy land. This

[1] For an account of this women's organization see pp. 172-3.

system is wasteful of labour since, on the ninety-day basis, a farmer has roughly four times more labour on his farm at any given time than he actually needs. Nevertheless, it is popular, particularly on large farms where a few morgen more or less do not matter to the farmer, because it involves no cash outlay. Since the Reserves are overcrowded, the system provides access to land for the African who wants to farm and thus reduces the pressure on the Reserves. It remains, however, an economic makeshift.

The part played by the system of payment for labour, either in part or in whole, by grazing and cultivation rights, may be gathered from the following facts about African agriculture on European-owned farms in 1955: Africans on such farms owned 1,292,000 head of cattle, 185,000 woolled sheep, 158,000 non-woolled sheep, 601,000 goats, 300,000 horses, mules, and donkeys, 165,000 pigs, and 1,760,000 poultry. They produced 872,000 lb. of wool, 2,906,000 bags (200 lb. weight) of maize, 213,000 bags of kaffircorn, 19,000 bags of wheat, and 870,000 lb. of groundnuts, as well as such vegetables as beans, peas, and potatoes.[1]

Under the supervision of the farmer, the African does all the farm labour. Milking, ploughing, fencing, dam-making, gardening, shearing, reaping are all in the day's work. There is practically no specialization, except that an African with an aptitude for machinery may be given all the jobs involving an elementary mechanical knowledge. Transvaal farmers some years ago asked that Africans should be allowed to obtain a motor-driving licence *even if they are illiterate*—a sign of the increasing mechanization of farming, of the dependence of the European farmer on African labour in spite of mechanization, and a reflection on the state of literacy among Africans.

Social life on a farm is much more like life in the Reserves than in towns, which is one of the reasons why the young men like to seek their fortunes in the towns. African and European children frequently play together on farms and become firm friends until they are separated at the age of 7 or 8, often to find their paths cross years later, in very different circumstances.[2] Tribal customs and superstitions have a stronger hold than in town, and African farm workers try to arrange for their children to undergo initiation ceremonies as part of their 'education'. On many farms no other form of education is available, though farmers are more and more making use of a system whereby, if the farmer builds a school and finds enough pupils, he may apply to the education department for a teacher. In 1957 there

[1] *Agricultural Census Report No. 24*, 1955.
[2] For a dramatic example see an excellent novel, *In A Province*, by L. van der Post.

were 1,405 such schools with a total enrolment of 143,000 children. This system is likely to become more popular, with the farmer if not with his workers, since the announcement by the Minister of Bantu Education, in the Senate on 2 June 1959, that any farmer who 'wishes to make use of the schoolchildren under supervision of the teacher to assist with certain farm activities' can arrange this and that such will be fitted in to the curriculum for farm schools.

Social life for adults on a farm is simple and monotonous. Births, marriages, and deaths, a weekly beer party with labourers from neighbouring farms, and an occasional visit to the market town are the highlights of social life. A few farmers, especially those living near a town, try to provide social amenities to compete with the glittering attractions of urban life.

Housing for African workers on farms is poor. The 'huts', or African quarters, are usually about half a mile from the European farmhouse. As a rule they are constructed of mud and do not keep out wind and weather effectively. The huts form a small hamlet or agricultural village of six or seven families, but the words 'hamlet' and 'village' should not mislead the reader into thinking in terms of English or Continental hamlets; hamlets are close to villages and not isolated, as the 'huts' on a South African farm are; and they have a village pub as a social centre, an institution almost wholly lacking in South Africa generally and certainly never found near the huts.

As a general rule, farmers treat their African workers in a patriarchal and kindly fashion. Physical ill-treatment is an exception; labour is scarce, and farmers who get a bad name are avoided by Africans seeking work. Nor do farmers, as is often suggested, habitually defraud their labourers by breaches of contract. Contracts are verbal, usually for six months or a year, or 'from harvest to harvest'. The unit of employment in the case of married men is the family, and the employer stipulates for the labour of the wife and children when required. This is traditional, and is also a fruitful source of dispute. But, quite apart from the fact that most farmers would scruple to defraud an employee, to do so would soon bring its own punishment in the shape of labour shortage.

On the whole, the lot of the African working on European farms is not positively unhappy. Nevertheless, there are disturbing features about it. Their diet is almost exclusively starchy and lacks protective food values; housing is poor and unhygienic, and it is only because of a favourable climate and plenty of space that there is not more disease. Social amenities and educational facilities are almost entirely lacking; pass laws and cash debts to the farmer tend to tie the worker to the farm. On the other hand, African labour is untrained and inefficient, and there is no incentive to improve efficiency and output, because wage rates make little distinction between efficient and inefficient labour and because cash wages are too low. Farmers have no real knowledge of what their labour is costing them because there is no effective method of accurately evaluating payment in kind; this militates against efficient farm management and the best use of labour.

There are various reasons for the inefficient use of African labour and for the poverty and low wages of the labourer. The belief persists that low-paid labour is necessarily cheap labour. Judged by its productivity, African farm labour is dear; but it is difficult to persuade farmers of this. The European farmer has always regarded the African as an inefficient labourer who cannot be paid a higher wage; he does not trouble to train him effectively, because he has a deep-rooted belief that the African can do what he is told, but will never 'think for himself'. What he requires from the African is absolute obedience to instructions rather than initiative. He pays accordingly, and the African acquires experience in carrying out instructions, but never becomes trained as an agricultural worker. There is little wonder that young Africans between the ages of 20 and 30 who are looking for work prefer not to go to the farms; and that Africans of that age, born and bred on a farm, prefer to go to towns to seek the opportunities they miss on the farms.

Africans on the Mines and in Industries

Every week five or more special trains arrive at Johannesburg with hundreds of Africans going to work on the mines. Some of them have been there before; many of them are coming for the first time from the simple, pastoral life of the Reserves to the rush and noise of a big city, and to a strange, machine-dominated existence in a highly organized industry. The train journey is the first unfamiliar experience; thereafter come the harsh compounds with their brick buildings and concrete bunks, the mass-produced, balanced diet, the shattering experience of being rushed to the bowels of the earth in a cage to work at a dangerous job. It is a big change from the small village community, where a man has a recognized place in the life of the community and where he is surrounded by familiar and kindly objects, to the anonymous vastness of a mining compound where he has a number instead of a name and where he hears the roar of mining machinery instead of the lowing of cattle on the hills.

Up to the end of 1955 the value of minerals mined in South Africa was £4,847,420,000. Of this amount gold accounted for £3,774,372,000, diamonds for £466,227,000, and coal for £294,126,000. The annual output of all minerals in 1958 was

£303,000,000 of which gold accounted for £220,000,000. The annual output of all privately owned industrial factories is over £500,000,000. This production of wealth from the mines and from industries was, and is, made possible by African labour.

On an average there are about 485,000 Africans and about 65,000 Europeans employed in mining.[1] Of the 360,000 Africans employed in gold-mining, only about one-third come from the Union itself: the rest are from territories that lie outside the political control of South Africa—Basutoland, Bechuanaland, Swaziland, the Rhodesias, Nyasaland, and Portuguese East Africa. Of all Africans employed in labour districts in South Africa (that is, chiefly in mining and in industrial undertakings) no fewer than 36 per cent are from outside the Union. South African mining and industrial development is to a great extent dependent on labour from outside her borders.[2]

There are three ways in which an African from the Union can become an employee on a mine. He can go to the mine and find work for himself; or he may go to the recruiting office nearest to his home and sign a contract for a fixed period under the Assisted Voluntary Scheme; or he may be recruited by the Native Recruiting Corporation, an organization that exists to recruit labour for the gold- and coal-mines from the Union, Basutoland, Swaziland, and part of Bechuanaland. Under the first system he can select his mine and need not bind himself for more than a month at a time. Under the second system he has his fare paid to the mine and can still select his mine, but he must contract to stay for a minimum of 180 shifts, or about six months. Under the third scheme his fare is paid and he must contract for a minimum of 180 shifts, but he is drafted to whatever mine needs labour at the moment. About two-thirds of Union Africans are employed under one of the first two schemes. Africans outside the Union and the High Commission Territories go to the nearest agent of the other great recruiting corporation, the Witwatersrand Native Labour Association. Since 1951 the Association has taken to flying its workers from Central African aerodromes to Francistown in Bechuanaland, whence they travel by train to Johannesburg. It now operates a fleet of nine Dakotas and one Skymaster, and carries about 88,000 workers each year.

Recruits are put through a stiff medical test at their place of recruitment and the percentage of failures is high, sometimes as much as 25 per cent, an indication of the extent of undernourishment in some of the Reserves. It is not unknown for the family of a potential

[1] These figures are averages taken from the *Monthly Bulletin of Statistics*, May 1958. Bureau of Census and Statistics.
[2] Not only on labour; nearly half (45 per cent) of the mining dividends are paid to shareholders outside the Union, chiefly in England.

recruit to 'fatten him up', at the expense of their own health, during the months preceding the examination. The recruit has a further medical examination when he reaches the mine and he is usually put on light surface jobs for some weeks before going on to the strenuous underground work. He must be medically examined every three months while employed on the mines. The diet on the mines is balanced and, unless they contract silicosis, Africans are usually in better condition when they leave the mines than when they arrived. Although the usual spell of work is 270 shifts lasting about ten months, Africans from Portuguese East Africa stay for 313 shifts, or about twelve months. There is, thus, a constant coming and going to and from the mines and the main labour force is not permanent. Having worked his shifts, the African miner returns to his home for a rest. Many return to the mines for further spells; if they come back within six months they receive a small monthly bonus.

The average cash wage for an African miner is 2s. 9d. a shift for underground work and 2s. 5d. for surface work; this works out at about £44 a year. In addition he receives free board and lodging, free medical attention, and a number of social services and amenities. The average annual wage of a European miner is £566. There is a deferred pay system, compulsory for Africans from Portuguese territory and voluntary for the rest, by which a portion of the wage is paid only when the African reaches home. Not a great many Union Africans make use of this, though they do remit money to their relatives at home; they prefer to spend their money in Johannesburg where they buy articles to take home—clothes, sewing-machines, musical instruments, blankets, etc. A certain amount of money is spent on visits to shebeens, on gambling, and on prostitution, but it is impossible to say what proportion of their wages this is.

Africans on the gold-mines are housed in barracks, called compounds, which consist of brick buildings round a quadrangle. The sleeping-quarters are fitted with concrete bunks, and each room may hold, in the best conditions, sixteen or twenty bunks, and, in the most crowded conditions, up to forty. There are about sixty such compounds on the Witwatersrand, each housing anything between 1,000 and 5,000 Africans. Under the Native Labour Regulation Act, which governs the employment of Africans in mines, hospital accommodation at the rate of at least one bed to forty Africans must be provided by the employers. Most mines have good hospital and medical facilities; others provide enough to satisfy the minimum standards laid down. On the whole, mine employers are well aware of the importance of the physical health of their workers and the industry spends more than £1,000,000 a year on medical services.

The Ernest Oppenheimer Hospital at Welkom, the centre of the Orange Free State gold-mining development, is the finest in Africa.

Rations include bread, coffee, sugar, mealie meal, beans and other vegetables, and kaffir beer, the daily ration containing 4,500 calories. The meat ration is 3 lb. a week, though the quality is poor. Recreational facilities provided are cinemas, concerts, athletic sports equipment, and facilities for tribal dancing and music. Workers are usually housed according to tribe, and tribal competition occasionally leads to faction fights. Mine managers, however, lay stress on competition between mines, rather than between tribes, and this lessens the chances of tribal friction.

A European 'boss' is in charge of each gang or working party of Africans, who do all the pick and shovel work; a small number are employed in drilling and in drill-sharpening, and in machine and hammer work. Skilled work is reserved for Europeans. The Mines and Works Amendment Act of 1926, the famous 'Colour Bar Act', prohibits Africans from obtaining certificates of competency to do certain skilled jobs, such as blasting and engine-driving, jobs that are done by Africans in Northern Rhodesia and the Belgian Congo without endangering the lives of their fellow-workers. African workers on the gold-mines are quite competent to do these jobs and the mining industry would, naturally, prefer to make a much wider use of African labour. The mine-owners are deterred from doing so by the fear that the European workers would strike, as they did in 1922, if they thought their jobs were threatened. As the law now stands, African miners cannot attain the skills and the pay of skilled jobs, but with the expansion of the gold-mining industry in the past ten years it has been increasingly difficult to find sufficient skilled labour, and it is probable that Africans are in fact performing skilled jobs with the tacit consent of all concerned.

Mining is hard work, and dangerous. The death and accident rate is slowly decreasing and the mine-owners do all they can to reduce it. Nevertheless more than 1,000 Africans lose their lives in gold-mining every year through accidents and disease. The Pneumoconiosis Act of 1956, which consolidated earlier laws, bases compensation on earnings; Europeans or their dependants receive either a pension and a lump sum, or a pension, while Africans or their dependants receive a lump-sum payment only, the maximum being £180. Compensation for accident is governed by the Native Labour Regulation Act, subject to the African's right to claim for compensation under the common law or under the Workmen's Compensation Act; but, once more, compensation is by lump sum, a system that operates unfairly for Africans.

4

The African miner is not considered as a town-dweller, but rather as a tribesman temporarily living in barracks. Accordingly, the Department of Bantu Administration and Development is responsible for maintaining law and order. Bantu commissioners, not magistrates, try petty cases, such as disobedience to orders, infringement of mining regulations, desertion, drunkenness, and assault. As we shall see later, African trade unions are not legally recognized. There are unions in some of the industries, but the mine-owners will not tolerate the suggestion of an African trade union on the mines. It is a criminal offence for an African mine-worker to take part in a strike or to absent himself from work. It would, indeed, be difficult to organize a responsible trade union on the mines because, unlike European miners, African miners are not a cohesive body of workers. Tribal differences, the transitory character of their stay at the mines, lack of a common language, and illiteracy would all militate against effective organization.[1]

The description given above of Africans in mining applies chiefly to the gold- and coal-mines of the Transvaal, where, mainly along the Witwatersrand, the largest mining concentrations are to be found. It may, however, apply, with a number of variations, to African workers in other mines and in industries. About 12,000 Africans are employed in diamond-mining. Over 440,000 are in industrial employment, and about half of them live in industrial compounds; 43 per cent of the industrial compounds are in the Transvaal, 44 per cent in Natal, and most of the rest in the Cape Province. These compounds are smaller and more dispersed than mining compounds; the food and accommodation are, on an average, not as good as on the mines, and there are fewer social amenities. On the other hand, industrial wages for Africans are anything up to 50 per cent higher than mining wages; in many industries these wages are statutory, being fixed by the Wage Board or by an industrial council. While Africans on the gold-mines are, with negligible exceptions, migrants, those in industry are tending to become permanent. On a few mining compounds there are married quarters for some of the surface workers; but mining policy is to employ migrant labour. On the new Free State mines, at Odendaalsrus and elsewhere, the quarters are a great improvement on the Rand compounds and the mine-owners were anxious to extend considerably the provision of married quarters; but government policy made this impossible.

The effects of mineral development on the economy of southern Africa—South Africa and all her neighbours—has been immense.

[1] The success of African trade unions on the copper-mines of Northern Rhodesia suggests that if the mine-owners would allow them to organize, African gold-miners would overcome these difficulties.

Mining has resulted in railway development, in the expansion of agriculture, and in the establishment of primary and secondary industries. South Africa is not a wealthy country. Contrary to popular opinion she is poor; and without mineral development she would have been immeasurably poorer. While the economic effects of this development have been great, the social effects on all races have been equally great. On the African, the effect has been shattering. His tribal economy has long since been destroyed, and his tribal customs and loyalties are in process of disappearing. This is particularly true of the industrial worker. On the miner, the effect of contact with Western civilization is violent and demoralizing, and he often returns to his tribal home having lost his natural dignity and simplicity and having acquired disease and a veneer of Western civilization. But he does go back to his tribal home. The permanent industrial worker has lost for good his former way of life. He and his family are having to readjust themselves painfully to their harsh and unsympathetic new environment.

3

The People *(Continued)*

THE EUROPEAN

THE EUROPEAN POPULATION OF SOUTH AFRICA IS ABOUT 3,067,000, of whom roughly 80 per cent live in urban areas. During the first three decades of this century it would have been true to say that the rural population was Afrikaans-speaking and the urban population English-speaking. Since the 'thirties, however, the Afrikaner has gone to town. This is, as we shall see later, a social and political fact of great importance.

The word Afrikaner requires some amplification. Until the first decade of this century it meant a white South African whose mother tongue was Afrikaans. Though that usage is still common in the rural areas of South Africa, the word has acquired a political and emotional significance associated with the rise of Afrikaner nationalism. Thus, Smuts and Malan grew up in the same Afrikaans-speaking rural village and would have been called Afrikaner boys. By the time of their death, however, most Nationalist Party speakers would have denied the title to Smuts, their political opponent, and granted it to Malan, their political leader. This appropriation of the term Afrikaner by the Nationalist Party was at first resented by Afrikaans-speaking South Africans who did not belong to that party; but, latterly, they have come to regard their exclusion with equanimity and to regard themselves as *Suid-Afrikaners*, the Afrikaans for South African. Though Afrikaner was a useful emotive word while nationalism was struggling to assert itself, some Nationalist writers are beginning to wonder whether its use is not too exclusive now that nationalism has triumphed. A word that excludes Smuts and Hofmeyr solely on the grounds of politics, and a Coloured poet, honoured by the Afrikaans Academy for his Afrikaans poetry, solely on the grounds of colour, may well be regarded as too exclusive. It is, however, doubtful whether the word will ever regain its original and more accurate meaning. It is still in a transition stage, and its use in this book will, it is hoped, be clear from the particular context in which it is employed.

About 57 per cent of South Africans have Afrikaans as their home language and 39 per cent English.[1] Probably 70 per cent are, to a lesser or greater extent, bilingual. The degree of bilingualism ranges

---

[1] See *Union Year Book No.* 24, 1948. The term 'South African' is usually applied to white citizens of the Union, though, legally, all citizens are South Africans.

from what is ironically called 'a working knowledge', through the ability to read and to understand the other language, to the fluent use of either language. Many more Afrikaners are, in common experience, bilingual than are English-speaking South Africans. But there is evidence that the position is changing in two ways: more English-speaking people are seeing to it that their children become bilingual; and fewer Afrikaners are attaining that proficiency in English that was common a generation ago. The rapid development of the Afrikaans language and literature during the past thirty years and the urbanization of the Afrikaner are responsible for this. With the increasing use of Afrikaans in commerce, there is now less incentive for the Afrikaner to learn English, and more incentive for the English-speaking South African to learn Afrikaans.

Both languages are official, and all public documents must be in both languages. Members of the public may use either language in official correspondence and in addressing an official. The rule in parliament is that either language may be used and that no interpretation is provided. *Hansard*, however, appears in both languages.

Afrikaners are wont to complain that, though Afrikaans is an official language, they have frequently, particularly in the large towns, to use English because the shop assistants, the railway booking clerk, the bank clerk, and others with whom they have to do business can speak only broken Afrikaans. On the committees of voluntary societies and of sporting bodies there frequently are members who cannot understand Afrikaans and for whose benefit the proceedings must be in English; but the exercise of tact and good will usually overcomes these awkward situations. Afrikaners tend to dissociate themselves from organizations that are so predominantly English-speaking that there is little hope of gaining recognition for Afrikaans. In some cases, such as youth movements and committees for adult education, parallel organizations have developed, one in English and the other in Afrikaans. Afrikaans cultural organizations urge their members to use Afrikaans only, and to patronize those businesses that cater for Afrikaners.

Since the Boer War the fight for the full recognition of Afrikaans has been an uphill one. The fight was not so much against English-speaking people as a fight to prevent the Afrikaner from becoming anglicized. The English language has an established international position, and in South Africa it was, and to a large extent is, the language of trade and commerce, of the professions, of amusement and recreation, and of urban society. The urge to learn English, and the temptation to regard it as the only cultured language, were strong. There was at the time a tendency among Afrikaners with pretensions to a more 'civilized' way of living to look down on Afrikaans as a 'patois' and as 'the *taal*', something of which to be slightly ashamed. Apart from English, the written and 'polite' language was Dutch, the language of the Netherlands. That was the language of the pulpit in the Dutch Reformed Churches. But Dutch was, in reality, merely the veneer covering the living and growing spoken language, Afrikaans.

After the Boer War of 1899-1902, a large number of English teachers and civil servants came to South Africa, and particularly to the ex-republics of the Transvaal and Orange Free State. They greatly strengthened the tendency to regard English as all-important. Afrikaners still speak about the generation that had its schooling in the first decade of the twentieth century as the 'lost generation', meaning that they had become anglicized.[1] Text-books were mostly in English, and English was the medium of instruction in practically all schools. Dutch, not Afrikaans, was the second official language, though only a small percentage of the population spoke the Dutch of Holland. Indeed, had the struggle been one between English and Dutch, the English language would probably have won. But the living and growing language of Afrikaans was waiting to push through the crust of Dutch. This happened during the second decade of the twentieth century, and it happened with all the force of a popular movement. Afrikaners began to write in Afrikaans and found an immediate and enthusiastic response. The movement was closely linked with the rise of the Nationalist Party under General Hertzog, and Afrikaans has never lost the strong political associations that accompanied its revival. A favourite text at that time was: 'The language of the conqueror in the mouth of the conquered is the language of slaves.'

From 1912 the Afrikaans movement gathered force. Afrikaans newspapers were established; the Bible was translated into Afrikaans; the new generation of parsons was trained in Afrikaans; Afrikaans text-books were printed and Afrikaans became the second medium of instruction in schools and universities. Dutch disappeared except as a modern language to be studied as such, and to be taken in universities as an adjunct to Afrikaans. A body of literature has grown up in prose, in poetry, and in drama. Much of this literature is preoccupied with past history, and particularly with the Boer War. But it is getting past that stage. The best Afrikaans writers no longer find it necessary to belong to a particular political party or to deal exclusively with the

---

[1] Other Afrikaners of that generation might be regarded as 'lost' in that they suffered a violent reaction, from which they do not appear to have recovered, *against* all things English.

rise of the Afrikaner and his fight against British imperialism. So far there has been very little satirical writing, which is possibly a sign that Afrikaans writers still take themselves and their work a little too seriously. Further, in their determination to keep the language 'pure' and elegant while expanding its vocabulary, Afrikaans academic writers have robbed it of some of its vigour and have created a gulf between the spoken and the written language. But these are, no doubt, passing phases.

The Afrikaans movement, coming when it did, has had profound social and political effects on South African life. After the Boer War the Afrikaner was, spiritually and socially, in very low water. The Afrikaans movement rehabilitated him, restored his self-confidence, and gave him a new hope. It brought him back into the life of the country on equal terms with the English-speaking South Africans, who represented England, the conqueror of the Afrikaner. Wise statesmanship on the part of Great Britain assisted the process by granting self-government and, ultimately, the independence of dominion status; but, considering the history of the relations between Britain and the Afrikaner, it is hardly surprising that Afrikaners tend to regard their survival and revival as, next to Divine Providence, the result of their own efforts. It is also not entirely surprising that Afrikaner nationalism has not yet completely shed its somewhat strident tones nor learned that it need no longer be always on the defensive. Those are marks of immaturity which the Afrikaner will no doubt outgrow.

By no means all who can be called Afrikaner joined in the nationalist movement of the second decade of this century. In fact, the Nationalist Party was a breakaway by General Hertzog from the main body of Afrikaners who were led by Generals Botha and Smuts. The policy of Botha and Smuts was 'conciliation'—to reconcile English and Afrikaner after their fight and to build up a united nation. Hertzog's argument was that a united nation could only be built on a basis of complete equality between English and Afrikaner. Therefore, the first task was to re-establish the Afrikaner. This could not be done by continually appeasing English susceptibilities, but only by insisting on language rights, by insisting on a separate flag, by insisting on South Africa's right to an independent existence and if necessary to secede from the British Empire. In 1933, when Hertzog had succeeded in securing these aims, he once more joined with Smuts. But by then nationalism had become a force that generated its own power, and it went on without him.

A phenomenon that has puzzled those visitors to South Africa who are astute enough to observe it is that the bitterest enmity exists, not between Afrikaner and English, but between Afrikaner and Afrikaner. The Afrikaner politician and editor reserve their sharpest darts for their fellow-Afrikaners. What is not always equally apparent is that the cause of this bitterness lies in the difference of attitude towards England and English-speaking South Africans. Possibly one-third of of the Afrikaner population, following in the Botha-Smuts-Hertzog tradition, desires co-operation with English-speaking South Africans, and sees in such co-operation the only prospect of a united nation. The rest of the Afrikaner population regards this attitude as a kind of treason to Afrikanerdom. If all Afrikaners would unite they could rule the country. Therefore, those Afrikaners who refuse to join the Afrikaner bloc are regarded as being untrue to their language and national traditions.

The Afrikaner who has grown up in a large town is, usually, indistinguishable in outward appearance from his English-speaking fellow-citizen. If he is an educated professional or business man, his accent, when he speaks English, can be detected, but his grammar and vocabulary are correct. If he is an artisan or an unskilled worker, his accent, grammar, and vocabulary will all deviate noticeably. In his amusements, his recreation, his occupation, and his general way of life there is little difference between him and an English-speaking South African who has grown up in similar circumstances.

There is a fairly marked difference between the Afrikaner farmer and the town-dweller, be he English- or Afrikaans-speaking. About 82 per cent of European farmers are Afrikaans-speaking. The word *boer* in Afrikaans is still commonly used to describe a farmer. By profession he is a *boer*.[1] By descent an Afrikaner farmer may be a Boer, with a capital letter, hence he is sometimes referred to tautologically as a Boer farmer.

The Afrikaner farmer is, usually, a kindly and leisurely man with a sense of humour that sucks the last ounce out of a situation. He is slow to anger; he has rugged common sense born of generations of struggle against the forces of Nature; he works hard and is not a 'planter' or 'plantation owner'; he does not easily part with hard cash and is convinced that townsmen are 'clever' ('slim' is what he would call it) and bent on defrauding him. He has many of the qualities and characteristics of the pioneer Trekkers, modified by the material progress of Western civilization; he is individualist in outlook and leisurely in habit; he has natural good manners and a dignified bearing. He will not tolerate equality with non-Europeans, but among those of his own colour he is no respecter of persons. He treats his labourers in a kindly and tolerant fashion and regards their many shortcomings

[1] In Afrikaans the word is pronounced like the German *buhr*, and *not* 'boor'.

as divinely ordained. The vagaries of the climate and his Calvinist religion have made him somewhat fatalistic.

Though there are many exceptions, the Afrikaans farmer is not progressive. A long tradition of large farms easily acquired, the presence of a relatively abundant supply of 'cheap' labour, and a contempt for 'experts' have induced bad economic habits and retarded scientific farming. Climatic conditions and out-of-date farming methods keep costs of production high, so that South African agricultural produce cannot compete successfully in the world market. The internal market is weak because 70 per cent of the population is too poor to be able to buy. Since the farming vote represents the most powerful single interest in parliament, all governments have found it expedient to subsidize agriculture. This is done by numerous control boards that guarantee high prices, by preferential duties and railway rates, and by subsidizing export. The expense to the country is enormous, in actual money, in inflated cost of living, in malnutrition, and in the continued production of subsidized crops on uneconomic soil.

It is interesting to note that, in recent years, urban Afrikaners have begun to complain about the favours shown to farmers, most of whom are Afrikaners. The fantastically high prices for wool in 1951 brought these complaints to a head. Letters to the Afrikaans Press, though careful to congratulate the wool farmers on their good fortune, complained that they were using their windfalls to evade supertax by buying up land at exaggerated prices. A leading article in *Die Burger*, the foremost Nationalist Party paper, explained how it was done. A farmer with a £20,000 wool cheque might have to pay £11,000 in supertax. To avoid this, he bought a farm worth £15,000 and paid £20,000 for it on condition that the payments should be in four instalments, but that the first three would be regarded as rent and, thus, deductible for tax purposes! The result of this was not only loss of revenue to the State. It meant that farms went out of production and that the price of land was artificially inflated, thus deterring younger men from being able to acquire their own farms. Another interesting, though less noticed, result is that reported by Dr. C. Neethling, head of the Department of Economics and Markets. According to *Die Burger* of 23 June 1959, Dr. Neethling said that 5,419 farms in Natal and 2,074 in the Orange Free State that had been occupied by whites in 1945 were today occupied by non-whites only. They were, of course still owned by white people on whose behalf they were being farmed by non-whites.

The determination to evade income tax and supertax may be a widespread characteristic. It may, in fact, be inherent in human nature not to regard tax evasion as immoral. It certainly is a fairly general characteristic of the Afrikaner farmer and it dates back to the eighteenth century, when 'good government' neither interfered nor taxed. At a Nationalist Party Congress in 1951 it was pointed out by one delegate that the only remedy lay in abolishing income tax and substituting a graduated land tax. It is, however, improbable that such an unpopular move would be lightly undertaken by any South African government. Meanwhile, agriculture in South Africa has many of the characteristics of a gigantic system of outdoor relief.

English-speaking South Africans are, for the most part, town- and city-dwellers, active in commerce and industry, in skilled trades, in mining, and in the professions. Isolated pockets of English-speaking farmers occur in three provinces, and in Natal the majority of farmers are English-speaking. In the large cities most of the capital and wealth is in the hands of English-speaking South Africans, many, though by no means all of them, Jews. In recent years so-called Afrikaans capital has increased. Even so, Afrikaner business-houses consider that they control only about 10 per cent of invested capital.

The contribution of English-speaking people to the development of South Africa is immense. The Afrikaner of the nineteenth century opened up the country and settled it; but for many years the main contribution of the Afrikaner to the material wealth of South Africa was agricultural. The English-speaking South Africans were responsible for mining and industrial development, for railway construction, for the establishment of towns and cities, for commerce and banking, for shipping and for harbour construction—in fact, for changing South Africa from an agriculturally backward community into a semi-industrial modern state. In this process the enterprise, the hard work, and the capital of the Jews played a very considerable part. It was not, however, only in material matters that English-speaking South Africans developed the country. In primary and secondary education, in the establishment and endowment of universities, in the building of libraries, in the development of the theatre and encouragement of the arts, in the spread of learning, in social welfare, and, last but not least, in the establishment of parliamentary traditions and of the rule of law, English-speaking South Africans have played a major part of which no Briton need be ashamed.[1]

In speaking about the contribution of the English-speaking South Africans it must not be thought that this was a contribution by 'foreigners'. It was a contribution by British men and women who had come to settle in South Africa and to make South Africa their home.

[1] For an excellent account of the part played by English-speaking South Africans in building up the country, see John Bond, *They Were South Africans*.

Many of them, and many of their children, married into Afrikaner families. Their children, and children's children, are the South Africans of today. Many of these, in whose veins flow Afrikaner and British blood, no longer care to describe themselves as Afrikaners or as English-speaking South Africans. They prefer to regard themselves simply as South Africans, and to look back with pride at the contributions which both their Afrikaner and English-speaking ancestors made to the establishment of Western civilization in South Africa.

It would be easy to exaggerate the social and political effects of having two official languages. Any description of the two language groups is apt to leave the impression that they are always and everywhere antagonistic, even if the antagonism is temporarily concealed. That is far from being the case. A great many ordinary men and women are, for most of the time, unconscious of belonging to any special 'group'. In situations where they do become conscious of it, most people manage to avoid friction and embarrassment by the exercise of common sense, good manners, and tolerance. Economic and social circumstances are, to an increasing extent, making people bilingual. During the last war Afrikaans- and English-speaking troops of all ranks found that they got on very well together; and unilingual English-speaking people discovered a new urge to learn Afrikaans, and to let their children learn Afrikaans, so as to lessen the points of friction between the two groups. During the war it was interesting and amusing to watch people switching with ease from one language to the other and, not infrequently, mixing the languages, to the annoyance of purists.

On the other hand, it would be equally easy to go to the opposite extreme and to imagine that language differences do not matter in South Africa. The danger in the situation is that the methods used while Afrikaans was fighting for full recognition may continue to be used after the battle is won. Afrikaners who saw the importance of Afrikaans found it necessary to insist on its use, to stress its importance even at the expense of English, to establish separate parallel organizations where Afrikaans could be used exclusively, to found cultural societies for the promotion of Afrikaans literature and culture, and to demand separate schools where Afrikaans was the only medium of instruction. In doing all this, the Afrikaner lost contact with the wider culture that could only be maintained through the medium of a world language. While he lost in this respect, he gained in the emotional stability which is a prerequisite to healthy citizenship. But there is no reason, now, why the Afrikaner should not have both—a healthy attachment to his mother tongue and an equally healthy contact, through English, with international thought. The present danger is that, by continuing to use the methods of a struggle for recognition, the Afrikaner will narrow his outlook unnecessarily. And the danger is real, because a vested interest, political and social, has grown up round Afrikaans. The cultural and linguistic struggle for Afrikaans has paid good party-political dividends and Afrikaner politicians are loath to relinquish a weapon that has served them so well. But unless they do, the Afrikaner himself will be the chief loser.

There are a few healthy signs that Afrikaans thinkers and writers are alive to the dangers of isolation from world thought. Though it is true that bilingualism is increasing, Afrikaans- and English-speaking teachers are gravely disturbed at the low standard of English being taught, particularly in the rural areas. Afrikaans-speaking students come up to the universities unable to express themselves grammatically in speech or writing. At the celebrations in 1959 of what was called 'The Wonder of Afrikaans', a great deal was spoken about the almost miraculous survival of the language, and Afrikaners were exhorted not to lose their heritage. But more than one speaker warned against the other danger—that of losing contact with the world by neglecting the English language.

THE COLOURED PEOPLE

One-tenth (or just over 1,405,000) of the population is officially classed as 'Mixed and other Coloureds' and is defined as consisting 'chiefly of Cape Coloureds, but includes also Cape Malays, Bushmen, Hottentots, and all persons of mixed race'.[1] 'Mixed race' means those who have some European blood in their veins, but are not of 'pure' European origin. Since the number of Hottentots and Bushmen is negligible, most people, when they refer to the 'Coloured People', are thinking of the mixed group that is to be found, for the most part, in the Cape Province. Nearly 88 per cent of Cape Coloured (or 1,243,000) live in the Cape Province, 102,000 in the Transvaal, and the rest in Natal and the Orange Free State.

This mixed race has its origin in the seventeenth-century slave population. The first batch of slaves brought to the Cape consisted of Negroes from the West Coast; the others came from East Africa, Madagascar, Ceylon, India and Malaya. In the earliest years of the settlement at the Cape, unions, regular or irregular, were frequent between Europeans and slaves, chiefly those from the East. During the first twenty years (1652-72) 75 per cent of children born to slave mothers had European fathers.[2] In 1685 marriage and intercourse with

---

[1] Estimate of Bureau of Census and Statistics, 30 June 1959.
[2] See Sonnabend and Sofer, *South Africa's Stepchildren*, South African Affairs Pamphlets.

slave women were prohibited, though marriage with half-breeds was still allowed. Since, however, there were far more European males than females at the Cape, this prohibition did not stop miscegenation. Although Europeans did not, in all probability, mix to any extent with Hottentots, whom they regarded with considerable contempt, the slaves and half-breeds did.

During the nineteenth century, and particularly after the liberation of slaves in 1834, colour consciousness grew. By then the new 'race' had been established, however, and it continued to increase as a separate group. A certain amount of miscegenation between Europeans and Coloured still took place, and, from the last quarter of the nineteenth century, there was a slight admixture of African blood.[1]

There is a great variety in physical features and in colour to be found among the Coloured people today. They vary from the typically Negroid types to types that are indistinguishable from Europeans. Many of them, in between these two extremes, could be taken for southern Italians. Except for the use of words of Malay origin, they have lost all trace of non-European language; they speak English and Afrikaans, according to the social environment of their employers, and, at the lower social levels, mix the languages in a kind of South African cockney. They have, too, a cockney sense of humour.

The cultural and recreational interests of the Coloured are those of the European. They are keen rugby footballers, cricketers and tennis players; and they follow the fortunes of their favourite European teams with remarkable loyalty. The greatest South African rugby players probably enjoy more popularity among the Coloured than they do among the European followers of that national game. In art and in literature there have, so far, been a few competent painters and writers, but no one outstanding. They have produced a number of top-rank ballet dancers.

The annual Coon Carnival, a purely Coloured institution, takes place in Cape Town on the second day of the New Year. For months beforehand songs are practised, costumes are prepared, and plans are made by the competing bands. On the second of January (traditionally known as *Tweede Nuwejaar*—second New Year—and universally accepted as a Coloured holiday) the 'Coons' march through Cape Town, watched by thousands of European and Coloured spectators, to the Green Point Common where singing competitions take place. It is a gay scene, full of life and vigour. Many of the songs are traditional Dutch songs, with variations, songs that have died out among the

[1] *Union Year Book No.* 24, 1948.

Europeans but live on, in somewhat mutilated form, among the Coloured. Other songs are composed for the occasion and show the influence of American popular music.

Coloured men find employment which would not be open to Africans. The building industry in the western parts of the Cape Province employs, today, more Coloured artisans than European; and in the printing industry there are a number of Coloured men. In other skilled trades it is more difficult for the Coloured to enter. In the numerous factories that have been established in the large urban areas of the Cape Province, Coloured men and women are employed as operatives. In the western Cape Province the bulk of farm labour consists of Coloured; and a great many of them are employed in domestic service, in hotels, and as office messengers. In many Cape towns the postmen are, traditionally, Coloured men. There are Coloured doctors, and, of course, many Coloured teachers; but it would be difficult for a Coloured man to make a living in any of the other professions, such as the law, engineering, or architecture. Coloured women may take up nursing, and in a city such as Cape Town they are increasingly employed as shorthand typists, dress-makers, shop assistants, and waitresses.

Though, in the nature of things, it is impossible to say how many Coloured have succeeded in 'passing'—that is, in being fully accepted as European—'passing' has certainly occurred. There are stories, some merely malicious gossip, others obviously plain statements of fact, about certain reputedly white families having 'Coloured blood'; others about individual members of a Coloured family passing for white and being, in their own interest, loyally ignored by the rest of the family. During the 1939-45 war there were cases of members of the same family serving in different regiments, one in a European regiment and the others in a Coloured battalion.

When so much social, political, and economic premium is placed on a 'white' skin, it is inevitable that those Coloured whose appearance makes it possible should attempt to 'pass'. There have been cases where, in entering children for a European school, the mother or father (as the case may be) has kept in the background; the children easily pass for white, but one of the parents might be too obviously non-white. More unhappy are the cases where children are admitted to European schools and, after the lapse of several years, malicious gossip reaches the ears of other parents and of the authorities. An investigation is then instituted and there is usually some publicity about these cases, particularly if the parents appeal against an adverse decision; but even if the case is kept out of the papers the child is forced to leave the school regardless of the psychological consequences of being thus 'stigmatized'. In one tragic case a young boy committed suicide because he had been evicted from a school in this way.

The Nationalist Party has for many years expressed concern about miscegenation and about 'passing'. In 1927 already, when the Nationalist-Labour Pact was in power, an Act was passed prohibiting extra-marital relations between European and African. From 1948, when the Nationalist and Afrikaner Parties came to power, they immediately set about passing legislation to prohibit illicit intercourse and marriage between European and Coloured. The existing Immorality Act of 1927 was amended to include Coloured, and a Prohibition of Mixed Marriages Act was passed which made marriage between white and non-white a crime and held marriage officers responsible for refusing to solemnize such marriages.

Since the passing of the Immorality Amendment Act of 1950 the annual number of prosecutions increased to such an extent that, in the latter part of 1959, there were signs that public opinion was becoming disturbed. A number of letters appeared in the Afrikaans Press; while many of the letter-writers advocated increased penalties for transgressors, a few openly questioned the value of a law that caused so much social damage and failed so patently to achieve its avowed object.

The Act has been strongly attacked from a number of points of view. Prof. B. B. Keet, of the Theological Seminary of the Dutch Reformed Church at Stellenbosch, twice raised the matter in *Die Kerkbode*, the official organ of the Church, arguing that it is impossible to approve of a law that makes an action immoral only when it occurs between people of different colours. Other critics have pointed out that the application of the Act entails snooping, tale-bearing, and other disreputable methods of law enforcement. Policemen shine torches into stationary cars at night and enter private houses and servants' quarters on suspicion. Since cases are difficult to prove, Coloured women have been induced to turn Queen's evidence and, as might be expected, have on occasion given perjured evidence. So bad had this become in a number of cases in which policemen themselves were accused that the magistrate trying the cases spoke strongly against the practice of relying on such evidence.

Apart from the unsavoury methods employed to gain convictions, and the malodorous publicity that accompanies cases under the Immorality Act, further hardships occur. In one case a European man and a Coloured woman had been living together for fifteen years and had three children. They were found guilty and sent to prison and the family was broken up. In another case, the parents were sentenced to imprisonment for four months but there was so much publicity that, after four days, they were released on instructions from the Minister of

Justice. Meanwhile the three children had been uncared for and were living on scraps of food. Such cases, though not frequent, do occur, and it is only when blatant injustice, legally perpetrated, is brought to light that the Minister is able to exercise his powers of pardon.

The Mixed Marriages Act has produced few prosecutions. The number of marriages between white and non-white, previous to the Act, was infinitesimal. Since the passing of the Act, no one who was obviously coloured would attempt to marry anyone who was obviously white. Such cases as come before the courts are, therefore, cases in which the marriage officer and both partners are genuinely convinced that there is no legal impediment. The police, probably on private and malicious information, suspect one of the partners, and a prosecution takes place.

In an attempt to prevent 'passing', the Nationalist Government passed the Population Registration Act. Though this Act had other objectives,[1] it provides for the issue to everybody of identity certificates showing the race of the holder—white, Native, Coloured, or Asian. The Director of Census is to compile a national register, based on the Census of 1951, in which citizens are classified according to race. Anyone may, on payment of £10, object to his own or to anyone else's classification; such an objection will be heard by a board of three appointed by the Minister of the Interior. According to the Act, a white person is one who (*a*) is 'obviously white in appearance', or (*b*) is white 'by general repute and acceptance'. If, however, he is (under (*b*)) *Coloured* by general repute and acceptance, he will not be considered as white even if (under (*a*)) he is obviously so. It is, therefore, not easy to decide doubtful cases, especially where documentary evidence, such as birth certificates, does not exist. Moreover, the Act opens the door wide to the common informer or to those who, for personal motives, wish to damage a reputation. Anyone dissatisfied with the decision of the board may appeal to the Supreme Court; but the expense and publicity involved acts as a strong deterrent to the exercise of this right. The identity certificate, once this matter of race has been decided, must be shown on demand to any authorized person. The Director of Census may at any time reopen a case if he thinks that a person has been wrongly classified. Nevertheless, once a man's race is registered it will be impossible to pass as a member of another group. The Act is not yet fully in force, but by 1958 the Population Registra-tion Appeal Board had tried some 3,000 white-Coloured borderline cases, and some 42,000 Coloured-Asian-African cases. It may be

---

[1] In *Die Burger* of 21 February 1950, Dr. Malan, then Prime Minister, was quoted as saying more than once that 'a national register is the basis of the whole policy of apartheid'.

imagined what mental suffering this has entailed in a country where freedom, security, economic and social welfare, and most of the things that make life worth living are dependent on a so-called 'race' classification from which there is no escape.

The political status of the Coloured people has received a severe blow in recent years. In 1853, when the Cape Colony obtained representative government, there was no colour bar. European, Coloured, and African males enjoyed the franchise on the same qualifications. These qualifications were, subsequently, raised in order to restrict the number of new non-European voters; but they were the same for all races. In 1910, with Union, the Cape franchise was entrenched in the South Africa Act. In 1930 the political influence of Coloured voters was diminished when European women were enfranchised by the Hertzog Government, and it is noteworthy, in view of subsequent legislation, that Malan, then a member of the Hertzog Cabinet, had earlier opposed votes for women unless Coloured women were included. In 1931, voting qualifications for European males were abolished, but retained for Coloured and African males, thus further weighting the scales in favour of the Europeans.

The Nationalist Party came to power in 1948 on a policy of apartheid, which included placing Coloured voters on a separate roll, and, in 1951, introduced a Bill to do this. The passing of the Bill, the storm it raised, and the constitutional crisis that followed are more fully described in chapter 4. The Separate Representation of Voters Act, which eventually became law in 1956, had several consequences. In the first place, Coloured voters are no longer able to participate in a general election and are thus to a large extent debarred from expressing an opinion, through the ballot-box, on questions of national importance. Secondly, where formerly they could exercise the vote in all fifty-five Cape constituencies, they are now limited to electing four members. Their influence had been considerable in some twenty-five constituencies and decisive in about seven; since, in recent years, they have usually voted for the United Party, these constituencies have now become possible Nationalist seats. In the third place, as experience with the separate representation of African voters in the Cape has shown, however capable the Europeans elected by Coloured voters may be, they will not be able to effect much for their constituents because they are too few in number.

Another aspect of the Coloured question about which the Nationalist Party has long been concerned is residential segregation. In Cape Town and its suburbs, and in many other towns in the Cape Province, there are districts where Coloured and European live side by side. These are usually, though by no means always, the poorer quarters.

Local authorities have tried to bring about separation by including a servitude in certain areas prohibiting the transfer of fixed property to non-Europeans. But, unless such a servitude existed, there has been nothing to prevent a Coloured man from acquiring property anywhere he liked. In 1950, parliament passed the Group Areas Act by which, after a fixed date, no transfer of property might take place between the different racial groups in demarcated areas without a permit. This policy of social and residential separation will take many years to enforce, if, indeed, it is enforceable. Almost every year since the Act was passed, the minister has asked parliament to agree to a large number of amendments giving him increased powers to coerce those local authorities that may be unwilling to face the enormous expense involved in applying the policy. In 1955 the Group Areas Development Act provided for the assessment of compensation in the case of forced sales and gave the Group Areas Development Board power to develop new areas for different racial groups and, if necessary, to do so without the consent of the local authority which has, nevertheless, to pay the bill. It remains to be seen whether adequate compensation is given for forced sales, and, even more important, whether the Coloured residential areas will receive adequate municipal services. Experience with African urban locations does not lead one to be optimistic on this latter point.

The City Council of Cape Town, where the largest concentration of Coloured peoples lives, has opposed the Nationalist Government's policies on race separation; but it is fighting a losing battle because both central and provincial authorities are tightening their control over all local authority. In the Cape Province, Coloured people still have a municipal franchise on a common roll, and in Cape Town there are Coloured city councillors; but the government has stated its intention of instituting separate Coloured municipalities and taking the Coloured voters off the common municipal roll. In Cape Town, too, there are Coloured traffic policemen and firemen serving with whites, but the Minister of Labour has decided, under recently acquired powers to reserve jobs, that no more Coloured shall be appointed. The City Hall in Cape Town and town halls in the suburbs of Cape Town are among the few places in South Africa where mixed audiences may watch plays or listen to music and where mixed meetings may be held; but this right is threatened by the Separate Amenities Ordinance, passed by the Cape Provincial Council in 1955. The full name of this Ordinance is the Reservation of Separate Amenities by Local Authorities Ordinance (Cape) and it empowers the Administrator, after consultation with a local authority, to direct it to provide separate amenities. If the local authority fails to do this, the Administrator may instruct the Provincial Secretary to do so, at the expense of the local authority. This ordinance must not be confused with the Reservation of Separate Amenities Act of 1953. Following a number of cases in which the courts ruled, in effect, that if separate public amenities are provided they must be substantially equal, this Act was passed empowering public bodies to provide facilities exclusively for one race or to provide separate but not necessarily equal facilities.

The Cape Peninsula is famed for its beaches which South Africans of all colours have always enjoyed and to which thousands of visitors from the northern provinces come in summer to acquire a tan that makes them almost indistinguishable from the Coloured people. Here, too, apartheid is gradually being enforced. The City Council has so far been able to stall on the ground that it was necessary first to establish definite high and low tide marks. This difficulty has now been overcome by empowering the Minister of Lands to disregard high and low water marks. A notice in the *Government Gazette* of 3 July 1959 empowers the Minister of Lands to divide the beach or the sea as bathing places and adds that a regulation by him may apply to 'the whole beach or a specified part of it, or to the whole sea or a specified part of it'.[1] With such sweeping powers given to the Minister of Lands, neither the City Council of Cape Town nor King Neptune will be able to prevent beach apartheid.

There is a great deal of poverty among the Coloured population. Inadequate housing, poor clothing, and malnutrition result in a high death-rate. The expectation of life of a Coloured male is forty years, as against fifty-nine for a European male. Tuberculosis is rife. The widespread drunkenness among Coloured people is both a cause and a result of poverty. There exists in the Cape Province a system known as the 'tot system' by which Coloured agricultural labourers are given a number of tots of wine during the working day as part of their wages. It has the weaknesses of the truck system of wages, and, moreover, it engenders and encourages the taste for strong drink. In the towns, Coloured people may buy wine and brandy at canteens and bottle-stores; there is an ineffective legal limit of four bottles a day in any one bottle-store, and the brandy is cheap and harmful. The result is seen in week-end drunkenness and all its consequences. Many people, of all parties, are concerned at this state of affairs, as are many of the Coloured people themselves; but the wine farmers and the liquor trade are a powerful political pressure group and nothing is done to improve matters. The abolition of the tot system is an obvious first step which no political party feels itself strong enough to take.

Although the Coloured people are, on the whole, cheerful even to

[1] Report in *Die Burger*.

fecklessness, educated men and women among them feel frustrated and embittered because they realize most clearly the colour-bar limitations that prevent them and their children from attaining good positions. Intelligent and hardworking as many of them are, they know that these characteristics will not ensure them an entry into most professional ranks, and even into many skilled occupations. Socially, they are debarred from European cinemas; they must occupy separate stands at football matches; they are not admitted to European restaurants and cafés, and have few of their own. They form a community of their own and have their own social life; but at the back of their minds is the realization that they are not full citizens in the land of their birth. Till 1956 they prided themselves on having the vote in common with Europeans; now that right has been removed.

While the Coloured people resent the colour bars that operate against them, they themselves have strong prejudices against the Africans. They have always cherished the fact that, unlike the Africans, they were administered on the European side of the colour line. During the last war, the Smuts Government set up a Coloured Advisory Council to advise the government on Coloured affairs. A proportion of Coloured people accepted this policy and were prepared to co-operate with the government; but the great majority of educated Coloured men and women would have nothing to do with it. They feared that the Council was an attempt to separate them, politically and administratively, from the Europeans. There were, they said, no Coloured affairs. Now, their fears have been realized: a Coloured Affairs Department and an elected Union Council for Coloured Affairs have been created.

Coloured leadership is divided, largely over the question of whether or not to co-operate with Europeans. At one extreme is a group, which includes a great many educated Coloured people, most of them teachers, that refuses to assist a European government to provide separate consultative and administrative machinery for Coloured people. The only Europeans with whom they will co-operate are those who stand for complete equality. Others are prepared to co-operate on the ground that there is more to be gained that way than by non-co-operation. When the Bill to place Coloured voters on a separate roll was before parliament, there was a temporary and uneasy union between all Coloured groups. But by now the division in the ranks of the Coloured has become embittered by personalities, and it will be extremely difficult to create a united Coloured front.

The Cape Malays are a distinctive group of about 40,000 Mohammedans. Their ancestors came from the East, largely from Java, some as slaves but most as political exiles, and mixed with European and Coloured and other groups. Though, in due course, they adopted the language of the Europeans, they retained their religion. It is that that has made them a distinctive group. For generations the Malays and their descendants were the skilled workers of the Cape—silversmiths, carpenters, coopers, cabinet-makers, and tailors; and Malay domestic servants helped to create many of the dishes that are today distinctively Cape dishes.

Although the Malays are classed, officially, as Coloured, their religion keeps them separate from the rest of this group. Marriage between the two groups does take place, but Malay parents prefer their daughters to marry Malay rather than Coloured men. If a Malay marries a Coloured girl she becomes a Mohammedan. The Malays consider themselves socially above the Coloured. Their temperate habits and their business acumen ensure that they are, for the most part, better off economically.

The Cape Malays mostly belong to the Sunni sect of Mohammedanism and look to Mecca for their religious leadership. Though their home language is usually Afrikaans, the language of the mosque is Arabic; and all religious feasts and fasts are scrupulously observed. In spite of colour bars, the Malays are psychologically better adjusted to life than the Coloured. Their religion and their social status are respected by Europeans; being Mohammedans, they have no desire to emulate the European Christians or to pass into their society.

THE ASIANS

When, in the 1860's, British settlers in Natal began to cultivate sugar they found that they could not get enough Zulu labour to work the plantations. So Asians were brought in as indentured labour. Many of these labourers stayed on after they had served their indentures, either as free labourers, or as independent small farmers, shopkeepers and traders, or domestic servants. Soon, their families and friends joined them to settle in a country which, colour bar or no, provided a better living than their native land. In 1911 the Indian Government put a stop to the recruiting of labour, and the South African Government, alarmed by Indian agitation for rights—an agitation led by Gandhi—prohibited free immigration. By that time the Asian population had grown considerably and South Africa was faced with an Asian 'problem'.

At that time, Gandhi was leading the passive resistance movement for Asian rights, and there were, already, various restrictions on them. They were not, and are not now, allowed to live in the Orange Free

State. In the Transvaal they might reside, but were forbidden to own land, a prohibition which was legally overcome by the formation of land companies or by persuading a European to act as nominal owner. In Natal they were allowed to own fixed property, but their parliamentary franchise, secure while Natal was under the final control of the British Government, was abolished when Natal achieved responsible government. In the Cape they suffered fewest restrictions.

By 1924 the 'Indian Question' became acute, particularly in the Transvaal. Municipalities complained, with some justice, that Asians created slums by sub-letting and that the value of urban property fell when they settled there. Asian trading-stores in the Transvaal and Natal were prospering and this may have added to European discontent. To meet that discontent, the Smuts Government introduced a Class Areas Bill for segregating Asians throughout the country. The agitation against the Bill, both in India and in South Africa, was furious, and when, in the middle of the controversy, the Smuts Government fell, the Bill was dropped. In 1926 the Hertzog Government introduced an even more severe measure, but, for the time, wiser counsels prevailed and à round table conference with the Government of India produced the so-called Cape Town Agreement which provided for assisted repatriation and, for those who remained, better conditions.

It is a misnomer to talk about repatriation. Asians in South Africa today know no other motherland. There are 450,000, of whom 20,000 live in the Cape, 61,000 in the Transvaal, and the rest in Natal. It is, accordingly, in Natal that the problem is most acute. In the first place, there is the usual colour prejudice that sees the rapid increase of the Asian population as a menace to European standards. Asians are by no means all wealthy, but some of them are extremely prosperous and, naturally, want to invest their money in real estate. In the second place, their way of life and their outlook on business are different from those of the Europeans who are their principal competitors in trade. The Nationalist Party regards the Asians as unassimilable, and most Europeans would agree with that description.

In 1946 the Smuts Government tried to deal with the situation in Natal by an Act which pegged property deals with Asians, while, at the insistence of the liberal element in his party which disliked the Act, it gave them the right to elect three European members of parliament. The Asians boycotted the elections and campaigned vigorously, in South Africa and at U.N.O., against the 'Pegging Act'. The passive resistance campaign in Natal never reached serious dimensions, but it attracted a great deal of publicity.

When the Nationalist Party came to power in 1948 it repealed that part of the Act which gave parliamentary representation but retained the restrictions on land purchase. In 1950 parliament passed the Group Areas Act which is described in chapter 7. The way in which the Act is being used in Durban and Johannesburg, and in small towns of Natal and the Transvaal, to deprive Asians of long-established rights and restrict their trading activities by forcing them out of areas which they have built up into trading centres, makes it hard to believe that the primary purpose of the Group Areas Act was anything else but an attempt to make life so intolerable to Asians that they would be forced to leave the country.[1]

The Asians in South Africa are a fertile, hard-working, ingenious people, and they are not likely for long to be content with the present situation. They will not voluntarily return to India or Pakistan, and the cost of 'repatriating' the entire population—a plan that has been seriously suggested in Nationalist quarters—will be far greater than any government could bear. A preliminary conference, held at Cape Town in 1950, at which the governments of India and Pakistan were represented, failed to reach an agreement on an agenda for a round table conference. Meanwhile, trade relations between the Union and her two sister Commonwealth states of India and Pakistan are at a standstill.

The Asians have further complicated the South African race situation. In 1949 South Africa and the world were startled by the suddenness with which the country's most serious race riot flared up in Durban. Starting from a trivial incident, in which a young African was knocked over by an Indian trader, a race riot developed in a matter of hours, and Africans killed as many Asians as they could find and pillaged and plundered the Indian quarter. All the evidence is to the effect that the riot was totally unpremeditated. There is, at the same time, considerable and reliable evidence suggesting that the Zulu in Natal had long resented the Asians for various reasons: Asian shops exploited the Africans; Asians could get licences to own and drive buses conveying Africans, while Africans themselves could not do so;[2] Asian men were accused of 'interfering' with African women. There is also evidence that the Zulu sensed the attitude of their European masters towards the Asians and thought that, if they attacked them, the Europeans would not really mind. Finally, it has been suggested that the riot was one of general discontent and that, in this case, the Asians stood between the Europeans and the Africans. Whatever the

[1] For fuller details of this aspect of the Group Areas Act, see a pamphlet by Alan Paton, *The People Wept*, and the excellent annual *Survey of Race Relations* by Muriel Horrell (South African Institute of Race Relations).
[2] This has since been altered.

truth of the matter, the riots were a warning of how inflammable race relations are in a country where the popular 'solution' to the problem of race friction is to separate, confine, and restrict the races and, thus, to diminish the chances of tackling the root causes of the friction—grinding poverty and overcrowding. The warning has not been heeded, and further riots in 1959 are but a sample of what may be expected unless wiser councils prevail. Within the first three months of 1960 major clashes between Africans and the police occurred at Cato Manor in Durban; Windhoek, in South-West Africa; Langa, in Cape Town; and Sharpeville, on the Rand. At Cato Manor the rioting was sparked off by a 'routine police raid' on a Sunday morning; at Windhoek, by the compulsory removal of Africans to a new African township; at Langa and Sharpeville, by a massed demonstration against passes organized by the Pan-African Congress, a breakaway group from the African National Congress which opposed the demonstration. The total casualties in these four clashes were about 80 people killed (including 9 policemen) and many more wounded.

4

Government

THE UNION OF SOUTH AFRICA CAME INTO EXISTENCE ON 31 MAY 1910 as a result of an Act passed by the British Parliament at the request of the four colonies that constituted the Union. This was the South Africa Act of 1909. Later, between 1920 and 1930 various resolutions of Imperial Conferences, which were meetings of Colonial and British prime ministers, were given legal effect by the Statute of Westminster (1931) and by the Status of the Union Act (1934). The first of these was an Act of the British Parliament, and its principal effect was to repeal the Colonial Laws Validity Act of 1865, as far as it concerned South Africa, by which colonial laws that were repugnant to British laws were, to the extent of the repugnancy, void. The Status of the Union Act was passed by the Union Parliament, and did no more than amend the South Africa Act so as to bring it into line with the position as established by the Statute of Westminster. By it whatever limitations there may have been on the sovereignty of the Union of South Africa were removed. In consequence, South Africa is an independent sovereign state, and the British Queen is also Queen of South Africa, being represented by a Governor-General, who, on behalf of the Queen, acts as a constitutional monarch on the advice of her South African ministers.

Unlike the federations of Canada and Australia, where the provincial and state parliaments have certain sovereign powers, South Africa is a union and sovereignty rests with the central parliament. This consists of the Queen, the House of Assembly and the Senate. The two Houses have equal legislative powers, except in financial matters, and all Bills must be passed by both Houses; a deadlock between the two is dissolved by joint session procedure. Parliament, being sovereign, may alter its own constitution (the South Africa Act); but that Act itself specified that three of its clauses might be altered only by a two-thirds majority of both Houses sitting jointly. These clauses were, firstly, a clause dealing with the recognition of English and Dutch[1] as official languages; secondly, a clause dealing with any alterations to the franchise that may diminish the voting powers of persons in the Cape Province by reason of their race or colour only; and, lastly, a clause empowering parliament to amend the Act by

[1] At the time of the Union Dutch (not Afrikaans) was one of the two official languages. In 1926 the South Africa Act was altered and Dutch was made to include Afrikaans. Technically, therefore, the Union has three official languages.

normal bicameral procedure except in the case of the two other clauses and of this clause itself. These were the so-called 'entrenched clauses'.

Until 1951 it was generally assumed that the entrenched clauses retained their validity, despite the altered status of the Union. In fact, when, in 1931, the Statute of Westminster was being discussed in the Union Parliament, Smuts raised this point. Hertzog was then Prime Minister, and he and his colleagues declared that the entrenched clauses were unaffected. These clauses were, they said, a matter of national honour and good faith. In 1936, when African voters in the Cape Province were taken off the common roll and given separate representation, the two-thirds procedure was followed. In 1951 Malan's Nationalist Government introduced a Bill to take Coloured voters in the Cape off the common roll. On that occasion, however, the two-thirds procedure was discarded. The United Party and Labour Party Opposition challenged this, and the Speaker ruled that, in effect, the entrenched clauses had ceased to be valid.

This ruling raised a constitutional issue of the first magnitude. Some constitutional lawyers supported the Speaker's ruling, while others vigorously disputed it. Most South Africans were not concerned about the strictly legal aspect of the matter, but a large section regarded the entrenched clauses as part of the solemn contract that established the Union. The validity of those clauses had been reaffirmed by leading statesmen in 1931, many of whom were, in 1951, members of the government that now denied that validity. It seemed, thus, as if the foundations of the constitution were being undermined. Mass protest meetings were organized against Malan's action, and more than 100,000 voters signed a petition against the Bill to remove Coloured voters from the common roll. Ex-Servicemen and women, seeing in the Bill a threat to democracy for which they had fought, organized protest meetings; and a commando of ex-Servicemen, led by the Battle of Britain pilot, 'Sailor' Malan, and an Afrikaner veteran of the Boer War, Commandant Dolf de la Rey, and joined by contingents from the other provinces, converged on Cape Town, where a mass meeting of 50,000 people was held. Before the meeting 10,000 ex-Servicemen and women marched with torches through Cape Town, and, later, a deputation presented resolutions to the leaders of political parties at the Houses of Parliament. This mass demonstration was a protest, not against the removal of the Coloured voters from the common roll, but against the threat to the constitution. The government was not, however, deflected from its course, and the Bill was passed by both Houses of Parliament sitting separately and received the assent of the Governor-General.

When the Act had been promulgated, four Coloured voters applied to the courts to have it declared invalid. The application was dismissed by the Cape Provincial Division of the Supreme Court, the Court holding that it was bound by a previous decision of the Appeal Court in the case of *Ndlwana* v. *Hofmeyr* in 1937. In that case the Appeal Court had held that, since the passing of the Statute of Westminster in 1931, the courts had no power to pronounce on the validity of Acts of Parliament. The Judge-President of the Cape Provincial Division expressed doubts as to the correctness of that decision but held, correctly, that it could be reversed only by the Appeal Court itself.

The case of the four Coloured voters went on appeal to the Appellate Division in February 1952, and, after a hearing lasting six days, the Appeal Court unanimously ruled that the Separate Representation of Voters Act was 'invalid, null and void and of no legal force and effect', since it had been passed bicamerally and not, as required by the South Africa Act, by a two-thirds majority of both Houses in joint session. The full text of this judgment is to be found in the *South African Law Reports*, 1952 May issue, and need not be discussed here. What is more important for our immediate purpose is to describe the political and constitutional implications of the judgment.

The immediate popular reaction was to regard the judgment as a political defeat for Malan's Government, and the Opposition parties called upon him to resign. When the Act was passed many people had felt that the Constitution of the Union had been violated and they now felt a sense of relief that its integrity had been upheld by the highest Court. This feeling was tempered, however, by the knowledge that the Nationalist Party Government would not accept the situation and that the real crisis lay ahead.

The Nationalist Party argument was, in essence, that the judgment restricted the sovereignty of parliament and, therefore, of South Africa; that if the courts were allowed to 'test' legislation they would, virtually, be in the position of being able to thwart the popular will and that government policy would be at the mercy of the courts. Malan and the Nationalist Party leaders and Press maintained that the South Africa Act of 1909 was an Act of the British Parliament, that the two-thirds majority entrenchment was inserted under pressure from Britain, and that, in effect, Afrikaner Nationalism was once more engaged in a bitter 'fight for freedom'.

The reply of the Opposition parties was that the Appeal Court judgment called in question, not the sovereignty of parliament, but the procedure adopted by parliament to express its sovereign will; moreover they said that the South Africa Act was indeed passed by the British Parliament but that this had been at the express wish of the four pre-Union parliaments and that there is no historical foundation for believing that the language and franchise clauses were entrenched under pressure from Britain. Finally, to evade the decision of the Appeal Court would be to destroy the foundations on which the Union was built and to shake public confidence in the courts.

In April 1952 the government introduced a Bill to provide for a 'High Court of Parliament' to consist of all members of parliament sitting together. According to this Bill, if the Appeal Court gave a decision which had the effect of declaring an Act of Parliament invalid, a minister might refer the matter to a judicial committee of the High Court of Parliament for review. This committee, whose members need have no legal training, would then recommend to the High Court of Parliament whether or not to set aside the judgment of the Appeal Court. This Act was to have had retrospective effect to 1931, the date when the Statute of Westminster was passed.

In a leading article on the Act, the Nationalist paper, *Die Burger*, of 25 April 1952 said that its object was to put beyond all doubt the sovereignty of parliament, including the right to place Coloured voters on a separate register. Once that had been done, said the article, it would be unnecessary for the new High Court to meet again. The article added that no one was enthusiastic about the new court and it was a pity that it had to be created, but there seemed to be no other way out of the difficulty. It was, therefore, evident that the object of the Act was to validate the Separate Representation of Voters Act before the next delimitation of parliamentary constituencies so as to ensure that at the next general election the Coloured voters would not be able to influence the elections in Cape constituencies.

The reaction to this move of Malan's Government was immediate. The United Party, the Labour Party, and the Torch Commando announced a united front against the government. Inside parliament the United Party and Labour Party fought the bill vigorously and took the extreme step of breaking off all 'pairing' arrangements with the government and of refusing to take part in the committee stage of the Bill on the ground that they would have nothing to do with the details of a Bill to set up what they described as 'an obviously fake court'.

Outside of parliament a widespread movement of protest was set on foot. Membership of the Torch Commando, which Malan described as a militarist organization under Communist influence, grew, and included a number of retired judges. In Natal a strong and growing movement was started to demand a new National Convention which would place the Constitution of the Union beyond all party-political interference.

Despite all protests, the High Court of Parliament Act was passed by parliament in 1952. It, too, was tested and declared invalid by the Appeal Court. Knowing that the prolonged constitutional crisis was bad for the country, and hoping that the Opposition would realize this and compromise, the government made two more attempts, in 1953 and 1954, to gain a majority of two-thirds in a joint session of both houses. The Opposition, however, refused to compromise and the government finally overcame its difficulties by passing two Acts, neither of which required a two-thirds majority. In 1955 the Appellate Division Quorum Act increased the size of the Appeal Court from 6 to 11 and laid down that in cases in which the validity of an Act of Parliament is called in question, all eleven judges must sit. In the second place, the Senate Act of 1955 altered the constitution of the Senate so as to give the government the power, by 'packing' the Senate, to create the necessary two-thirds majority of both houses in joint session. Having thus prepared the way, the Senate was enlarged, and in 1956 the requisite two-thirds majority was found to pass the Separate Representation of Voters Amendment Act and the South Africa Act Amendment Act. The first of these two enactments placed Coloured voters in the Cape Province on a separate electoral roll to elect four European members of parliament, and the second removed the entrenchment of voting rights from the South Africa Act.

To return to the constitution of parliament: the House of Assembly consists of 163 members, who must be Europeans. Of these, 150 are elected by European voters throughout the four provinces and a handful of Coloured voters in Natal; 6 are elected by European voters in the territory of South-West Africa; 4 by Coloured voters in the Cape Province; and 3 by African voters in the Cape Province. In 1959 parliament abolished the representation of Africans in the Cape Province, and when the term of office of the present three members expires in 1960, Africans will no longer be represented in the House of Assembly.

Those entitled to vote are: (i) all European citizens over the age of 18[1] unless disqualified by reason of insanity or criminality. Immigrants to South Africa must have five years' residence (six, if they are not British subjects), after which they may apply for citizenship; the grant of citizenship is, however, not automatic, but lies in the discretion of the Minister of the Interior, who may, according to the Citizenship Act of 1949, take cognizance of secretly sworn information in coming to a conclusion; (ii) a limited number of Coloured males in Natal who

[1] The age was lowered from 21 to 18 in 1958.

were entitled to be and were registered as voters before the Separate Representation of Voters Act. These people voted in the European constituencies, and the Separate Representation of Voters Act provided that those on the roll would remain but that no new Coloured people would be added; (iii) in the Cape Province, Coloured males who are 21, who are literate, and who occupy property worth £75 or earn £50 a year, elect four representatives who must be European; (iv) in the Cape Province only, African males who are literate, and who either earn £75 a year or own fixed property to the value of £50, may be registered on a separate roll to elect three European members. This representation ceases in 1960.

For the purpose of European elections, each province of the Union is divided into constituencies of which there are, in all, 150. Until 1951 provision was made for delimitation of constituencies after every five-yearly census. From 1951, the census will be decennial, and so will the delimitations.[1] At the time of Union it was felt that the rural areas, with their sparse population, might be outvoted by the more densely populated urban areas. Constituencies were, therefore, 'loaded'. That is to say that when the Delimitation Commission has decided on the quota for each province, i.e. the number of voters required to form a constituency, it may take sparsity or density of population into account to the extent of 15 per cent above and below the quota. In other words, an M.P. in a rural constituency may represent 26 per cent fewer voters than in an urban constituency. As long as the main political parties enjoyed roughly the same support in the rural areas, this system had no marked political effects. But since the strength of the Nationalist Party in the rural areas has steadily increased at the expense of its main opponent, the United Party, the Nationalist Party now has a distinct electoral advantage. In the general election of 1948 the Nationalist and Afrikaner parties polled 140,000 fewer votes than their combined opponents, but returned seventy-nine members against their opponents' seventy-one. In the 1958 elections, after making allowances for uncontested seats, the number of votes cast for the Nationalist and United parties was about equal, yet the Nationalists returned 103 members to the United Party's 53.

The size of a South African constituency may vary from under 9,000 to over 12,000 voters. In South-West Africa, however, it is much smaller. By the Act of 1950 which provided for representation in the Union Parliament from that territory, South-West Africa was entitled to return six members to the Union House of Assembly, while the total number of registered voters was about 24,000.

[1] A delimitation was, however, made in 1957 and another will probably be required because of the lowering of the voting age to 18.

The newly constituted Senate consists of 89 members of whom 18 are nominated by the Governor-General; theoretically, half of these must be selected on the ground of their knowledge of the reasonable wants of the non-white races. Four are elected, through a complicated system of indirect election, by Africans, but this representation ceases in 1960. Two are elected from South-West Africa, and the remaining 65 are elected in the four provinces in the following way: an electoral college consisting of the members of parliament and members of the provincial council in each province elects a number of senators equal to one-fifth of the number of M.P.s and M.P.C.s from that province, provided that the number of senators from any province shall not be less than eight. At present the Transvaal has 27, the Cape 22, and Natal and the Orange Free State 8 each. Voting is by direct ballot and the senators from any province are all members of the political party that has a majority in the electoral college.

There can be few people who regard the Senate as at present constituted with equanimity. It has been the subject of denunciation, irony, sarcasm, and special pleading. To most people it remains an uneasy reminder of an expensive and not very worthy essay in South Africa's constitutional history. Even those who owe their membership of the Senate to the Senate Act have been known to scoff at its constitution, and it was with relief that the country heard, in the latter half of 1959, of the government's intention to reconstitute the Senate, reducing it to about one-third the size of the House of Assembly. Senators are, nominally, elected or nominated for ten years; but the government may dissolve the Senate within 120 days after a dissolution of the Assembly. The Assembly is elected for not more than five years. (See footnote, p. 97, on the Senate.)

South African parliamentary institutions are modelled closely on those of Great Britain. The procedure in the Union Parliament would, with minor exceptions, be familiar to anyone accustomed to the House of Commons in London. Cabinet responsibility; the control of the executive through finance; the election of the Speaker; procedure for public and private bills; question time—all these are features of the South African Parliament, as they are of all popular assemblies that derive from the Mother of Parliaments at Westminster.

PROVINCIAL GOVERNMENT

The four provinces of South Africa are controlled, subject to the approval of the central government, by administrators, provincial executives, and provincial councils. The administrator is appointed by the government and is assisted by an executive committee of four which is elected by the provincial council. The council is elected by parliamentary voters, and the number of constituencies is the same as for parliament, except that a council must have a minimum of twenty-five members.

Provincial councils have power to make ordinances governing a number of matters such as primary and secondary education for European children (their most important function), provincial roads, control of municipal and other local governing bodies, and general hospitals. They also have powers of taxing, but these are severely limited by the central government which prefers to pay subsidies to the provinces from general revenue.

Provincial borrowing for capital expenditure is strictly controlled by the central government which also jealously guards all sources of revenue but tends to allow the provinces to levy the more irritating forms of taxation—amusement tax, licences, and wheel tax. The result is that the provinces are unable to raise more than about 40 per cent of the revenue they must spend if they are to carry out their functions. The balance is provided in the form of subsidies from the central government for education and hospitals. Apart from the financial unsoundness of bodies elected on purely party-political grounds being responsible for raising less than half only of the money they spend, an even unsounder result is that provincial councils, being chronically short of revenue, tend to pass on to municipal councils certain functions involving expenditure that are properly provincial or national, and would be more efficiently run if they were conducted over wider areas.

To avoid overlapping and too great a divergence in provincial policies, an Inter-provincial Consultative Committee meets from time to time. This consists of representatives of the central government, including two ministers, the administrators, the directors of education, and the high provincial officials. This in itself is a recognition of the fact that the provincial system of South Africa is not an entirely satisfactory method of administration. Nor has the Consultative Committee succeeded in doing much more than iron out a few inequalities. There are disadvantages in the provincial system as at present constituted. At the time of union it was hoped that the provincial councils would be elected on non-party political lines; but from the first election onwards, elections followed national party divisions. It can thus happen that a majority in a provincial council may not be of the same party as that in power in parliament. This would not matter much if, as in a federal system, the provincial councils had sovereign powers in their domestic affairs and were not dependent on the good graces of the central government. As it is, the provincial councils are either pale reflections of the central parliament or are implacably opposed to its policies. In neither case are they able to follow really independent policies.

The provinces retain the boundaries they had, before union, as colonies. These boundaries are historical and anachronistic. Business organizations, national sporting bodies, and even the state-owned South African Railways disregard provincial boundaries when establishing branches; to do otherwise would be uneconomic. Administratively it would be far more efficient to divide the country into nine or ten natural regions, and this could easily be done without doing violence to local susceptibilities. As it is, the provincial system has all the disadvantages, and few of the advantages, both of a unitary and a federal system. There are other cogent reasons for a constitutional change that would alter the provincial system, but these will be discussed in a later chapter.

The administration of South-West Africa is slightly different from that of the provinces. South-West Africa received a new constitution in 1950, and has an administrator, an executive committee, and a legislative assembly that has more power than the provincial councils. The territory taxes itself, and the Union Government has agreed not to interfere. At the same time, the Union Government is responsible for raising loans for the territory and has taken over the railway system, thus relieving South-West Africa of a considerable financial burden.

LOCAL GOVERNMENT

There are officially listed, as urban areas, 780 distinct units, the large majority of which are small villages with populations of anything up to 2,000. Only 127 have populations exceeding 5,000. There are also 54 rural townships of which only 4 have populations of more than 1,000.[1] Large or small they all have some statutory form of local government. The smallest may be classed as public health area, local area, local board area, health committee, sub-urban area, quasi-urban area, and rural township; as some of the names indicate their main preoccupation is with health—sanitation, water supply, etc. Slightly larger areas may have a township board, village council, or village management board, depending on what province they are in. A village can aspire to achieve municipal status (still called borough in Natal) and will then be governed by a municipal council, usually called a town council or a city council. The South African Municipal Yearbook of 1958-9 shows that there are 288 municipalities in South Africa, varying in population from Kentani, with 195 inhabitants, to Johannesburg with 976,000. From the stage of township upwards the boards or councils are always elected. In all provinces except the Transvaal

[1] Bureau of Census and Statistics, *Special Report No.* 200, based on 1951 census.

6

there is a small property, or occupation of property, qualification for the municipal franchise. In the Free State and Transvaal, all non-Europeans are excluded; in Natal, Coloured, but not Africans or Asians, have the vote on the same terms as Europeans. In the Cape, all races may qualify, but only a small number of Africans do because of the restrictions against their owning land in European areas; Coloured and Asians not only have the vote, but a number of Coloured councillors have been elected on the Cape Town and Port Elizabeth city councils. The government has announced its intention of instituting separate town councils for Coloured people who will then cease to be on the common roll or to be eligible to election to a common town council.

Various Acts of Parliament and provincial ordinances govern the constitution, functions, and powers of local authorities, whether of municipal status or not. It should be noted that in the Cape Province there is an additional unit of local government, the divisional council, which embraces several smaller units and has limited taxing powers.

The most important services which local authorities are empowered to provide—and in some cases must provide—are the environmental services: removal of rubbish, sewage, water supply, inspection of food, prevention of pollution of streams and the air, economic and sub-economic housing, and slum clearance. Then there are personal welfare services, which include libraries, parks, and art galleries. These services can only be afforded by the larger municipalities. There are, too, personal health services such as vaccination and the isolation of cases of infectious diseases. There are protective services such as traffic control and fire brigades; and, finally, the services of convenience—streets, lighting, transport, electric power, swimming-baths. Two important functions of English local authorities, education and police, have in South Africa always been regarded as belonging to the provincial and central governments respectively.[1]

Most of these functions of local authorities are permissive and not compulsory. Thus, slums may be cleared, but the municipality is not compelled to do so. Theoretically the provincial authorities can compel a local authority to provide an efficient water supply and system of sanitation. In practice, these services are for the most part poor. It was estimated some years ago[2] that, among urban local authorities below the status of municipality, 58 per cent had no piped water supply, 15 per cent had no proper sanitary services, and 20 per cent had no system of refuse-disposal. The Social and Economic Planning Council

---

[1] Except in Natal where the police (though not education) were formerly under the borough.

[2] *Social and Economic Planning Council Report No. 8*, U.G.40/1945.

considered that, while most of the municipalities provided fairly complete environmental services, these services were restricted and inferior when supplied to the non-European inhabitants. While, for example, most municipalities had reticulated water supplies for the European quarters, the non-European quarters were normally restricted to public taps. The Department of Public Health, in its annual reports, has drawn attention to the lack of proper sanitation for the non-European communities in urban areas. And in many of those towns where civic amenities are lacking in the non-European areas, the European areas are well supplied with services of a non-essential character.

In chapter 2 we saw that local authorities had fallen very far behind in the matter of housing for Africans but that, under pressure from the central government, great progress had been made since 1951. The same is true, to a slightly lesser extent, in regard to European housing and slum clearance. So great and rapid has been the influx into urban areas that municipalities have been quite unable to cope effectively with the situation, particularly for the lower income groups who require sub-economic housing. The result is that rents are high, and take about 25 per cent of a man's earnings.

The most important items of revenue for local authorities are from property rates, sanitary rates, municipal trading in electricity, gas, water, and transport, and fees, fines, and licences. The percentages that each of these items form of the total varies greatly from municipality to municipality. The figure for municipal trading is usually high, and financial experts have condemned this method of raising revenue as a form of concealed taxation. A surprising fact is that provincial and government subsidies amount to about 5 per cent of local revenue. In Britain, subsidies provide about 40 per cent of local revenue, and in most European countries the figure is much higher: the assumption in paying high subsidies to local authorities is, of course, that very few of them can be financially self-sufficient, and that the functions they are performing are, in reality, national rather than local and should be paid for out of national revenue. But many of the duties imposed on local authorities in South Africa under the Public Health Act, the Housing Act and the Natives (Urban Areas) Act among others, are in fact of a national character, and it is unreasonable to expect local authorities to find the necessary money from their own resources. To make matters worse, what subsidies are available are paid on a pro rata basis rather than by block grant, and this presses hard on the smaller municipalities. Also, government property, such as public buildings and schools and hospitals, is exempt from the rates. In Cape Town, for example, government property is valued at about

£68,000,000, on which the City Council of Cape Town receives no rates.

With negligible exceptions, every town and village in South Africa has its European and its non-European populations. The pattern varies. Thus, in the Western Province of the Cape, the European, Coloured, and African populations will be roughly in the proportions of 5 to 5 to 1. Further east and north the ratio between Coloured and African in urban areas gradually changes, the number of Coloured decreasing and the number of African increasing, until, in the Free State and Transvaal, the Coloured have almost disappeared and there are usually slightly more Africans that Europeans in any one centre. In Natal the pattern is different, and, in numbers though not in occupation, Asians largely take the place of the Coloured of the Cape. This is a very general picture; but what is important is that, just as the government and the provincial councils have to think in terms of different colour groups, so each local authority, large and small, has perforce to deal with the problems that arise from this multi-racial society. A large number of local authorities have three groups to deal with, and the problem is aggravated by the suspicion and fear with which, in general, Asians and Coloured regard the African. The different groups are at markedly different cultural and economic levels, and social customs and manners differ at each level; where the Asian is concerned, there is a strong religious difference as well.

It is at the stage of local government that many of the problems and difficulties of a multi-racial society are best seen. It is there that national policies impinge most directly on the individuals of all population groups, and that the various laws that constitute national policy, or reveal its absence, are given personal significance. The regulations drawn up under these laws by distant departments of state have here to be carried into the lives and homes of human beings in day-to-day administration. It is in the sphere of local government that the social effects of the laws and regulations are felt. In order to give the reader a clear picture of local government from this point of view, we propose to describe in some detail a particular urban area. It is an area of medium size, and, to simplify the picture, one in which there is no Asian population and only about 800 Coloured people. The town is a real town, which we shall call Middeldorp, and the figures are chiefly those taken from the South African Municipal Yearbook of 1958-9.

In 1921 the European population of Middeldorp was 4,300. By 1936 it was 5,300, by 1946 it was 7,700, and by 1958 it was 12,500. The African population in those years numbered 4,500, 7,500, 12,800, and 25,000, most of them employed by Europeans. Thus, since 1921 the European population has almost trebled and the African population has increased to more than five times its original size—a feature typical of the urbanization of the past four decades. Middeldorp is a thriving semi-industrial, semi-market town, on a main railway line and on the national road. It has rateable property valued at over £10,000,000; its revenue and expenditure balance at about £650,000, and it has a municipal debt of close on £2,000,000.

The town council consists of nine members elected by the European voters. Councillors are unpaid and devote a considerable amount of time and energy to their voluntary job; each councillor is on at least two, and usually three or four, committees of the council. One such committee is the Native affairs committee, responsible for the African location which is about two miles from the outskirts of the town. All municipal by-laws affecting Africans must be approved by the Minister of Bantu Administration and Development, and each municipality must keep a separate Native revenue account which is credited with money received from pass and registration fees, rents of stands (or small plots) on which the Africans' houses are built, rentals from trading-sites, fines, and a portion of the money collected by the government under the Native Services Levy Act. Against this revenue, the account is debited with charges for municipal services, such as water, lighting, and sanitation, and with interest and redemption on money borrowed on behalf of the African location.

The revenue from the location is about £75,000, from which the town council must provide services and amenities for 25,000 Africans, as compared with the £650,000 for 12,500 Europeans. Unlike most local authorities, Middeldorp may from time to time spend £1,000 more on the location than it receives from it; but local European opinion, as throughout South Africa, cannot persuade itself to regard the African location as an integral part of urban society. This may be a convenient myth to excuse the outmoded system of making the poorest section of the community pay for its own municipal services, and get nothing more than it pays for. But whatever the explanation, the town councillors of Middeldorp would not be able to persuade ratepayers to spend good 'European' money on African locations. The total municipal revenue and expenditure of local authorities throughout the Union is about twenty-five times greater than the revenue and expenditure of the African locations controlled by those local authorities. Expenditure on African locations for the whole of the Union is, in fact, slightly in excess of revenue, which means that a few of the largest municipalities are beginning to accept a measure of responsibility for their African citizens.

The difference between Middeldorp's £650,000 and its location's £75,000 is immediately apparent. The European town has water-borne sewage, electric light and power, paved streets and sidewalks, a fine town hall, a public library, parks and public gardens, and plenty of playing-fields. In keeping with these are the things not paid for by the town council but made possible by the enterprise of Middeldorp's white citizens and the labour of its black: fine houses, large schools where education is free and compulsory, cinemas, shops, hotels, and churches. The African location has no water-borne sewage; electricity lights the streets inadequately; streets are dusty and full of potholes; there is a poorly built community hall where cinema shows are held three times a week and which contains, in a room at the back, a few hundred cast-off books that serve as a library; there are no beautiful parks or gardens and only a few rather straggling trees; there are a few recreation fields that look like very poor relations of the beautiful fields in Middeldorp. Again, in keeping with these things are small, overcrowded houses, far from weatherproof; a few dingy shops; a high school and four primary schools, all overcrowded and able to take only 60 per cent of the children of a schoolgoing age—the rest play in the streets while their parents are both at work. There are as many churches as in Middeldorp, but through the simplicity of poverty, many of them are not as ugly as those of the white town.

It must not be thought that every African in the location is poorer than every European in Middeldorp. As one walks from the centre of Middeldorp towards the location, the quality and the size of the houses become progressively poorer; there are a number of men in the location—a doctor, schoolmasters, a few builders, the top clerks at the Native affairs department—who have better incomes, houses, and furniture than the poorest whites. There is an African middle class, small as yet, whose standard of living is higher than that of the poor white section of Middeldorp. Nevertheless, the people of Middeldorp, rich or poor, all regard themselves as 'superior' to the African, poor or rich.

An official of the municipality, called the location manager, is in charge of the administration of the location. His office is on the outskirts of the location, and he and his staff of European and African clerks issue passes and permits and administer the Natives (Urban Areas) Act and the various regulations under the Act that aim at controlling the movement of Africans into towns. They also administer poor relief, housing, and health regulations, all products of national or provincial legislation; and they collect the taxes and maintain, under the town council, the Native revenue account. The manager of Middeldorp urban location is an excellent official who understands the needs of the people he must rule, and is sympathetic to their aspirations. Lack of funds, and the need to carry out national policy with which he, as an individual, does not necessarily agree, have not discouraged him as they have so many of his colleagues in other urban locations. A heavy responsibility rests on him, and he stands between his African wards and the European ratepayers as represented on the town council, the one clamouring for improved conditions and the other clamouring for 'economy'.

One of the most difficult tasks of the manager is to administer the regulations that attempt to control the entry of Africans into urban areas. Middeldorp is one of the 'closed' urban areas into which no African may enter to live without permission. He will, on entering Middeldorp, apply to the manager for a permit to seek for work. If he obtains work, a service contract with his employer must be registered with the manager; if he does not find work, he must leave within seven days. The permit to seek work and the service contract are passes that must be produced on demand by the police. With the small staff at his command, the manager finds it impossible to carry out these regulations adequately. There is no fence round locations; and in most locations it is impossible to trace Africans who fail to report. Criminals, who fear that they might be up against the police on other grounds, usually manage to get a forged or a borrowed pass. The manager of Middeldorp location has a comparatively easy task, because the population is not large. But if you were to ask two different officials in Johannesburg or in Cape Town what the African population in their locations is you are likely to get widely differing answers. They just do not know with any degree of accuracy. Even in Middeldorp the manager is attempting to do the impossible when he tries to administer the regulations.

Another very difficult task for the manager and his staff is to prevent the illicit sale or brewing of strong drink. It is against the law to sell any alcoholic liquor to Africans, who may, however, drink kaffir beer. This is a traditional African drink, brewed by African women from fermented kaffircorn and containing a maximum of 2 per cent of alcohol. Socially, it is closely connected with African customs and traditions; scientifically, it has some nutritional and anti-scorbutic value. In Middeldorp the system of home brewing is allowed and each family is permitted to have not more than four gallons on the premises at any one time; but like all restrictions on the individual, this regulation is difficult to administer. In an attempt to do so, periodic beer raids are carried out by the police. Needless to say, these are bitterly resented by the Africans. Middeldorp, however, has a comparatively easy time of it, because home brewing is popular and not frequently abused. Other municipalities have followed the alternative policy allowed by law—municipal brewing and sale in municipal beer halls. This is unpopular and leads to considerable illicit brewing, and to the brewing of stronger concoctions that make the consumer fighting drunk. Profits from beer halls are large, and are usually used for social, recreational, and welfare purposes.

During the past ten years the job of the manager has become more and more difficult. In the first place, African discontent and ambition have, as elsewhere in Africa, increased, and Africans no longer ask only for a little more generosity, a few more crumbs from the white man's table, a little more second-hand charity. Many of them now clamour for rights as citizens. Secondly, the response to these more insistent and strident demands has been, at the national level, increasing doses of apartheid and, to implement it, of measures to 'control' Africans. The location manager has been at his job for a long time and looks back nostalgically to the days when things were 'easier', when his relations with his wards were less troubled. Today, though he is in municipal employ, he and his council must carry out laws and regulations which they did not make and of which they may disapprove, and they are no longer allowed that measure of discretion which might soften administratively the harshness of legislation. It is the Nationalist Government's policy to try to curb the continued growth of urban African population except as migrant labour; and to this end it has made a law by which no African is regarded as a permanent resident unless he was born in an urban area such as Middeldorp, or has been in continuous employment there for ten years or has resided there continuously for fifteen.[1] Not being permanent, he may not have his wife and family with him for they are presumed to be resident 'somewhere in the Reserves'. The location manager has, on every working day of his life, to deal with Africans who are unable to produce evidence that they have complied with all the regulations but who, nevertheless, are in fixed employment and want to have their families with them. He knows that many of them have come from smaller towns or from farms and have never had any contact with Reserves; he knows, too, that some of them are unable to produce evidence simply because a previous employer has left the town or has died or, in a more relaxed period, had omitted to register his service contract. He knows these things and he sympathizes with the husbands and fathers who want to have their families with them. But he knows full well that he dare not be too lenient with such applicants.

One of the most hateful tasks that the location manager at Middel-

[1] Native Laws Amendment Act, 1957.

dorp has had to perform in recent years is to issue reference books to African women. Africans have always resented and resisted the carrying of 'passes' by their womenfolk, and they regard the reference book as a pass despite the fact that it was made compulsory by an Act called the Natives (Abolition of Passes and Co-ordination of Documents) Act of 1952. That Middeldorp escaped the demonstrations and riots that occurred elsewhere when the reference books were issued was due to the fact that the manager is a sympathetic man who went about his distasteful task in a reasonable and kindly manner. This did not however save him from the anger and hatred that Africans felt for all who were associated with reference books.

Then came the application of the Group Areas Act. Middeldorp has only 800 Coloured inhabitants but there was an area somewhere between the town and the location where Coloured, white, and Africans lived in fairly close proximity and the Group Areas Board called upon the town council to make proposals for separating these people. Dr. Dönges, then Minister of the Interior and in charge of the Group Areas Act, had said in parliament that the Act would be carried out with justice towards all sections; but it was rather much to expect of town councillors that they should recommend the removal of white voters when they could solve their problem by removing African and Coloured non-voters. Once more, the location manager was the man who had to carry out the policy.

Since legislation of this kind is bound to produce discontent, and since Africans no longer suffer in complete silence, it is only natural that there should be 'agitators'. There have for many years been laws that restrict freedom in order to restrain 'agitators', and during the past ten years these laws have been tightened up, and new laws added, to such an extent that individual liberty has come to depend largely on the good will and permission of government or of those to whom its authority has been delegated. By suitable definition of such words as 'undesirable', an African may now be moved from Middeldorp even if he was born there; and, to prevent vexatious legal delays, he is prohibited by law from applying to the courts for an interdict until he has been moved to some place perhaps a thousand miles away from his home town.[1] It is the central government rather than the local authority that normally uses these powers, but it is hardly surprising that the location manager of Middeldorp, hard

[1] Natives (Prohibition of Interdicts) Act of 1956. It is impossible, in a book not solely devoted to that purpose, to deal with the extent to which civil rights have become privileges at official discretion. Readers who want further information are referred to Brookes & Macaulay, *Civil Liberty in South Africa*, and to the annual *Survey of Race Relations in South Africa*, by Muriel Horrell, South African Institute of Race Relations.

pressed as he so often is these days, sometimes yields to the temptation to use this supposedly easy method of getting rid of a 'trouble-maker'.

It is no wonder that the location manager sometimes sighs for the 'good old days'. He can recall the time when looks were not sullen; when Europeans from Middeldorp used to move in and out of the location freely to co-operate with Africans in running child welfare, social clubs, night schools, and other welfare activities. Now, the location is a prohibited area and entry is by permit only. Moreover, the government dislikes 'mixed' committees, and no organization that draws public funds may function on the basis of practical co-operation between black and white.

Like all other urban locations, Middeldorp has a Native Advisory Board of six African members, three elected by the African inhabitants, and three nominated by the manager, who is chairman of the board. The functions of the board are purely advisory; all regulations affecting the location must be laid before the board before being sent to the provincial Administrator or the Minister of Bantu Administration and Development for approval; and the board may suggest amendments or new regulations. The manager at Middeldorp is a man who can get the most out of his board, and he uses it in a friendly way to keep in touch with the people. But it has little authority or power, and he finds, like most other people in his position, that the system of advisory boards has been a failure, and that few Africans are interested in them.

The real trouble with such boards is that they have no executive power and no financial authority. There have been many suggestions for improving them, but none of these have overcome this fundamental weakness. The truth of the matter is, of course, that Africans and Europeans are, whatever the theories may be, inhabitants of the same town; and no system of local self-government that does not recognize this fundamental fact is likely to have anything but a novelty value which disappears as the novelty wears off. In the Promotion of Bantu Self-Government Act of 1959 provision is made for linking Africans in urban areas such as Middeldorp with the Bantu authorities in the Reserves by allowing the latter to nominate, in consultation with the minister, Africans to act as their representatives in the urban areas. This is, in accordance with Nationalist Party policy, an attempt to strengthen tribalism even in the towns, and it seems likely that this will be officially regarded as a suitable substitute for the Native Advisory Boards which have of late been outspokenly critical of government policy.

Such, then, is Middeldorp. It is a fairly representative town, full of kindly, friendly people, black and white. It has its quota of saints and sinners. Its town councillors are mostly business men, though an occasional professional man or woman may be elected. They do their work without pay. From time to time there is talk of bribery; and councillors have been known to become wealthy by buying land at the right time and place. Though all of them are under social pressure to see to it that the wealthier parts of the town have the best streets, they do not always yield to this pressure. It is only since the 1940's that party politics have begun to play a part in council elections. When the Royal Family visited South Africa in 1947, the Mayor of Middeldorp was a Nationalist who acted with traditional Afrikaner courtesy and hospitality, though the party to which he belonged had not favoured a royal visit.[1]

As a social organism Middeldorp is typical too. The organism is divided into black and white by two miles of land. In both halves social divisions based on wealth and occupation are evident; but the working class in the town does not combine with the working class in the location. The location exists almost entirely to serve the needs of the other half. A few teachers, ministers of religion, African clerks, small shopkeepers or hawkers—perhaps 200 all told—serve their own African fellow-citizens; the rest are all employed by the Europeans in the town as domestic servants, unskilled labour, messengers, and office-cleaners, at wages that are about one-sixth of those of Europeans. The European knows the African as a servant; the African knows the European as a master. The African sees the European at home; the European hardly knows what the African's home looks like, and does not realize that he has pressing social and domestic problems. He does not even know his surname.

There are in Middeldorp, as elsewhere, points of contact between the two groups apart from the master-servant relationship. European men and women are found who give freely of their time and thought to assisting Africans to run welfare societies, Scouts and Guides, and night schools, though their activities have been curtailed by various apartheid laws. There is a Joint European-Bantu Council on which intelligent Africans and Europeans meet to discuss race relations and African welfare in the location. The Christian churches initiate and support much of this kind of work. But these things do not touch the mass of the European or the African population.

It is a curious organism in which each half lives its own social life, but in which the two halves are intimately connected by economic ties. By day the two halves coalesce; by night they separate. Each half is suspicious and afraid of the other because neither half knows the

[1] There is a story told that at one such reception—it was not at Middeldorp—the official host, to make his position quite clear, told the Queen that he was a Nationalist. Her Majesty is said to have disarmed him by replying: 'Oh! Yes, I know all about that. You see, I come from Scotland.'

other as human beings. A social organism built on such lines cannot thrive. Justice and fair-dealing, common sense and human kindliness, do not die; but they cannot function freely in such an atmosphere.

Middeldorp is in little a slightly simplified version of what the whole of South Africa is. The problems of a multi-racial society are not easy to solve. Europeans in South Africa have the ultimate responsibility because they have the political power, and, faced with the problems, they have not so far succeeded in evolving a workable policy. They have failed because they have ignored the fundamental human needs of those whom they govern. The social organism that is Middeldorp will always be weak and liable to disruption until the European inhabitants learn to regard the Africans as fellow citizens who can, themselves, take a pride in belonging to Middeldorp.

This leads to one final observation: for years the white inhabitants of Middeldorp have shuffled off their civic responsibilities on the ground that the African inhabitants of Middeldorp were migrants for whom it was a waste of good ratepayers' money to provide decent housing and social amenities. For years the citizens have insisted, through their town council, that the major responsibility for migrant Africans rests with the central government. They invited and welcomed control by the central government because they never regarded Africans as fellow-citizens. Once the central government had come in to control the black half of Middeldorp it was a short step to control of the white half; and Middeldorp is finding that the local liberty on which it prided itself has been sapped. Middeldorp town council has become the rubber stamp of the central government. The white citizens will regain their own liberty only when they have learnt to regard all who live and work in Middeldorp as citizens.

Note on the Senate

In February 1960 a Bill to alter the constitution of the Senate was tabled. By this, the number of senators would be reduced to 54 of whom 11 will be appointed by the Governor-General, including 1 to represent Coloured voters and 2 from South-West Africa. In each province the M.P.s and M.P.C.s will elect a number of senators, on the single transferable vote, proportional to the number of M.P.s and M.P.C.s in that province. At present the numbers of senators would be: Transvaal, 14; Cape Province, 11; Orange Free State and Natal, 8 each; 2 will be elected by the M.L.A.s and M.P.s for South-West Africa. All the Opposition parties in parliament opposed the Bill, mainly on the grounds that it made no provision for representing Africans or Asians, that the Senate would become merely a reflexion of the Assembly, and that the Bill disregarded the original intention of the National Convention of 1908 to give equal representation to the provinces and to make the Senate an effective house of revision.

5

Administration

THE PUBLIC SERVICE OF SOUTH AFRICA HAS TREBLED IN THE LAST THIRTY years. In 1959 there were over 90,000 white and 30,000 non-white posts in the service, and these figures included the police force, the Permanent Defence Force, and the Department of Posts and Telegraphs; they did not, however, include railways and harbours which employ 112,000 whites, 108,000 Africans, 11,000 Coloured, and 650 Asians. Nor did they include teachers, of whom there were about 21,000 European and 28,000 non-European. The provincial public services employ another 13,000 servants.

The number of Europeans regularly employed by the central and provincial governments is about one in six of employable Europeans between the ages of 18 and 60. Though comparable figures for non-Europeans are not available, a conservative estimate is that one in fifty employable non-Europeans are in the public service. What is significant about these figures is that a high proportion of the European or voting population is dependent on public employment and is thus precluded from taking public part in party politics. This produces a state of affairs which political parties and the public services are both under strong temptation to exploit at elections. In the second place, the public services find it difficult to fill the posts on the establishment and have to put up with low standards of education for new entrants. The obvious remedy is to make greater use of non-Europeans, but public opinion is opposed to this except in the lowest grades, and the policy of the Nationalist Party has always been to appoint Europeans rather than non-Europeans—the so-called 'civilized labour policy'. In effect, South Africa is trying to run her public services by drawing their employees, as far as possible, from 20 per cent of the population. This constitutes an intolerable burden on the small European population. A more widespread use of non-Europeans in the public service would relieve the pressure and would release Europeans for commerce and industry, which urgently need them.

The public service is divided into twenty-two departments of state in charge of sixteen ministers (including the prime minister) and four deputy ministers, a recent and welcome innovation designed to relieve the pressure on ministers. Ministers and deputy ministers are responsible to parliament, and the organization of departments is much the same as in Britain—secretaries, under-secretaries, boards, commissions—and it is unnecessary to describe them in detail. A few major differences may, however, be noted. The air, land, and sea forces are directly under one Ministry of Defence; the police force is controlled by the Department of Justice and not by the Department of the Interior, which would be the equivalent of the Home Office in Britain; the Minister of Education[1] controls university and technical education, but not primary and secondary education, which are provincial matters. It should be noted, too, that African primary and secondary education was formerly a provincial matter, while university education fell under the Minister of Education; but in 1953 African primary and secondary education was taken over by the (then) Department of Native Affairs, and in 1958 it came under the newly created Department of Bantu Education with its own minister. The Extension of the University Education Act of 1959 placed African university education in the charge of this department.

Entrance into the public service, the questions of authorized establishment of departments, discipline, administration and interpretation of public service regulations, promotions and new appointments, reorganization of departments, and other public service matters are under the control of the Public Service Commission. This consists of three officials appointed by the Governor-General. The Commission makes recommendations on all these matters and reports annually direct to parliament. No increase in establishment may be made without the approval of the Commission; and the expenditure involved is subject to Treasury approval. No recommendation of the Commission regarding an individual appointment may be altered or rejected by the government except with the sanction of the Governor-General. Such an alteration, approved by the Governor-General, is reported to parliament by the Commission.

In theory the whole public service is outside politics, and appointments and promotions are made without reference to party political affiliations or to personal relationships. In practice this is not invariably so. South Africa is—in terms of European population—a small country where many people are related. In the two republics, before the Boer War, it was considered only pious for someone in office to 'assist' relatives and friends. This tradition has not entirely died out. It is not long since a politician was asked at a public meeting whether he had helped to get his aged father a particularly lucrative job. His reply was: 'Naturally. What son wouldn't?' Nevertheless, there has not been a great deal of nepotism in the public service, though the idea of 'rewarding' a faithful political follower dies hard, not only in South Africa.

Appointment, and particularly promotion, of public servants goes

[1] The full title is the Minister of Education, Arts and Science.

on without regard to party political affiliations until a fundamental difference in policy manifests itself, when it breaks down. During the last war there was such a difference between the United Party under Smuts and the Nationalist Party under Dr. Malan. The Nationalist Party was totally opposed to South Africa's participation in the war, and Smuts could not take the risk involved in promoting known Nationalists to key positions. When, in 1948, the Nationalists came to power they reversed several of these war-time promotions, notably that of the General Manager of Railways, and recompensed public servants who had been interned and had, therefore, missed promotion.

Another such fundamental cleavage occurred when the Nationalists came to power in 1948 on a policy of apartheid.[1] When the position of Secretary for Native Affairs fell vacant the government overrode the recommendation of the Public Service Commission and appointed someone known to be in sympathy with government policy. The present government has expressed itself very clearly on the need for fully bilingual personnel in the public service and is unlikely to promote people who do not wholly sympathize with that policy or are not reasonably bilingual. But this alone can hardly be called party political interference in the public service since bilingualism is a nationally accepted policy. Much, however, depends on the practical interpretation of the word bilingualism and on whether the policy is applied sensibly. There appears to be a strong reluctance on the part of English-speaking boys and girls to join the service and this is said to be due to the belief that they would have small hope of promotion against Afrikaans-speaking competitors. This reluctance may, however, be partly due to the superior attractions of commerce and industry. Whatever the cause, the fact remains that the lower levels of the public service are today staffed by young men and women whose knowledge of written and spoken English is minimal, and in the absence of serious competition it is they who will in due course receive promotion to the higher ranks of the service. The belief that the Nationalist Party favours Afrikaans-speaking public servants probably arises from the government's policy of applying periodic bilingual tests in the service, those who fail being given a period of time in which to become proficient. Most of the failures have been senior English-speaking officials who have not had the time or the opportunity to become proficient in Afrikaans and whose promotion is therefore delayed. All this has given rise to the saying that, for the present government, to be bilingual means to be able to speak Afrikaans. It is difficult to establish the actual facts, apart from individual hard cases; but whatever the facts, the results are unfortunate. The field from which the public

[1] See chapter 7.

service is drawn is already limited by racial policies that exclude four-fifths of the population from making that service a career; its further limitation, on what are in effect party-political grounds, will have a disastrous effect. Already there are ominous signs that there are not enough efficient public servants for effective administration and that the remedy is being sought in greater numbers rather than in better quality.

Until 1952 it was possible to say that there had been only a few flagrant cases of partisan appointment to the judiciary, by both major political parties, and that such appointments had not been so outstandingly successful as to encourage the belief that partisan appointments were in the public interest. Since 1952, however, there have been a number of appointments to the bench in which factors other than legal eminence must have been predominant. That, at any rate, is the considered and publicly expressed view of the Bar Council. By tradition, only Q.C.s are appointed to the bench, and the exceedingly brief time that has, in several cases, been allowed to elapse before a newly appointed Q.C. is offered a judgeship has caused serious misgivings to those who value the high reputation that the South African judiciary has enjoyed. Moreover, public disquiet has not been allayed by the considerable number of junior judges who have, since 1952, been appointed to senior positions over the heads of those with many more years of judicial experience.

There are two departments that require description in some detail because of their importance in a multi-racial society. They are the departments of Bantu Administration and Development and of Justice.

DEPARTMENT OF BANTU ADMINISTRATION AND DEVELOPMENT

The Department of Bantu Administration and Development is in many ways an *imperium in imperio*, a government within a government. By custom, from convenience, and by policy, administrative and legislative matters affecting Africans have been taken away from the department normally concerned with such matters and placed under the control of what was known, until October 1958, as the Department of Native Affairs. At that date the department was split in two: the Department of Bantu Administration and Development, and the Department of Bantu Education. We shall here deal only with the former of these two and leave the latter for discussion in chapter 8.

The Department of Bantu Administration and Development is responsible for the control and administration of all Reserves, with a population of about 3,650,000. In the Reserves it administers justice through Bantu Commissioners' courts and through recognized chiefs;

it collects taxes and administers Native Trust Funds; it is responsible for soil conservation and for fostering industries; it administers social welfare Acts; and it controls the recruitment of labour to work outside the Reserves. Since the passing of the Bantu Authorities Act of 1951 an important function of the department has been to set up and control the tribal, district, regional, and territorial authorities envisaged by that Act. Parliament has in the past delegated to the Governor-General-in-Council (in practice, the Minister) wide powers to legislate for the Reserves by proclamation. The department, thus, both legislates and administers; in fact, it performs in the Reserves the work of parliament and of a dozen departments of state. Outside the Reserves, in the European areas, the department has, in collaboration with local authorities, a general responsibility for African welfare and administration. Until the early 1950's this responsibility was discharged by supervising the local authorities rather than by active participation in urban affairs. But a number of new Acts, and amendments to existing legislation, have brought the department so thoroughly into urban affairs that local authorities find themselves unable to take any decisive step without prior approval of the Department of Bantu Administration and Development. To a large extent local authorities have lost the power of independent action in connexion with their African populations.

In the past this system had, in so far only as it applied to tribal areas, certain advantages. It removes from party-political debate, though not from parliamentary control through the minister, the details of African administration and places it in the hands of sympathetic officials; it enables African customary law to be applied by men who understand it; in general, it makes possible the application of special techniques in the government of people, many of whom are to a large extent still tribal and primitive. The system has, however, its dangers, the greatest of which is to be found in the wide powers which the minister is given. By the Native Administration Act of 1927 (and amendments) the Governor-General is regarded as supreme chief over all Africans, and the minister, acting on his behalf, exercises all the powers that a despotic chief was assumed to have among the Zulu. These powers are exercised by proclamation which cannot be called in question before any court of law. The minister and his officials may compel tribes, or portions of tribes, to remove from one area to another; he may prohibit an individual from leaving his usual place of residence without permission or he may order him to leave an area and stay in another area; he may cause the arrest, and detention in gaol, on no specific charge, of any African who he has reason to fear may disturb the peace. All these powers to banish have been

7

freely exercised. For example, eighty-one Africans, including several chiefs, were served with removal orders between 1948 and 1958, and in October 1959 an African trade union organizer, Mrs. Mafekeng, was summarily served with a banishment order from Paarl, where she had lived for thirty-two years. Clashes between the police and non-whites occurred on the day she was to have been removed, but she eluded the police and escaped to Basutoland.

Such autocratic powers, uncontrolled by the courts, are dangerous when employed in simple law enforcement and day-to-day administration. They become far more dangerous when employed in the task of persuading people that a particular *form* of government (as distinct from day-to-day administration) is what they really want. The autocratic powers are then used, not to administer and enforce necessary laws, but to silence critics, to banish those who do not accept the official policy, and to encourage waverers to support policies of whose excellence they are not convinced.

The whole theory of Native Reserves and their viability in a modern economy was critically examined in chapter 2 where it was pointed out that the Tomlinson Commission had postulated individual, instead of tribal, tenure of land and intensive industrial development within the Reserves, with the aid of European enterprise, if the Reserves were to become an effective homeland for the African population. It was pointed out, too, that in rejecting these postulates the government had destroyed the props on which its policy might have been built. The existing policy, then, is to restore the power of the chiefs, to bolster up tribalism and tribal authority, and to attempt to resuscitate it even in the urban areas. Since 1952 it has been a major task of the Department of Bantu Administration and Development to persuade Africans in the Reserves to accept this policy by agreeing to the establishment of district, tribal, regional, and territorial authorities as provided in the Bantu Authorities Act of 1951. So that the normal work of the department should not suffer, a whole new section was created, under a senior Native commissioner, to attend to this special job, and it was given resources of propaganda in the shape of a well-produced monthly journal and a staff of information officers whose function appears to be twofold: to give information to chiefs and headmen and tribesmen, and to report confidential information back to headquarters.

There is no need to describe in detail the functions that the various Bantu authorities are being asked to assume. They are the normal functions of local government and administration, under the control of the department, that are to be found in any colonial system in Africa and that were, in fact, already in operation in most of the

Reserves. It is, however, necessary to try to find out why there was, and still is, so much opposition to a system that was, superficially at any rate, not new and that offered chiefs and headmen a restoration of powers they had gradually lost. That there was, and is, opposition is an observable fact; but even if it had not been observed it would have had to be assumed because of the lengths to which the government and the department go in trying to popularize the idea. It is probably true, as the government asserts, that there would have been less opposition in the Reserves had it not been for the implacable opposition of African organizations in urban areas. All this proves, however, is that African townsmen will have nothing to do with a policy that denies them citizenship in one part of South Africa on the grounds that they may, at some future date, achieve it in another, and that Africans (including chiefs) in the Reserves are in closer contact with urban African opinion than was supposed, and are susceptible to influences coming from the urban areas. The constant flow of labour between the Reserves and the urban areas has ensured this.

Agreeing to the establishment of tribal authorities involves acceptance of the Nationalist policy of making the Reserves the only permanent home for Africans. This policy is rejected as impracticable and undesirable by most Africans and by a large number of Europeans, and it is little wonder that chiefs and tribesmen are hesitant about accepting it however attractive it was made to appear. A steady stream of propaganda is directed at chiefs and tribesmen to show the advantages of acceptance. The argument is advanced that no man can develop properly unless he has a home base and unless he is proud of his tribal traditions and his mother tongue, even though that might be a minor dialect spoken by a few thousand people. Great emphasis is laid on tribal differences and tribal, as distinct from African, nationalism. If, after a great deal of persuasion, a tribal authority is accepted, effective use is made of this by the ceremonious installation of the chief at which compliments and presents and staffs of office are exchanged, cattle slaughtered for a feast, and much kaffir beer drunk, all photographically recorded for the Press and for the official journal of the Department of Bantu Administration and Development.

Persuasion has not stopped at promises of future benefits. The department has invoked its autocratic powers in order to isolate the Reserves from undue outside influences. Chiefs who showed clearly that they were not to be persuaded have been refused official recognition or else quietly banished; schoolmasters who openly oppose the policy find themselves redundant; Europeans, travelling on their lawful occasions through the Reserves, are not allowed to leave the main road without permission; the entry into the Reserves of urban

African 'agitators' is carefully controlled; and, as happened in a few cases, when the police are called into a tribal area to deal with a minor revolt, the Press is kept out. In the process of establishing tribal or district areas a good deal of ethnological reshuffling had to be done to ensure that the right subjects had the right chief. One way and another, some of the tribesmen had got mixed up and this had to be put right even if it meant moving Africans from one place, in which they had been content to remain, to some other place; or even if it meant appointing a chief whom many of his subjects failed to recognize as such. It was in such cases that the police had to be called in.

As a result of all this activity the minister was able to announce in September 1958 that 1 territorial authority, 8 regional authorities, 26 district authorities, and 298 tribal authorities had been established, and estimates for expenditure for the year ending 31 March 1959 made provision for the payment of 500 recognized chiefs and 1,200 headmen. By the end of 1959 the most important acceptance of Bantu authorities occurred in the Transkei which accounted for the one territorial and most of the 26 district authorities. The next most important were the Ciskei and Zululand.

In the Cape Province, as early as 1894, a policy was begun of establishing local, district, and regional councils in which the chiefs had, as such, little part, a policy deliberately aimed, in fact, at destroying the power of the chiefs and of introducing local government on an elected basis. This policy, generally known as the Transkeian system, constituted South Africa's most original contribution to the science of governing Africans. In the Transkei there were twenty-six district councils, each composed of six members, four elected and two nominated, with the magistrate (a European) as chairman. Three African representatives from each district council, one nominated and two elected, formed the basis of the Transkeian Territories General Council. The Chief Magistrate of the Transkei was chairman; twenty-six magistrates were *ex officio* members; and the chiefs of Western and Eastern Pondoland and of Tembuland were *ex officio* members, constituting the only survival from tribalism in the General Council.

The General Council (usually called the Bunga) dealt with an annual revenue of about £200,000 derived from quitrent and from a hut tax of 10s. Its functions were to make roads and dipping-tanks, to maintain agricultural institutions, and to support education. It made grants to the district councils, which had no revenue of their own. The Bunga was an advisory body and might discuss any subject it liked, whether of national or of local interest. Resolutions on national affairs were transmitted to the Governor-General and were seldom acted on; but its decisions on local affairs were usually carried out.

Its great difficulty, as with urban locations, was the lack of funds owing to the poverty of the inhabitants of the Reserves.

As a method of training Africans in local self-government the Transkeian system had a fundamental weakness: the district councils had no original taxing powers and were, thus, dependent for their small budgets on grants from the General Council, which was itself lamentably short of funds for the work it was expected to do. Britain found, in her African colonies, that tribal treasuries are an essential feature of indirect rule; and, though the Transkeian system was not technically indirect rule, since it was not based on tribal institutions, the same principle holds good.

In April 1955 the Transkeian Territories General Council decided to accept the Bantu Authorities Act and was subsequently proclaimed a Bantu Territorial Authority. The new Authority is distinguished from the old Council in three ways: it will have original taxing powers; no European magistrates will be members, a chief taking the chair instead of the Chief Magistrate; and its members will no longer be indirectly elected but their appointment will be strictly controlled by the Department of Bantu Administration and Development. Chiefs throughout the Reserves hold office at the pleasure of the minister, so that control over the composition of the Authority will be a simple matter. The example of the Transkei was followed by the Ciskei. In Zululand the Paramount Chief has, after much hesitation and delay, accepted the Bantu Authorities Act, but it is uncertain to what extent tribal chiefs under him have done so. While much publicity is given to acceptance, not much is known about rejections. It may be assumed, however, that if there had been widespread acceptance by the Zulu people, a territorial authority, such as in the Transkei, would by now (February 1960) have been established.

There are Reserves in the Transvaal and Natal where tribalism still has a fairly firm hold, though there are signs that there, too, it is weakening. The Nationalist policy might conceivably work in such areas for a time; but it is doubtful whether it would, in the long run, be possible to maintain a system that is so contrary to Western economy. Chiefs, headmen, and councillors are, notoriously, the most conservative element in tribal life. A system of government based on them has no room for the growing class of progressive, educated Africans. And no system that ignores this class can hope to prevail.

There are superficial similarities between this policy of reviving and bolstering up tribal authority and the policy of indirect rule which Lord Lugard and Sir Donald Cameron made famous in other parts of Africa. But there are two vital differences—the motive of the policies, and the social and economic circumstances in which they are applied.

When indirect rule was beginning to be introduced in Nigeria, in Tanganyika, in Northern Rhodesia, tribal life in those areas was still vigorous. It had not suffered the violent disruption that had occurred in South Africa as a result of European settlement and of the discovery of diamonds and gold. It was, therefore, still possible in those colonies to find enough land, to recognize and develop, rather than to revive, tribal authorities, and to make them an integral part of local government.

In South Africa conditions are radically different. Tribal life has been largely disrupted, or is being disrupted, and there is not enough land available on which to base tribalism. Further, the motive in the British colonies was to find a system of administration which would train Africans in local government and—most important—would lead them gradually to take part in central government. In South Africa the declared policy of the Nationalist Party is that Africans shall never play any part in central government. Even, therefore, if indirect rule as a system of local government were possible in South Africa, it is a truncated form of that policy from which one of the main motives has been removed. Under indirect rule in British colonies tribalism is made to serve a temporary, transitional purpose. Under the Nationalist Party policy it becomes an end in itself. This, alone, would condemn it to failure.

Under indirect rule a Department of Native Affairs must, if the policy is successfully applied, play a diminishing part; in South Africa, the Department of Bantu Administration and Development has to carry an ever-increasing burden of responsibility. And the more it takes on, the more difficult does it become to divest itself of paternal authority. In the early days of the 1959 parliamentary session the Prime Minister, Dr. H. F. Verwoerd, made an important speech on policy which was widely acclaimed in the Nationalist Press as a 'new vision', the details of which were subsequently sketched in by the Minister of Bantu Administration and Development, Mr. D. de Wet Nel. The gist of the argument was that such progress had been made in the Reserves that the time had arrived when increasing doses of self-government could be administered to Bantu authorities and the Union Government could consider successive steps of 'creative withdrawal'. Parallels from British colonial history were freely, if somewhat mistakenly, drawn; Africans in their homeland Reserves would learn to manage their own affairs, to tax themselves, to make their own laws; they should no longer be spoonfed by the Europeans. Since the Europeans had a moral responsibility to help Africans develop their homeland, a Bantu Development Corporation would be set up, as, indeed, it subsequently was with £500,000 to encourage

Bantu industries—most of any further capital required would, it was thought, come from the Africans themselves. Bantu self-government had already advanced so far that it was no longer necessary for Africans to be represented in the Union Parliament, and that representation would, therefore, cease in 1960. In order to maintain close contact with African opinion in the Reserves, however, the Union Government would appoint five or more commissioners-general to represent it in the Reserves, and these commissioners-general were compared to the resident commissioner in a British territory. Finally, if at some future date the Africans in the Reserves reached a sufficiently high standard of self-government, there was no reason why they should not, ultimately, become semi-independent states and, with the Union, form a sort of commonwealth.

Closer examination of the present administration and development of the Reserves and of the stubborn facts of economic life in South Africa leads to one of two conclusions: either the new policy is a fantasy or those who advocate it are setting about things in a manner least calculated to achieve their object. In effect, the government is proposing to create 'colonies' so that it can withdraw from them. But what sort of colonies? And what preparations are there for withdrawal? Bantu self-government turns out to be, in practice, the restoration of a decaying and outworn tribalism in which the elective principle is noticeably absent and the main characteristic is authoritarianism exercised by the white government. 'Taxing themselves' is the name given to tribal levies which, if not voluntarily offered after official encouragement, may be compulsorily instituted by the minister. To those who know the poverty and economic backwardness of the Reserves, the £500,000 to develop industries, and the idea that additional capital would come from African 'investment', hardly merit comment. As for representation in the Union Parliament, the policy neglects the fact that more than half the African population no longer lives in the Reserves. In short, it is hard to avoid the further conclusion that the traditional South African policy of regarding the Reserves as reservoirs of labour is being streamlined to make them less of a financial burden on Union revenue. Reservoirs of labour they will remain, but the employers of that labour will be relieved of as much financial responsibility as possible.

One probable result of the attempt to restore the power of tribal chiefs may well be as unexpected by the protagonists of apartheid as it will be unwelcome by all who hope for a reasonable adjustment of race relations. Chiefs who are recognized as such by their tribal followers have several choices: they may accept the government's policy of Bantu Authorities willingly or unwillingly, with or without the approval of their followers; or they may reject it. If they accept the policy, their actions are so closely controlled by the Department of Bantu Administration and Development that they become, in effect, tools of the Administration and their influence over their followers is bound to wane. If they reject the government's advances and refuse to become tools, they are supplanted by nominated chiefs whom the tribe does not recognize. In any event, tribal discipline—the very quality that the Bantu Authorities Act wishes to preserve—will slacken, and the Act will defeat its own purpose. Though evidence is hard to pin down, it seems as if something of this nature is taking place, particularly among the Zulu, where a noticeable deterioration in tribal discipline and cohesion appears to be setting in. The attempt to revive tribal institutions in modern conditions may, therefore, have the unwelcome result of speeding the decay of those institutions before more suitable substitutes have had time to take root. That is what has happened in urban areas, with tragic results.

JUSTICE

The other department that must be briefly described is that of justice, and, with it, the judicial system. South Africa has an independent judiciary. Judges are appointed by the Governor-General-in-Council and may be removed from office only on an address from both Houses of Parliament praying for such removal on the ground of misbehaviour or incapacity. This has never yet happened, nor is it likely to happen. The Supreme Court of South Africa consists of an Appellate Division, presided over by the Chief Justice, and six provincial divisions, each presided over by a Judge-President. The Appeal Court has no original jurisdiction; it is purely a court of criminal and civil appeal from the provincial divisions. The provincial divisions have criminal and civil jurisdiction and have appellate jurisdiction from the lower courts.

Throughout the country, and not only in the Reserves, there are native commissioners' courts to try civil cases between Africans and Africans, and in trying such cases the native commissioners' courts are given a discretion to apply Native law and custom. The Supreme Court in each province retains its inherent jurisdiction to hear cases between Africans only but discourages the institution of such actions unless the issues are intricate or the subject-matter is of substantial value; costs are much lower in the native commissioners' courts. There are three Native Appeal Courts and a Native Divorce Court. Appeal from Native Appeal Courts to the Appellate Division of the Supreme Court is in the discretion of the courts themselves or of the Minister of Justice, who may want a Supreme Court ruling for future guidance. Appeal from the Native Divorce Court to the Supreme Court is an absolute right.

Each provincial division of the Supreme Court has an attorney-general who, unlike the Attorney-General in England, is not a politician. He is responsible for directing prosecutions, subject to the ultimate control of the Minister of Justice. There are also a State Attorney and a number of deputy state attorneys who are full-time salaried men performing much the same functions as those performed by the Treasury Solicitor in Great Britain.

The magistrate in South Africa is a paid official and, in addition to his judicial functions, performs a host of administrative duties. He is, except in Pretoria, the senior representative of the government in his district. There are 266 magisterial districts, and in most of them the magistrate's office acts on behalf of all state departments. Registration of births, deaths, and marriages; collection of revenue; payment of fees and licences; the issuing of permits; administration of old-age pensions and of poor relief—all these, and many more, are the responsibility of the resident magistrate and his office.

Judicially, the magistrate has jurisdiction to try all criminal cases except murder, rape, or treason, but his punitive powers are limited to fines of £100, imprisonment for six months, and a maximum of ten strokes, unless the attorney-general remits the case to him with increased jurisdiction. Because of his limited punitive powers, more serious cases are investigated by him by way of a preparatory examination. The magistrates also try civil cases where the sums involved are below a certain limit. They may not try cases involving disputes about a will, or divorce suits, or cases involving the mental capacity of a person. In an effort to relieve the overburdened Supreme Court, regional courts were set up in 1952 with increased jurisdiction of £300, three years' imprisonment, and a maximum of ten strokes; subject to these limits of punishment, regional courts may now hear rape cases. The same magistrate may sit in both the magistrate's court and the regional court, but usually only experienced magistrates sit in the regional courts.

The jury system is used in South Africa in criminal trials only and not in civil cases. Further, the accused may choose whether he prefers to be tried by a jury or by a judge, with or without assessors, except that in certain classes of cases the minister may direct that the trial should not be heard by a jury; and the Minister of Justice may direct that a case, or certain classes of cases, be tried by a judge and two assessors. The judge normally sits with two assessors though he is not obliged to do so. The law, giving the accused the option, was introduced because of a number of flagrantly wrong verdicts by juries where black and white were concerned in a case. Juries are composed of Europeans only, and jury service is obligatory for European males who are qualified, and a right to be specifically applied for by European women; but men and women may not sit together. (Women have not yet exercised their rights in this matter.) The jury is composed of nine, and a seven-to-two majority decision is required for conviction or acquittal.

The death sentence must be passed for murder unless there are extenuating circumstances, when the court has a discretion; it may be passed for treason, rape, aggravated cases of robbery where grievous bodily harm has been inflicted or threatened, and for aggravated cases of housebreaking where the housebreaker carries a dangerous weapon or threatens or commits assault. Crime statistics show a steady increase in the proportion of the total population prosecuted, sentenced, admitted to prison, or sentenced to death. Between 1947 and 1958, 979 people were sentenced to death and of these 549 were executed. Corporal punishment, which has recently become obligatory in certain cases, rose from 4,406 cases in 1950 to 17,498 in 1957 and to 18,542 in 1958, the large majority of these being Africans and Coloured, though the number of Europeans and Asians who received corporal punishment has risen steeply.

A special criminal court of two to three judges, without a jury, may be set up by the minister to try cases of treason. There have been a number of famous treason trials in South African history, but the one that has attracted most international attention is, at the time of writing (February 1960), still proceeding; comment would therefore be improper. The bare facts are that, commencing on the night of 4/5 December 1956, 156 men and women, from all racial groups and from different parts of the country, were arrested on charges of high treason and sent to the Fort in Johannesburg. The accused included doctors, lawyers, journalists, clergymen, and teachers, and the basis of the charge was incitement and preparation for the overthrowing of the existing state by revolutionary methods involving violence. The preparatory examination before a magistrate opened on 19 December and, a few days later, all the accused were released on bail.

The preparatory examination lasted (including various adjournments) till January 1958, and during the last adjournment in 1957 the Crown announced that the charges against 65 of the accused and against a printing establishment had been withdrawn. The remaining 91 were committed for trial before a special court of three judges. This trial began on 1 August 1958 and was marked by frequent adjournments on exceptions and on applications by the defence to have the indictment quashed. Eventually the Crown withdrew the charges against 61 of the accused (though they may be re-indicted) and altered the indictment against the remaining 30 so that charges under the Suppression of Communism Act were withdrawn and only the charge of high treason remained.

Immediately after the arrest a public fund was opened, under the auspices of the Archbishop of Cape Town and a number of public men and women, to provide for the adequate defence of the accused and for the support of their dependants.

An important question that remains to be discussed is whether the machinery of justice works smoothly in a multi-racial society, and whether justice not only is done, but whether it appears to be done. Leaving aside for the moment the fact that there are a number of laws that discriminate between European and African and Asian and Coloured, we may inquire whether the non-European gets a square deal in the courts, and from the police before he comes to court. These discriminatory laws will be discussed in chapter 6; but it is necessary to say here that at least 50 per cent of the offences which bring Africans to the courts are statutory offences which, when committed by a European, would not be a 'crime'. These are offences against the pass laws, the masters and servants laws, municipal and location regulations, curfew regulations, and against the various Acts that control African movement and labour. For such offences by Africans the police have powers of summary arrest. A police official may stop any African male and demand to see his pass; failure to produce it is an offence rendering the African liable to arrest.

This point has to be stressed, because it is the exercise of these powers that constitutes an important element in the fear and hatred that most Africans feel for the police. When something like half a million Africans a year are arrested for offences under laws that apply solely or principally to Africans, it would be surprising if the African community felt anything but antagonistic to the policeman, black or white, and did not regard his appearance as a source of safety but as an omen of evil. This relationship between the Africans and the police is a bad basis on which to build a system for maintaining the peace. In the police force itself it breeds the attitude that regards all Africans as potential criminals who will perjure themselves if necessary. European policemen share the colour prejudices of the community in which they grow up; and their experiences in carrying out the law among Africans do nothing to alter these prejudices. In 1959 the police were instructed not to arrest Africans for statutory offences where they think the African will obey a summons to appear in court. If these instructions are reasonably carried out there would be a great easing of tension; but the laws and regulations themselves are bad, and until they are repealed it is doubtful if there will be any real improvement. In any case, it will take many years of altered conditions and attitudes before Africans will be persuaded into regarding the police as anything but sworn enemies.

There is considerable evidence of ill-treatment by the police of non-European witnesses and of prisoners awaiting trial. Cases of this kind come before the courts from time to time, and both non-Europeans and European legal men allege that only a fraction of the actual cases ever become public.[1] Non-Europeans are afraid to give evidence against the police; and, in any case, accusations of excessive violence are very difficult to prove. The behaviour of the police in making arrests and in quelling disturbances is not above criticism. Considerably more force than appears necessary is used, and policemen are too apt to use their revolvers when their own safety seems to be threatened or when trying to prevent escape. In explanation, it must be added that the task of a police force in a multi-racial society is no easy one. The laws of the country are such that they tend to destroy any incentive on the part of non-Europeans to observe the law. European policemen grow up with a prejudice against, and a fear of, non-Europeans. These are no bases on which to build a system of keeping the peace by mutual trust. The non-European population has little faith in the impartiality of the police, and without that faith the task of the police force becomes increasingly impossible to perform. The roots of this undoubtedly serious evil lie deep in the social structure of South Africa.

There are signs that the relationship between the police and the public, of whatever colour, is not improving and that the conditions that make for mutual trust between police and public are, in fact, deteriorating. Since 1948 many new laws have been passed that have two main objectives: to enforce apartheid at all levels and to provide for the security of the state. Most of this legislation gives police officials the right to enter premises without a warrant if they suspect that a law is being broken or is likely to be broken. A policeman may enter a house or a room, by force if necessary, where he suspects that the Immorality Act is being infringed. The police may raid offices and private homes, and the Security Branch (in plain clothes) may attend any meeting, even in a private home, on the plea that someone

---

[1] In reply to a question in the Senate, the Minister of Justice stated that from 1 January 1949–30 April 1951, 347 members of the police force had been found guilty by the courts of assault, and 52 had been found guilty departmentally. The assaults were: 54 on Europeans and 345 on non-Europeans. *Cape Argus*, 22 June 1951. Figures given at a later date by the Minister showed that, from 1956–8, 69 European policemen were found guilty of assault on Europeans, and 475 of assault on non-Europeans.

who has been banned under the Suppression of Communism Act may be present or that the security of the State may be endangered by such a meeting; and in most cases it is the police themselves who are the sole judges of whether the supposed threat is sufficiently serious to warrant police action. Members of the Security Branch regularly attend 'mixed' gatherings such as those held by the Liberal Party, the Civil Rights League, and similar organizations. Since these meetings are normally attended and addressed by highly 'respectable' citizens —city councillors, barristers, ex-judges—the reason for such constant attention by the Security Branch is probably to frighten would-be protesters against government policy. No one, particularly in South Africa, likes to feel that he is being watched by the police. In 1959 the students at Witwatersrand University discovered that the Security Branch had persuaded a woman undergraduate to accept money in exchange for confidential reports on student activities. She happened not to be blonde, but the country at large was entertained for some weeks by the hilarity with which students greeted and treated this discovery. It is, of course, no laughing matter though it is better that the young should ridicule such things rather than be cowed by them.

Such wide and arbitrary powers would be dangerous in the hands of the most upright and highly trained police force. Unfortunately, however, the police force in South Africa finds it extremely difficult to obtain recruits and is often compelled to accept the second best. In some cases it has accepted young men of doubtful suitability who have themselves had criminal convictions; in a case in the Transvaal, early in 1959, a policeman was charged with assault and the Press was unable to publish his name because, by law, the names of persons under eighteen, who are involved in criminal charges, may not be published. When, during the course of 1959, there was a spate of cases in which policemen were the accused, and the Minister of Justice was asked in parliament whether all those found guilty were discharged from the force, he replied that disciplinary action was taken but that they were not always discharged. As he explained, 'We try to rehabilitate them'. It is not surprising that when men of weak character are given wide powers they succumb to the temptation to abuse them. Nor is it surprising that, even though only a small percentage of the police force is at fault, public distrust tends to spread to the whole force. In any society such distrust would be dangerous. It is doubly dangerous in a society rendered unstable by the ease with which racial passions can be roused.

When an accused African appears before the magistrate he suffers, with few exceptions, from serious disadvantages. The magistrate is, as we have seen, an extremely busy administrative officer; faced with

a long roll of statutory offences, he cannot waste time. English and
Afrikaans are the official languages, and the African accused may be
familiar with neither; worse still, he may have a smattering only of
one, so that an interpreter will be deemed unnecessary. If the African
is not yet an experienced town-dweller, and has but recently come from
tribal life, the procedure of the court will be utterly foreign to him.
His tribal court, to which he is accustomed, is a leisurely affair in
which anyone takes part; hearsay evidence is admitted and importance
is attached to evidence of character. In the European court the African
habit of illustrating remarks by similes would contravene the rules of
evidence. He does not understand the rule by which he must plead
guilty or not guilty before the trial commences. When he pleads
guilty he may merely mean that he has heard what the prosecutor has
to say. Finally, if it is a case of his unsupported word against that of a
European witness, his master, or the policeman, it is improbable that
his word will be taken. Since the African is too poor to engage legal
defence, and since the idea of prisoners' aid is in its infancy in South
Africa, the accused has little chance of conducting a successful defence.
The prosecutor is either a police sergeant who is out to secure a conviction, or the public prosecutor, who knows every twist of procedure,
and can turn an African witness inside out.

When it comes to the punishment for statutory offences, the sentence
may not be any greater than it would be for a European. Compared
to their relative incomes, however, it is far greater. A fine of £2
may represent a day's pay to a European; to an African farm labourer
it may be a month's pay, and to an urban African it may be a fortnight's
cash wage. In most cases, therefore, he accepts the alternative of
imprisonment for a week or a fortnight, either in gaol or at a government road camp.

Offences against masters and servants laws, or against property
such as sheep and cattle, are much more severely punished. A South
African small town is surrounded by farms. The magistrate is on
friendly terms with European townsmen and farmers, largely in his
capacity as representative of the central government. An unpopular
magistrate may be transferred on petition, and an unpopular magistrate
is often one who is too lenient in his sentences on African labourers,
or who takes the word of the African before that of his master. The
magistrate is under constant social pressure to uphold 'white prestige'.
This explains why the sentence imposed by the magistrate is so
frequently reduced by a judge on review: sometimes the review is
accompanied by caustic remarks on the severity of the sentence.

A trial before the Supreme Court is almost invariably conducted
with scrupulous fairness, and the bench in South Africa has a deservedly

high reputation in this respect. Judges are hampered by popular colour prejudice when a European stands accused of a crime against a non-European and elects to be tried by jury; but even with this occasional handicap the judges are scrupulously careful to see that the African accused or aggrieved party is not prejudiced in his case. In any serious case before the Supreme Court such miscarriages of justice as may occur are not related to colour. In the matter of sentences, however, there is still a considerable difference made between European and non-European. Sentences passed on Europeans for assaulting Africans are always lighter than those passed on Africans for comparable assaults on Europeans.[1]

In explaining, though by no means defending, the discrimination that justice makes between European and non-European—and particularly the African—there are a number of things to be said. To most Europeans the African appears to be a source of potential physical danger, particularly when they think of him—as they do—in the mass, as 'the Africans'. Therefore, when an African commits a crime of violence against a European, and more especially against a European woman, European public opinion feels that 'an example should be made'. South Africa has, fortunately, been spared lynch law; and, though it may be a harsh saying, it is no small thing that unequal laws are administered by due legal process, and that the rule of law—though it is bad law—is maintained. When judges and magistrates come across cases of ill-treatment of prisoners awaiting trial, they are outspoken in their condemnation and severe in their sentences. The trouble is that a great many such cases never come before the courts.

Many Europeans are aware of the situation and openly condemn unequal justice. Newspaper editors draw attention to bad cases of unequal punishment. And the judges themselves, and many magistrates, try to mitigate some of the harshest laws. But most Europeans still regard the African as not far removed from barbarism, as someone who understands severe punishment only and to whom a light sentence is no deterrent, and as someone to whom a sentence in gaol is neither a hardship nor a disgrace. Those who know the African intimately realize that these assumptions are almost fantastically inaccurate; but most Europeans do not know the African as a human being.

The history of the United States of America shows that there are powerful social and economic forces in a multi-racial society that

---

[1] Cases may be found almost daily in the Press and could be quoted if that would serve any purpose. Quoting brutal cases, however, tends to give a distorted view of the situation unless all the circumstances are known.

militate against the impartial administration of justice. Even in the homogeneous societies of Europe it is only since the latter half of the nineteenth century that harsh laws and sentences against socially inferior classes have come to be regarded as unjust. In South Africa, social distinctions are intensified by differences in colour. Those who have political power use it to entrench their social and economic position. In such circumstances, justice is poisoned at its source and cannot flow in a clear stream.

6

The Colour Bar

IT IS IMPOSSIBLE TO SPEND EVEN A FEW DAYS IN SOUTH AFRICA WITHOUT realizing the distinctions that are made between European and non-European. On railway stations and on trains and buses, at airports, post offices, and all public buildings, in banks, at race-courses and sports grounds, on the beaches, and in graveyards, there are separate 'facilities' for European and non-European, and the notices 'Europeans Only' and 'Non-Europeans Only' are ubiquitous. The 1959 version is 'Whites Only' and 'Non-Whites', but there are so many of these signs up and down the land that it will take much time, and a great deal of paint, before the old notices are replaced by the new. Restaurants, hotels, tea-shops, cinemas, and theatres make the same distinction but it is unnecessary to put up notices to that effect. The social, economic and political life of South Africa is based on these distinctions and it is well to find out what lies behind them, what their real extent is, what their purpose is, and whether they fulfil that purpose.

The distinction made between white and non-white is usually referred to by the comprehensive name of the 'colour bar', and for purposes of closer identification an adjective is added: thus we have industrial colour bars, political colour bars, social colour bars, colour bar in sport, and so on. A great deal of social discrimination is the result of custom rather than of legislation or regulation. The great social gulf between the white settlers and the aboriginals with whom they came into contact acted as a deterrent to social mixing; and though in the early days, the deterrent was not strong enough to prevent miscegenation, it gradually became the social custom to frown on Europeans who defied the conventions to the extent of intermarriage. The whites were heavily outnumbered and had a strong incentive to keep together against the danger of having their more progressive civilization swamped by the numerically superior group. Though the social gulf has grown narrower it is still wide enough to account for the dislike, amounting to physical aversion, that most Europeans feel for intermarriage. The very narrowing of the gulf powerfully reinforces colour prejudice on the part of the whites who, being outnumbered by the non-whites, fear that if social distinctions disappear political distinctions could no longer be maintained.

Fear and dislike of mixed marriages are the strongest expression of colour prejudice, and a great deal of social discrimination is justified popularly on the grounds of its potential danger to the 'purity of the race': it may lead to mixed marriages. 'How would you like your sister to marry a Native?' is the popular, if illogical, expression of this prejudice. Lincoln's reply, that because he wanted justice for a Negro woman it did not mean that he wanted to marry her, has little effect on this deeply rooted anxiety. It is probably this fear of miscegenation that explains why colour prejudice is strongest against social activities where physical contact is close and intimate. Europeans and non-Europeans go to the same race-meetings, but to different enclosures; they do not play football together, or swim in the same public baths, or (normally) bathe from the same beaches; they buy goods at the same shops but do not go to the same restaurants and hotels. Since many towns in the Cape Province cannot support more than one cinema, European and Coloured people customarily attended the same performance but sat in separate blocks of seats—a practice now forbidden by law unless an annually renewable permit has been granted to the proprietor. White and non-white will watch the same rugby or cricket match,[1] though from different stands; but they do not go to the same boxing-match which takes place at night and in a hall; boxing between black and white is unheard of,[2] and films showing such boxing are censored. Even among many 'advanced' Europeans, mixed dances are not regarded as desirable.

South Africans do not, however, object to non-European servants who perform the most intimate domestic duties for them. The vast majority of adult Europeans in South Africa were looked after by non-European nursemaids. African or Coloured servants waken their employers with early morning tea or coffee; they prepare their food for them; make their beds for them; wait on them at table; do their laundry for them. This is, of course, only an apparent inconsistency. Domestically, the non-European is a servant and the European a master. In a public restaurant or at a cinema, that relationship would not exist; European and non-European would pay the same and would, in fact, be equal.

Social colour prejudice as it exists in South Africa is known in other parts of the world. The Southern States of America provide one example. Other parts of Africa provide further examples. Even in Britain, as recent years have shown, colour prejudice is not unknown. There is, of course, a great difference between the Africans whom people in Britain meet and the mass of Africans in South Africa. The former are mostly educated men and women who are studying

[1] Except at Bloemfontein, the capital of the Orange Free State, where the town council recently erected a giant stadium and, despite the opposition of white sporting bodies, decreed that no non-white spectators would be admitted.
[2] Until January 1960, when it was forbidden by law, white boxers frequently used black sparring partners.

overseas, and they have adapted themselves to European ways and manners; and the ordinary educated Englishman associates with them easily, though, sometimes, a little self-consciously. In South Africa, too, many Europeans will meet educated Africans on terms of equality. But there is this difference, that while English people meet the few educated Africans and so fail to understand why South Africans are colour-conscious, South Africans see the few educated Africans against a background of ignorance and semi-barbarism, and they are afraid to distinguish between them lest the small trickle of friendly association becomes a swollen river of social amalgamation.

Until 1948 social colour bars were, generally speaking, conventional. Political and economic discrimination, on the other hand, is for the most part the result of legislation. We saw in chapter 4 that only Europeans are eligible to sit in parliament or in the provincial councils, and that while Europeans enjoy universal suffrage from the age of 18, it is only in the Cape Province that Coloured males, from the age of 21 and with certain property and educational qualifications, are directly represented, by Europeans elected on separate electoral rolls. Africans in the Cape Province with the desired qualifications elected Europeans, on a separate roll; but that representation was abolished in 1959. In Natal a negligible number of Coloured voters are enrolled both for parliamentary and provincial elections. The Separate Representation of Voters Act, 1956, however, provides that no new Coloured names shall be added to the roll. In municipal government, again, it is only in the Cape Province that non-Europeans may qualify to vote, and there is no legal bar to their election to a town or city council. The government has however announced that, as soon as the Group Areas Act has been put into effect, there will be separate municipal councils for Coloured people who will then be taken off the common municipal roll.

Other chapters in this book describe the administrative differentiation between European and non-European, and the increasing discrimination involved in the policy of apartheid. Such Acts of Parliament as the Group Areas Act, the Population Registration Act, the Immorality Act, the Mixed Marriages Act, the Extension of University Education Act, and the Industrial Conciliation Act, all discriminate between different 'racial' groups in South Africa. While some of the provisions of these Acts do entail serious economic hardship, their main purpose is to achieve as much social separation as possible, even at the expense of economic efficiency. There are, however, laws specifically designed to prevent non-whites from working at what jobs they like or where they like. The Industrial Conciliation Act, for example, empowers the Minister of Labour to reserve jobs for different racial groups, and a debate in parliament in 1959 made it clear that one of the objects of this was to safeguard the position of white workers in times of unemployment.

By the Land Act of 1913, Africans were prohibited from acquiring land except in the Reserves. The courts decided that the Act did not apply to the Cape Province, but the Natives Trust and Land Act of 1936 removed that exception. It is, of course, equally true that Europeans may not own land in the Native Reserves, but, since the land open to European occupation is about 87 per cent of the area of the Union, this is not a serious restriction on Europeans. Until 1950, Coloured and Asians could own land where they liked in the Cape Province except in a Native Reserve; but the Group Areas Act of 1950 has put a stop to that. The right of Asians to hold land in Natal and the Transvaal has always been severely restricted.

The laws that restrict freedom of movement of Africans are popularly known as the 'pass laws'. A law of this kind was introduced into the Cape Colony by the British Government, in the early nineteenth century, with the object of controlling roving Hottentots. It was subsequently abolished at the Cape, but the system was extensively used by the Boer Trekkers in the new states they founded, and it was carried over into Union. The Natives (Abolition of Passes and Co-ordination of Documents) Act of 1952 abolishes the pass laws in the technical sense in which they were used in the Transvaal and Free State. Nevertheless, an African needs a permit to enter an urban area where he is allowed to stay for seventy-two hours only without further permission; if he goes to an urban area to undertake employment (not to seek it) he must have the prior permission of the labour bureau in his home area; as soon as he takes up employment his service contract must be registered; and he must have a permit to be outside the location after curfew hours. All these permits and registrations are entered in his reference book which he must carry with him at all times; reference books for African women are not yet compulsory but will become so as soon as their issue is completed. Passes in the popular sense are not required by Africans in the Cape Province, but all the regulations just mentioned apply to them as well as in the rest of the Union. Whatever name the law may give to permits and documents and reference books, to Africans they are 'passes', that is, papers connected with restriction of movement, not carried by all races, and having to be produced on demand.[1] Any

[1] The official Bantu Education Journal for September 1959 carried a notice to the effect that the department had been at pains to coin vernacular equivalents of the words 'reference book', and employees of the department and pupils were encouraged to use these rather than the objectionable word 'pass'. It is doubtful whether this will have more than a superficial effect on popular usage.

police official may at any time demand to see any one of these papers, and failure to produce it is an offence involving a fine or imprisonment. It has been said that the number of technical offences of which an African may be guilty is such that any police official can at any time arrest any African and be sure of obtaining a conviction.

There are few aspects of European administration that Africans resent so bitterly as the pass laws and regulations. They consider passes as badges of inferiority; they resent the constant interference of the police; the fines imposed are out of all proportion to the offence or to the income of the offender; and the conviction stands as a 'previous conviction'. There can be few adult Africans living in European areas who have not, at some time or other, offended against the pass laws. In January 1960 the Minister of Justice, in reply to a question in parliament, gave details of the instructions issued to the police in regard to the treatment of Africans accused of minor offences (see p. 112 above). From these instructions it is clear that the policy is to make that treatment dependent on the possession of a reference book which, as the Minister said, would be regarded 'as a guarantee of the honesty and bona fides of the holder' who 'may consequently be treated with more consideration than those who do not possess reference books'. It is difficult to see how the new regulations, thus framed, can have anything more than a very minor effect in easing the situation. All Africans regard the reference book as a 'pass' that must be carried day and night and can be demanded by a police official. The most law-abiding African citizen who has left his reference book at home will still be liable to arrest on the charge that he has committed a minor offence.

The reasons advanced for maintaining the pass laws are that they help to control the influx of Africans to overcrowded areas, that they prevent desertion from service, and that they enable the police to trace criminals. These arguments do not hold water. About 90 per cent of prosecutions under the pass laws occur on the Witwatersrand, an area notorious for crime, for overcrowded slums, and for desertion. Since passes are reasonably easy to forge, the African criminal makes quite sure that, if he is stopped, he will not be arrested because of the absence of a piece of paper. And the pass regulations do not effectively control the entry into crowded urban areas. In the European rural areas the pass system does, indeed, enable farmers to prevent African labourers from leaving their service. But, on the whole, the pass laws do not achieve their object. What they do achieve is an interference with the mobility of labour, and an enormous number of prosecutions and imprisonments for technical offences. Since no African regards the pass laws as other than unjust, their administration has no moral support from the African public. To have laws to which 80 per cent of the population are bitterly opposed is unlikely to inculcate a regard for law.

There are a number of Acts on the Statute Book that discriminate against the African as a worker. The most famous of these has given its popular name to the whole system of discrimination. It is called the Colour Bar Act. The Mines and Works Act of 1911 empowered the government to regulate the issue of certificates of competency in skilled occupations in mining and engineering. The first attempt to apply it was in 1923, when government proposed to prevent Africans from obtaining certificates. The regulation was tested in the courts and declared *ultra vires*, but the European trade unions agitated until the Nationalist-Labour Government passed an amending Act in 1926. This was the Colour Bar Act, which prevents Africans from performing a large number of skilled mining jobs.

The object of the Colour Bar Act was to reserve skilled jobs in mining for Europeans, and it was confined to mining until 1956 when the Industrial Conciliation Act (and subsequent amendments) gave the Minister of Labour unfettered power to reserve any job or any class of job for members of any race. The first reservation decrees were declared invalid by the courts, but that loophole was stopped. The same object of reserving skilled jobs for Europeans is achieved by refusing to enrol Africans as apprentices, thus effectively preventing them from acquiring skill. European workers, having achieved certain standards of living and of skill, fear that an influx of Africans into the skilled trades would enable employers to reduce wages and so lower trade standards. The skilled trade unions will not admit Africans to membership, and it is only in some of the semi-skilled unions that mixed membership obtains. The Industrial Conciliation Act prohibits the establishment of further mixed unions and an amendment limits the activities of existing ones by compelling them to organize separate branches, hold separate meetings, and elect Europeans only to their executive committees.

The regulations between employers and their African workers are regulated by various masters and servants laws and by the Native Labour Regulation Act. Under these laws it is a criminal offence for an African to refuse to obey an order or to break his contract. For Africans employed on more than daily or weekly contracts, this effectively limits their right to strike. African trade unions have no legal status, and, with the severe limitations on the right to withhold labour, effective combination becomes difficult. The gold-mines prohibit African trade unions altogether. In secondary industries Africans perform a great deal of semi-skilled labour, and, though their trade unions do not have legal recognition, they have succeeded in gaining wage increases by strike action.

The original Industrial Conciliation Act of 1924 provides machinery, retained in the Act of 1956, for the establishment of industrial councils; but it specifically excludes 'pass-bearing Natives'. Since most industries employ Europeans and Africans, an industrial council may ask the Minister to fix African wages in that particular industry. The Wage Act of 1925 provides machinery for fixing wages of unskilled and unorganized labour, European or African; but, like the Industrial Conciliation Act, it does not apply to farm labour, to domestic servants, or to government employees. Moreover, since the Wage Board carries out its investigations separately in different trades and in different areas, progress is slow. In many cases the last minimum wage-levels were fixed twenty years ago, before World War II, and though wages have been increased by a statutory cost-of-living allowance, this has been too small to cope with the actual increase in cost of living.

There are many Acts of Parliament that do not contain a colour bar, but do, in administration, discriminate between European and non-European. All social welfare legislation is administered on the assumption that it costs more to feed a European than it does a Coloured, and more to feed a Coloured than it does an African. Mothers' pensions, old-age pensions, assistance for the blind, school-feeding are all graded in this way. Then, again, the Stock Theft Acts contain severe penalties irrespective of race, but in practice the punishment of the African—both absolutely and relative to his economic state—is many times more severe than that of the European. Moreover, a recent amendment to the Stock Theft Act discriminates against non-Europeans by empowering the Minister to proclaim areas in which every sale of stock must be accompanied by a document from the seller to the buyer; if the seller is a European he may sign this document himself, but if he is a non-European (other than a landowner) he must get a certificate from an employer, a policeman, a chief or headman, or some other person mentioned in the amendment.

The various forms and sources of colour discrimination may be summed up as follows:

(1) Long-standing convention or custom, deeply rooted in the habits of European and non-European, and not dependent on any legal sanction, lies behind all social segregation, including that of organized sport. There were signs that strict social segregation was beginning to break down, but since 1948 the Nationalist Government has amended existing laws and made many new laws to prevent this from happening, and has applied legal sanctions to what were formerly

matters of convention. Social contact between the races was much more difficult in 1959 than it was in 1948.

(2) There are laws with no colour bar, but colour discrimination is applied in their administration or, in their very nature, they press more hardly on African than on European offenders. There are many examples of this: different pension scales for different races; inferior public service for non-whites; harsher sentences for assault or rape; fines that would not be seriously felt by a white man but press hardly on a non-white.

(3) Laws containing a specific colour bar have either a social purpose, or an economic purpose, or, more commonly, both. The Mixed Marriages Act has a social purpose; the Colour Bar Act has an economic purpose; the pass laws and the laws regulating African labour have a social and an economic purpose.

(4) Finally, there are colour bar laws in which the political motive dominates but where economic and social reasons, frequently obscured, play an important role. Examples of this are the various Acts providing for the separate administration of Africans; the various franchise Acts that have placed Coloured and African voters on separate rolls with much reduced representation; and the South Africa Act itself—an Act to constitute the Union and passed by the British Parliament.

It is clear, then, that with small and significant exceptions which will be noticed presently, South African national life is based on colour distinctions that are as strong and rigid as the class and social distinctions that were characteristic of Europe until the nineteenth century. The immediate and obvious effect of this is that, economically, the whole country and all its people are suffering from the reckless waste of manpower and of land. Muscles and skills that could be harnessed to increase the prosperity of the country are kept untrained and idle. The mass of the population is unable to produce enough or to earn enough for sufficient food and housing, and medical reports are unanimous in asserting the disastrous results in high mortality rates and susceptibility to deficiency diseases.

The political results of the colour bar are not so immediately apparent, though equally far-reaching. Parliament does not represent the people of South Africa, and most members of parliament are out of touch with the needs and wishes of the non-Europeans, who constitute about 80 per cent of the population. It is possible that the majority of Africans have not yet advanced sufficiently from tribalism to be able to exercise the franchise usefully in a multi-racial society; but many Africans are fully capable of doing so. To cut them off from the opportunity of making their influence felt in the legislature is to weaken parliament by making it too narrowly representative. Further, the policy of apartheid expressly excludes Africans from ever having political influence in parliament. The effect of this is to induce an anti-European African nationalism that cannot but weaken the country in peace and in war. Failure to give the non-European an effective stake in the country and in sound government must, in the long run, lead to revolt.

Another result of the political colour bar is that, in order to retain political control, European South Africa has resorted to policies and laws that have progressively disregarded the standards of justice and of Western civilization. This has been done on grounds of so-called 'self-preservation'. In 1936 the Hertzog-Smuts Government removed African voters in Cape Province from the common roll on which they had been registered since 1853; this was done by a law passed, as required by the South Africa Act, by a two-thirds majority of both houses in joint session. In 1956, parliament deprived Coloured voters in the Cape of their common roll rights, but in passing the Bill, disregarded the two-thirds majority rule, thus denying the validity of the procedure entrenched in the constitution. That the object of this measure, and the method used to secure it, were to retain political control has not been denied. To abandon standards of justice in the name of self-preservation, for selfish group ends and with the consequent disregard of the rule of law, is dangerous in all societies but incalculably so in a multi-racial society.

It is chiefly in urban areas that non-Europeans become acutely aware of social colour discrimination, though even there it is probably a minority who actively resent this. So deep-rooted is colour discrimination that most people, European and non-European, accept it unquestioningly as part of the natural order of things, and many non-Europeans who bitterly resent economic and administrative discrimination, accept social discrimination. There are, however, growing numbers of educated non-Europeans who have adopted European civilization and who are ambitious for themselves and for their children. These people, the natural leaders of the non-Europeans, resent more or less bitterly a scheme of things in which they are made to feel inferior and are treated, at best with condescension, and at worst with injustice. They have few rights in their only native land and are made to feel that what they have are privileges rather than rights. The result is a dissipation in rebelliousness and non-co-operation of what would otherwise be socially constructive energies.

The policy of social and political discrimination has adversely affected South Africa's Commonwealth and international relations, particularly since the end of the Second World War. At a time when world opinion was moving away from racialism and towards greater freedom for non-European colonial dependencies, the Nationalist Party came to power in South Africa on a policy of apartheid which demanded an even more stringent application of colour bar legislation, at variance with modern world trends. She has, as a result, regularly been attacked at United Nations meetings and has found herself in the position of prisoner at the bar of world opinion. At first she had friends who agreed with her that internal affairs should not be debated at U.N.O. but her friends have become markedly less enthusiastic, and for a time South Africa withdrew from sessions of the United Nations. Some of the accusations against her have been well founded, while others have been marked chiefly by exaggeration and a lack of understanding of the difficulties of a multi-racial society. Her defence, particularly against the latter kind of charges, has usually taken the form either of saying, 'This is our private affair' or of the counter-accusation, 'You are no better than we are'.

The result of being out of step with world opinion has produced a sense of isolation, and in defending herself against world criticism South Africa has not escaped the danger of regarding isolation, not with concern, but with defiant pride—the more so when the criticism is uninformed and therefore regarded as malicious. Afrikaners in particular have to a large extent come to regard themselves as maligned and misunderstood, standing alone against an unsympathetic world. In May 1951, the then Prime Minister, Malan, said in a public speech that the continued criticism of South African policy by the British Press would drive South Africa to become a republic. He used an illuminating parallel. Just as, he said, the Voortrekkers had left the Cape Colony in 1838 because of the false accusations constantly made against the Afrikaners by the British, so the modern Afrikaner would have another Great Trek, a trek not to another country, but to an independent republic. The implication is that South Africa can protect herself against the blasts of international criticism by wrapping herself in a cloak of isolationism. The fiercer the storms, the more precious to the wearer does the cloak appear to be.

It is not only the government that has found itself at odds with world opinion. The Dutch Reformed churches have officially supported the policy of apartheid, while Calvinist and other Protestant churches in Holland and the United States of America, as well as elsewhere, have expressed their disapproval. A few Dutch Reformed Church ministers are disturbed about this break in Christian unity; but most of them are closely allied with the Nationalist Party's interpretation of Afrikaner sentiment and accuse disapproving outsiders of being ignorant of the situation in South Africa.

Even the South African medical world has felt the repercussions of this policy. In 1950 the South African Medical Association proposed to invite the British Medical Association to a joint meeting and was asked by the B.M.A. to ascertain from the government whether any difficulties would be placed in the way of delegates on racial grounds. The then Minister of the Interior, Dr. Dönges, refused to commit himself in advance to granting visas to members of the B.M.A., saying that each case would be judged on its merits. The B.M.A. would not accept an arrangement that might lay its members open to being refused admission on the grounds of colour: and the joint meeting was called off. The South African Medical Association, and numerous other public bodies, protested against the action of the government, but to no avail; and without government co-operation the meeting could not be held. For this reason South Africa is often denied the opportunity and the privilege of being host to international conferences.

Repercussions of South Africa's apartheid policy have been felt in the world of sport. In 1959 government permission was granted for a West Indian cricket team to tour South Africa to play against non-whites only. Many Coloured and Asian enthusiasts were anxious to have such a tour, but so much pressure was brought to bear, both in the Union and in the West Indies, against conniving at an apartheid tour that it had to be dropped. Again, a few non-white associations have applied for international recognition on the grounds that, not only did they have more members than their white counterparts, but unlike the latter they had no colour bar. Thus the South African Table Tennis Board (non-white but with no colour bar) has been internationally recognized as the controlling body in South Africa, with the interesting result that the white table tennis players have to obtain its permission before inviting teams from other countries. A few years ago such permission was sought to bring a team of white Australian players to South Africa and the Board agreed on two conditions: there should be no colour bar among spectators and two matches against non-whites should be arranged. The white South African players felt themselves unable to accept these conditions and gave as their reason that they had been told by the Minister of the Interior that matches between white and non-white were not allowed. In strict fact, this excuse was not valid because there is no law (at present) forbidding such a match. That the excuse was used is indicative of the fear that many Europeans have of going counter to government policy as distinct from the law of the land.

There are other examples of the difficulties being caused in inter-national sport by South Africa's customs and policies. The Olympic Games Governing Council, the controlling board of international association football, and other bodies will be under continuing pressure; so, of course, will the white organizations in South Africa be. Possibly the most serious situation, from the South African point of view, arises in rugby football. When South African teams (the Springboks) tour New Zealand they play against Maoris without losing caste; but in deference to South African customs the New Zealand Rugby Board has thus far excluded Maoris from their teams to tour the Union. A New Zealand team, ironically enough known as the All Blacks, is due to tour South Africa in 1960, and the South African Press has given much publicity to the protests in New Zealand against excluding Maoris. It is interesting to note that a number of ex-Springboks who had played in New Zealand publicly expressed the view that Maori players would be welcome; whether the government would grant the necessary visas is another matter. At the time of writing it seems as if the All Blacks will tour South Africa in 1960, without Maoris; but it also seems probable that that will be the last time that the New Zealand Rugby Board will be allowed by New Zealand public opinion to have the composition of its national rugby team dictated by considerations other than merit.

There is another respect in which South African colour bar policy is a hindrance to progress. As the state in Africa that has by far the biggest European population, it is natural that the Union should play a prominent part in the development of Africa south of the Sahara. She does, in fact, play a considerable part in promoting co-operation with other territories to tackle common problems such as locust destruction; and she desires to maintain good relations economically with the other territories. The populations of these territories are overwhelmingly African, and, except for Southern Rhodesia and Kenya, include a mere handful of Europeans. The policies of the European mother countries that govern these territories differ, but they have this in common: they all envisage a time when Africans will share fully in the common task of government. To this the Nationalist Party policy of apartheid is entirely opposed, and the result is that in political matters the governments of those colonial territories and the vast majority of their subjects are deeply suspicious of South African Native policy, and political co-operation towards working out a solution of Africa's problems is becoming increasingly difficult.

It is difficult to estimate the real strength of colour bar institutions and to assess the forces that are working against them. The great majority of South Africans of all colours approve of some degree of social separation, the degree varying with the individual and his social sphere. The English-speaking churches have all declared themselves opposed to separation in matters of religion, and there is no colour bar at synodical and similar meetings. In practice, however, there are very few churches where all races habitually worship in common. Again, though the universities of Cape Town and Witwatersrand may no longer enrol non-European students, the principle of academic equality is accepted by the overwhelming majority of staff and students at those two institutions; yet it is doubtful if the majority would favour full social equality outside the lecture rooms. A great many Europeans are opposed to the Nationalist Party's policy of apartheid, not because they favour social equality or miscegenation, but because they do not believe that such matters can, in the long run, be determined by legislation and regulation. They feel that popular sanction for social separation is so powerful that legislation is unnecessary and vexatious.

Government policy and administrative pressure have tried to prevent any form of social contact between white and non-white. In spite of that, social and political contact has increased since 1948 because men and women on both sides of the colour line who have not shut their eyes to what is happening in the world, and particularly in Africa, have come to realize the vital need for such contacts. Long-established bodies such as the South African Institute of Race Relations and the National Union of South African Students have redoubled their efforts to maintain old contacts and encourage new ones; and the Liberal Party and the Civil Rights League in Cape Town, founded to oppose Nationalist policy, are interracial in membership. The Black Sash, a body of women established to protest against what they regarded as the breaking of the constitution, has gone on from that point to practical and positive work in defence of civil liberty. While it consists of voters, and has therefore no non-white members, its work inevitably brings it into contact with African women and their organizations. Multi-racial conferences, sponsored by men and women of standing in the different racial communities, have been held and widely attended. The leaders of the South African Bureau of Racial Affairs, which has white members only, have continued to meet African and Coloured leaders in spite of ministerial disapproval; and students at Afrikaans universities have had Coloured and African speakers to address them and have themselves paid friendly visits to Fort Hare University College.

It is probably in the industrial and commercial spheres that the strongest forces against economic colour bars are to be found. The demands of secondary industries and of commerce have increased, and are increasing, so rapidly that Africans and Coloured are already widely employed as operatives and in semi-skilled jobs. And the demand is becoming more insistent for the progressive abolition of the colour bars which prevent non-Europeans from being trained and used in skilled work. All but the most extreme supporters of apartheid now recognize that strict economic separation cannot be carried out: and even the extremists tacitly admit the country's dependence on the work of all races when they say that the Europeans must be prepared to make sacrifices for the ideal of race purity.

As we saw, it is on the mines that the Colour Bar Act is enforced.[1] With rising costs, the mine-owners would like to abolish the colour bar and to use Africans in skilled jobs; but the European miners' unions are too powerful. It is the same in the building and other skilled industries. European workers are afraid of being undercut, as, indeed, they must be unless the state were to guarantee both full wages and full employment. Probably the majority of European skilled workers is English-speaking, so that support for economic colour bars is not purely Afrikaner.

Skilled trade unions are not, of course, the only obstacle to the removal of the industrial colour bar. They are backed by the force of public opinion which regards the colour bar as traditional and has not yet become fully aware of its effect on economic production. An illustration of the force of such public opinion is to be found in the fact that the Nationalist Party consistently accuses the United Party opposition of planning to abolish the colour bar in industry, and regards the accusation as effective political party propaganda. That the United Party regards it in the same light is shown by its strenuous denials that it is planning anything of the sort. Despite the denial, however, it is among those who normally support the United Party that there exists a growing body of opinion favourable to the gradual relaxation of industrial colour bars. That it should be gradual is essential, for to abolish them suddenly, and all at once, would have catastrophic economic results in unemployment and in lowered industrial standards.

Among the forces making for the relaxation of economic colour bars is the African worker. Coloured workers are found mostly in the Cape Province, where they are still admitted to a variety of skilled trades. The industrial colour bar does not, therefore, press as hardly on them as it does on the Africans, who constitute something like 80 per cent of the labour force in South Africa and are becoming increasingly aware of their importance to the economy of the country. Thus far their organization has been weak; but there are plenty of signs that it is improving. More and more the African industrial worker is losing touch with the Reserves. Where, formerly, he still

[1] There is evidence that, even on the mines, the colour bar is being relaxed.

regarded his urban or mine cash wage as supplementary to his stake in the Reserves, he is now an industrial worker and nothing else. This increases the incentive to improve his skill and to obtain higher wages. This demand from below, coupled with the economic needs of industrial employers, constitutes the most serious threat to the industrial colour bar.

Probably the best illustration of the newly felt power of African workers is the famous bus boycott that took place in Johannesburg and Pretoria in 1957. In its bare essentials, the story is that African workers decided to walk to and from their work rather than pay an increased bus fare that had been sanctioned by the Road Transportation Board. The government took an extremely serious view of this and regarded it as a challenge that must be met. The Minister of Transport appealed to employers not to be lenient with late-comers or tired workers, and he more than once stated that he would break the boycott which, in his view, was a political threat organized by the African National Congress. Police harassed the walking Africans by demanding to see their passes and, when they were given lifts by sympathetic Europeans (a common occurrence), by stopping the cars on the pretence of searching for wanted men or for permits. Despite every threat and discouragement, something like 45,000 Africans walked distances of 18 to 20 miles a day, and kept it up for ten weeks until the Chamber of Commerce and the Johannesburg City Council intervened. The African workers had won their fight and had done so without any organizational machinery except for *ad hoc* committees, chosen as need arose. Moreover, the boycott revealed a new phenomenon: Africans were no longer content to let Europeans, or Africans nominated by Europeans, negotiate on their behalf; negotiations were to be with their own boycott leaders or not at all.

It is in political affairs that colour distinctions attract most attention, in and out of South Africa. Those among the non-Europeans who are educated, who have discarded tribalism, and who live among Europeans are the people who demand representation in parliament. There are a great many Europeans who feel, in a somewhat confused way, that there is something wrong about denying the vote to such people. Among the most thoroughgoing supporters of apartheid, for example, the argument is as follows: you cannot, in common decency and in justice, allow people to work in your industries and then deny them a say in the government; but we cannot allow them to vote because they will swamp the European vote; therefore, there is only one just solution: complete territorial apartheid. This argument involves a recognition of the justice of the African's demand for the franchise.

The United Party Government, under Smuts, passed an Act in 1946 giving Asians the right to elect three European members to parliament on a separate roll. This was done in spite of opposition within the party, chiefly from the province of Natal itself, where most South African Asians live. The Asians refused to co-operate and failed to elect their members; and, in 1948, the Nationalist Party Government repealed the Act on the ground that the Asians are an unassimilable element and should have no part in government. Nevertheless, the fact remains that a South African parliament had recognized the need to grant more non-European representation.

The question may well be asked: why is it then that, despite the existence of a not entirely unsympathetic sentiment, the political status of the non-European has deteriorated? This deterioration is not solely the result of the Nationalist doctrine of apartheid; it began in the 'thirties when Coloured and African women were omitted from the Act that instituted universal suffrage for Europeans, and it continued in 1936 when African voters in the Cape were taken off the common roll. What apartheid has done is to remove Coloured voters in the Cape from the common roll, to kill by slow degrees the small Coloured vote in Natal, to abolish the incipient Indian representation, and to abolish the existing Natives' representation of three members. On the face of it, the record of both parties does not reveal much 'sympathetic sentiment'; nevertheless, the sentiment exists. What stultifies it is the overriding fear of being swamped by non-European voters. Europeans have an uneasy feeling that they cannot, for ever, postpone giving political representation to non-Europeans, and they are trying, desperately, to put off the 'evil' day. They are unable to rid themselves of the conviction that Africans, if given the vote, will automatically vote 'black' against 'white'. What they fail to realize is that the longer they withhold the franchise the more likely are their fears to prove justified.

The purpose of political and economic colour bars in South Africa is to ensure that effective control remains with the Europeans. In that way, and in that way only, most Europeans believe, will the standards of Western civilization be maintained. It is a deep-rooted and genuine belief. But the truth of the matter is that the more effective the present application of the colour bar is, the less likely is it to achieve its long-term objective. Western civilization cannot be maintained by denying rights, but only by extending them.

7

Politics, Policies, and Parties

POLITICS IN THE UNION OF SOUTH AFRICA ARE DOMINATED BY TWO
facts: English-Afrikaans relationships are always present; and the
majority of the population is practically unrepresented in parliament.
There are other elements in the situation: personalities play a large
part in South African politics; so do differences of outlook between the
new, hustling, pioneering Transvaal and the older, more relaxed,
settled Cape; economic factors are always present and sometimes
decisive; even a prolonged drought may affect the result of an election.
But the two dominant factors remain, like submerged rocks that give
ever-changing shapes to the waves and currents. Properly understood,
these two elements, constantly reacting on each other, will give a
clearer idea of the shifts and turns in South African politics and of the
way South Africa is going. The Union Parliament reflects European
public opinion and in this respect resembles the parliament in England
immediately after the Reform Act of 1832, when it was elected by
landowners, by urban employers, and by the top layer of workers,
while the mass of the population had to wait for later reform Acts to
enfranchise them. Within the Union Parliament that reflects European
opinion only, party alignments, defections, and realignments are the
result of what people feel and believe about English-Afrikaans relationships and about the unrepresented millions who are neither English
nor Afrikaans and on whose labour the wealth of the country rests.

The first Union Cabinet, in 1910, was formed by General Louis
Botha after elections that had been fought provincially rather than
nationally. In Natal, for the first and last time, all candidates stood
as independents. In the other provinces the Unionist Party, led by
Jameson from the Cape, was predominantly English, and returned
39 candidates. The Labour Party had 4 members. The Afrikaner
parties in the Transvaal, Free State, and the Cape had the support of
many English-speaking people and elected 66 members. It was only
after the first parliament had met, however, that political divisions
began to sort themselves out, and Botha became leader of what was
then called the South African Party.

Botha's policy was one of conciliation between English and
Afrikaners, and it soon became clear that a great many Afrikaners in
the Free State and Transvaal did not support that policy. By 1912
the differences between Botha and Hertzog became so great that a
split occurred and Hertzog formed the Nationalist Party. There was a

great upsurge of nationalism linked with the growth of the Afrikaans language and based on a 'South Africa First' (that is before the Empire) policy. The outbreak of war in 1914, and Botha's determination to stand by Britain, inflamed nationalist opinion still further. The Rebellion, though officially frowned on by the Nationalist Party, stirred Afrikaner memories and added many members to the party. In the general election of 1915 the Nationalists polled 77,000 votes to the South African Party's 95,000. Botha, with 54 seats, had the strongest party but did not command an absolute majority, and was forced to depend on the good will of the Unionist Party which had 40 seats. The Nationalists, with 27 seats, were a cohesive and growing party, and they became in effect the Opposition. In the same year in which Hertzog formed the Nationalist Party, a conference of African leaders, alarmed by the colour bar in the South Africa Act and by the evident tendencies of Union policies, met in Bloemfontein and established the African National Congress—a little-noticed portent of the shape of things to come.

Botha died in 1919 and Smuts became Prime Minister. During the war (1914-18) the government had failed to cope with rising costs of living or to exercise any reasonable control over commodities and food. This question became the main argument in the 1920 general election, but as always in South Africa, nationalist sentiment played a big part. It was because South Africa was tied to the Empire, said the Nationalists, that people were having economic difficulties. By the election the Nationalist Party became the strongest party with 44 members; the Labour Party gained largely from the Unionists, who returned 25 members, while Labour had 21. Smuts's South African Party had 41, and he decided to carry on with the help of the Unionists and of 3 Independents; but it was a precarious and unstable position. Even before the election there had been talk that the Unionists and South African Parties would unite. Smuts, knowing the importance of Afrikaner support, was anxious to avoid an out-and-out alliance with the Unionists. The part he had played as imperial statesman during the First World War had enabled the Nationalists to taunt him with being the 'handyman of the Empire'. Smuts never took notice of personal taunts, but his party could not afford to alienate Afrikaner sympathy, so he made an attempt to bring about a reconciliation between the Nationalist and South African Parties. This failed, partly because by now the Nationalists were convinced that they would eventually gain the upper hand in South Africa, and partly because the two groups could not agree on the question of the right of secession from the Empire. So Smuts decided to combine with the Unionists. The two parties merged under his leadership, retaining the name of

South African Party, and another general election was held in 1921 at which the Nationalists got 45 seats and Labour lost 15 of its previous seats to the new South African Party, thus giving that party a clear majority of 22.

During the next three years Smuts's Government was faced with problems that had been slowly ripening and whose growth had been accelerated but obscured by the war. The so-called 'Rand Revolution' of 1922 illustrates one of these problems clearly. Faced with rising costs and shortage of labour, the gold-mines proposed to use Africans in certain skilled work—in other words, partially to abolish the colour bar on the mines. The white miners at once struck, and within a few weeks strikes had turned into a rising directed by a Communist Council of Action which had as its principal slogan: 'Workers of the World, fight and unite for a White South Africa.' The Defence Force was called out and the rising was suppressed, but Smuts's Government was identified, both by the Nationalists and by the Labour Party, with the Chamber of Mines and with large-scale capitalism that was not interested in protecting the white race. From now on the 'Native Question' was firmly in the political arena. The influx of Africans to urban areas, to work in the new industries, was one very important aspect of this problem. It created difficulties for local authorities, and it helped to draw labour from the farms where Nationalist Party strength lay. Trade unions saw in the influx a threat to their standard of living, and the Smuts Government, whose support increasingly came from urban industrialists, seemed to both Nationalists and Labourites to be either unwilling or powerless to do anything about it. It was at this time, too, that white politicians began to take note of an organization of African workers formed in 1919 by Clements Kadalie, a native of Nyasaland and a remarkable man. This was the Industrial and Commercial Workers' Union of Africa, commonly known as the I.C.U., and though it was short-lived it succeeded in giving South Africa a bad fright. The leaders of the Nationalist Party, Hertzog and Malan, thought it worth while to keep on friendly terms with the I.C.U. in the Cape Province, where Africans still had the vote on the common roll; and both Hertzog and Smuts handled Kadalie and his organization with great care but with equal determination not to allow it to get the upper hand.

Thus it came about in 1924 that a predominantly English-speaking party, the Labour Party, and a predominantly Afrikaner party, the Nationalist, formed an election pact. The Nationalists undertook to respect Labour's attachment to Britain and not to speak about secession, while Nationalist fears were set at rest by the assurance that Labour did not aim at socialism. The common ground was nothing positive; it was dislike of Smuts and his supposed association with finance capital. At the general election the Nationalists had 63 seats, Labour 18, and the South African Party 53, with 1 Independent, and General Hertzog formed a cabinet which included two, and subsequently three, Labour ministers.

The Pact Government, as it was called, remained in power till 1933, having again achieved a majority at the 1929 elections. During its terms of office there were two Imperial Conferences, in 1926 and 1930, at which Hertzog represented South Africa. The decisions of these conferences were to have far-reaching effects on political align-ments and on constitutional history. When Smuts came back from Europe in 1919 he had talked about the new and higher status that South Africa had achieved—dominion status. He was laughed to scorn by the Nationalists under Hertzog, and a popular Nationalist cartoon depicted a baboon (South Africa) tied to a pole (Great Britain) by a chain that was long enough to enable it to climb to the top of the pole—but still chained to Britain. At the Imperial Conference of 1926 Hertzog, mindful at once of his Afrikaans followers and of his pro-British Labour supporters, persuaded the Conference to put into writing the new relationship in the Commonwealth. With this document he returned to try to persuade the Afrikaners that South Africa had really achieved independent status. He succeeded up to a point; but already there were murmurs from the extreme Nationalists that Hertzog had given in to the Empire and had lost his republican ideals. When the next Conference, in 1930, agreed to give legislative effect to the Balfour Declaration on dominion status, as was done by the Statute of Westminister a year later, Hertzog declared himself satisfied with the constitutional position. From now on the breach between him and his more republican-minded followers widened.

The great economic depression of 1931 was directly responsible for the next shift in party alignments. When Britain went off the gold standard in 1931 the Pact Government in South Africa, in order to show its independence of Britain, refused to follow suit. The debates on the gold standard illustrate very well the point made at the beginning of this chapter—that the question of Afrikaans-English relationships, the miscalled 'racial' question, has always dominated politics. The Nationalist Party stayed on gold because Britain had gone off, and for a while economic considerations were entirely subordinated to nationalist sentiment. A flight of capital took place and the depression deepened. Then, at the end of 1932, Tielman Roos, an Appellate Division judge who had been a Nationalist Cabinet Minister, resigned from the bench and stumped the country in the interests of a national government that would deal with economic

problems in an economic way and not on 'racial' grounds. The effect
was instantaneous because Roos put into words what a great many
people were feeling. In 1933 Smuts and Hertzog formed a coalition
government with Hertzog as Prime Minister, and received an overwhelming majority at the subsequent election.

Malan had not been enamoured of coalition, and was utterly
opposed to a union of the two parties. Though he refused a cabinet
position, he remained in the coalition for a short time and then
withdrew with his supporters to form what was called the 'purified'
Nationalist Party—purified, that is, of un-Afrikaner elements. On
the other extreme, Colonel Stallard formed a Dominion Party as a
sort of watchdog of the Empire. Hertzog and Smuts formed the
United Party, with Hertzog as leader. Thus, the Afrikaner front was
broken for the second time. Hertzog had broken away from Botha in
1912; Malan broke away from Hertzog in 1934. Hertzog and Smuts
had travelled by different roads to achieve reconciliation between
English and Afrikaner; and in his long journey Hertzog had shed
republicanism as an immediate practical policy. He still believed that
a republic was the most suitable form of government for South Africa;
but he also believed that it would only come when English-speaking
South Africans were ready for it.

The new Cabinet was not fundamentally a united one. Economic
revival in mines, agriculture, and industry papered over the cracks;
but the cracks were there. Hertzog may have given up republicanism
but he was as determined as ever that South Africa should not be
bound to Britain or feel herself in any way unfree. Though he was
opposed to secession he maintained South Africa's right to secede if
she wished to. Hertzog and Smuts, both Afrikaners, differed in this
respect: Hertzog always looked over his shoulder to see if the
Afrikaners were following him; Smuts looked to see if the English-
speaking South Africans were following him. So the Afrikaners
distrusted Smuts, as the English did Hertzog. Five years after the
United Party had been established it split wide open on the war
question. Hertzog proposed benevolent neutrality; Smuts was for
full participation on the side of Britain and the Commonwealth.
Smuts won by 80 votes to 67 and became Prime Minister of a Cabinet
in which he included Labour and the Dominion Party.

The Nationalist Party was jubilant that Hertzog and his followers
had stood firm on the question of 'fighting Britain's war'. There was
much talk of a political reuniting of Afrikaners who held similar views,
but it was soon evident that while Hertzog and his lifelong friend
and lieutenant, Havenga, were not prepared to go all the way with
Smuts, they were equally unprepared to go all the way with Malan

and the purified Nationalist Party. During the five years preceding the outbreak of war, Hertzogites and Malanites had attacked one another with all the fury reserved for family quarrels; and it was not easy to forget the hard words and accusations of disloyalty to ideals. Besides, Hertzog had genuinely arrived at the stage where immediate republicanism no longer played a dominant role in his political thinking. He had become convinced that co-operation between the two European sections of the population was an essential prelude to a republic. His life's policy had been based on the assumption that such co-operation must be between equals and was only possible once the Afrikaner people had been thoroughly rehabilitated. That stage, he felt, had been reached. Co-operation could now take place on a basis of equality, and he was no longer politically at home in a party that had begun to think in terms of domination by the Afrikaners.

The Nationalist Party, on the other hand, regarded an Afrikaner republic as nearer to achievement than ever before. They banked, some consciously and others subconsciously, on a German victory and entertained the illusion that Hitler's Germany would favour an Afrikaner republic. The rapid progress of the German armies made them feel that the dissolution of the Empire was at hand and that this was not the time for Hertzog's gradualism. They were, therefore, not inclined to appease English-speaking sentiment but proclaimed their belief in the republican ideal with Afrikaans as the first language and English as the second, or subsidiary, language.

At the same time, both Malan and Hertzog felt the strong popular expectations among their followers—expectations that there would be a happy reunion of all 'true' Afrikaners. For a short while the two groups, Hertzogites and Malanites, were combined, rather than united, as parliamentary opposition under Hertzog. The new party was called the *Herenigde Nasionale of Volksparty*; but it was an uneasy alliance which had still to be cemented by a constitution and a programme of action. After months of discussion, complicated by intrigues against Hertzog's leadership on the part of the younger Nationalists, the two groups failed to agree. Both parties agreed on a republic as the desirable aim, but Hertzog insisted that it could come only in co-operation, on a basis of full equality, with English-speaking South Africans, and only by the 'broad will of the people'. The Malanites maintained that the Afrikaner would never get co-operation from the English-speaking South Africans and that a simple majority in parliament was sufficient authority to proclaim a republic. Once the republic was established the English would see that their advantage lay in co-operation.

Hertzog and Havenga resigned from the party and formed the Afrikaner Party, but the majority of Afrikaners remained with

Malan in the *Herenigde Nasionale Party*, and Hertzog presently retired from active politics leaving Havenga to lead the new party. No doubt the question of party leadership had entered into the situation. Had Hertzog been fully readmitted to the Nationalist Party it could only have been as leader, which would have ousted Malan whose reputation as an undeviating Afrikaner republican was unsullied and who had the firm support of the younger Nationalists. But the split, or rather, the failure to heal the split, went deeper than personalities. There is little doubt that the Nationalist leaders hoped for an immediate republic and regarded Hertzog as an embarrassment to their aims.

The general election during the war, in 1943, gave Smuts a sweeping majority. The Nationalists were uncompromising in their anti-war attitude and Malan had gone as far as to say that if Germany won it would be to South Africa's advantage to have a Nationalist government in power to conduct the peace negotiations—a government, that is, that would be *en rapport* with the German Government. Moreover, a draft republican constitution, not officially sanctioned but not officially repudiated, was made public. This constitution envisaged clearly a dominant Afrikaner republic from the civil benefits of which un-Afrikaans elements would be excluded. All this was too much for the bulk of the electorate who, wherever their ultimate sympathies might lie, felt that it was too late in 1943 to stop the war.

The post-war Smuts Government was faced with a multitude of problems that had been allowed to lie hidden while more pressing matters were afoot, or that, in the relaxed atmosphere of victory, were thought to be capable of solving themselves. Cost of living, acute housing shortage, scarcity of materials, rising expenditure, were none of them dealt with in an effective way, and discontent among government supporters was rife. The continued and accelerated flow to the towns, of Africans and of Europeans, aggravated the situation, and the Native question once more became acute: there had been a strike on the gold-mines that was suppressed by shooting; Africans were demanding better wages and more rights, and the African National Congress was growing in numbers and in influence. Moreover, the Natives' Representative Council, a body set up in 1936, had grown tired of passing resolutions of which the government took no notice. The Council had become, as one of its members aptly said, a 'toy telephone'—an inevitable result because, if the Council really represented African opinion, it was bound to ask for rights which no government was prepared to grant.

Since the danger from conquest by Germany was over, government supporters and Nationalists alike felt they could afford the luxury of a change of government. The Nationalist Party cleverly exploited the weak spots in the United Party's armour. A somewhat half-hearted policy of immigration was pictured as a threat to jobs, as an attempt to flood the country with unassimilable elements, and as an aggravation of the housing shortage. Above all, the Nationalist Party accused the United Party of having no clear-cut Native policy and, thus, of allowing the 'threat' to European civilization in South Africa to develop. They tried to persuade Havenga and his Afrikaner Party to join them in ousting Smuts, but Havenga would, at that stage, go no further than an election agreement and a coalition. Finally, the republican issue was put into cold storage and Malan announced that it was not a plank in his electoral platform; nevertheless, election propaganda played heavily on Afrikaner sentiment and on the damage Smuts had done to that sentiment by taking South Africa into the war on Britain's side.[1]

The result of the general election in May 1948 was a victory for the Nationalist-Afrikaner Party coalition. There were 70 Nationalist and 9 Afrikaner Party members, as against a combined opposition of 65 United Party, 6 Labour, and 3 representatives of Africans—79 to 74. Malan formed a cabinet with Havenga as Deputy Prime Minister and Minister of Finance, and three years later the two parties coalesced to form *Die Nasionale Party* with Malan as leader. Thus, for the first time since the establishment of Union in 1910, a party was in power that drew its support almost exclusively from one only of the two major white population groups. In opposition there were: the official Opposition, the United Party, which was more broadly based on English and Afrikaans support but whose main strength was urban and whose main weakness was a constant trimming of urban progressive sails in a vain attempt to recapture the rural conservative breeze; the small and dwindling Labour Party based on urban industrial labour and largely English-speaking; and three Natives' Representatives elected by African voters in the Cape Province. In 1949 the Government was strengthened by six M.P.s elected under the South-West Africa Affairs (Amendment) Act.

When Smuts died in 1950 the United Party chose Mr. J. G. N. Strauss as its new leader, and in the general election of 1953 it made a strong bid to unseat the Nationalists, and to this end had an agreement with the Labour Party and with the Torch Commando, at that time still a strong extra-parliamentary force. In spite of all opposition efforts, however, the Nationalist Party increased its parliamentary majority though it did not yet have a majority of votes. This defeat

---

[1] This view is still held by Nationalists. A leading article in *Die Burger* of 3 September 1959 reflected on the outbreak of the Second World War and maintained that, by his actions, Smuts had shown that he cared more for Britain than for his own Afrikaner people.

set in train movements within the United Party that reduced its parliamentary strength still further, though it is arguable that they increased its internal coherence.

In the first place, a number of people had always found the United Party unsatisfactory on race questions but had supported it on the ground that the great and immediate danger was Nationalist policy. These progressive-minded opponents of the Nationalist Party were now in the same dilemma as young Liberals in England during the first decade of this century: should they break away from the Party or remain and try to liberalize its policies? There were strong arguments for the latter course, and most followed that for the time being. A smaller number were moved by three principal considerations: in the interests of race harmony it was essential for some public demonstration that all white South Africans did not accept current policies; it was necessary to provide a political home for those young men and women who could no longer accept United Party policy; if the policy of white domination were ever to be challenged, it was a matter of urgency to have a non-racial political party (as distinct from society or association) from whose platform liberal views could be asserted. Accordingly, the Liberal Party was founded in 1953 and Mrs. Margaret Ballinger, M.P., who represented Africans in parliament, was persuaded to lead it. Without money and without a press (until it established a fortnightly called *Contact*) the Liberal Party attracted to its ranks a small band of South Africans of all races who threw their energies and abilities into propagating liberalism. Most of them were newcomers to politics or to public life, but a few were well known (or became so) even beyond the confines of the Union: Mrs. Margaret Ballinger, M.P., Mr. Walter Stanford, M.P., Senators Leslie Rubin[1] and William Ballinger, Mr. Jordan Ngubane, Mr. Alan Paton, and Mr. Patrick Duncan were and still are members of the Liberal Party.[2] The Party has fought a number of elections and has lost all except those seats representing Africans; in European constituencies it has thus far been decisively defeated though not disgraced, and it has had some measure of success in making South Africa aware of a possible alternative policy to that of white domination. The main plank in its programme is a common citizenship based on a common franchise, and there are differences within the party on the extent to which the franchise, though common to all races, should have property and educational qualifications.

A second defection from the United Party was the Federal Party

[1] Senator Rubin resigned in November 1959 to take up an appointment in Ghana.
[2] Mr. Walter Stanford resigned from the Liberal Party in 1959 and joined the Progressives.

whose main strength is in Natal where there is a strong feeling that the United Party is unsound on the questions of republicanism and of provincial rights. When the Torch Commando disintegrated after the electoral defeat of 1953, many of its members in Natal combined to form the Federal Party. The Party has as yet no parliamentary representation, but people outside Natal are beginning to turn their attention to the possible advantages of a federal, as opposed to a unitary, state in the circumstances that prevail in South Africa. It is therefore possible that the idea of federalism, rather than the Federal Party itself, may become of increasing importance.

A third defection took place in 1954 when a group of six (subsequently increased to seven) right-wing conservative United Party M.P.s rebelled against the Party leadership and policies and founded the National Conservative Party. All these M.P.s subsequently either joined the Nationalist Party and so retained their seats, or they were defeated at the next general election, and the event is of little significance except as showing the dominating part played by white-black and English-Afrikaans questions: the conservative rebels left the United Party because they found its race policy too liberal; but in many statements made at the time the main stress was on the fact that they, as Afrikaners, no longer felt at home in the United Party.

Malan retired from active political life in 1954 and there was a sharp struggle in the Nationalist Party over the question of his successor. It was common knowledge that Malan's advice was to choose Havenga, leader of the former Afrikaner Party and an elder statesman who had served under Hertzog for many years; indeed, it was generally understood that when the two parties had merged in 1951, Havenga had been promised the premiership when Malan retired. Despite all Malan's considerable influence, the Transvaal Nationalists nominated a more extreme and uncompromising Afrikaner, J. G. Strydom, and succeeded in defeating Havenga. Some years later, in 1958, a similar crisis occurred when a successor to Strydom had to be found. The two strong claimants were Dr. Dönges (a Cape and a Malan man) and Dr. Verwoerd (a Transvaal and Strydom man), and before his death, Strydom, fearing that the rivalry might cause a split in the Party, urged the election of Mr. C. R. Swart, Minister of Justice,[1] who, as leader of the Party in the Orange Free State and the most senior leader of the Party as a whole, might have been expected to hold a balance between the Transvaal and Cape rivalries. The withdrawal of Dr. Verwoerd and Dr. Dönges would have had the additional advantage for the Party that its leader would then have been chosen unanimously. Nevertheless, the Transvaal Nationalists did not accept

[1] Mr. Swart was appointed Governor-General at the end of 1959.

Strydom's death-bed advice, and when this became clear the Cape Nationalists decided to nominate Dr. Dönges. In the three-cornered fight that ensued Mr. Swart was eliminated on the first count, and on the second count Dr. Verwoerd defeated his Cape rival, thus becoming leader of the Party and, therefore, Prime Minister. Once more the moderate candidate nominated by the previous leader was rejected by the Party in favour of a more extreme Afrikaner. The Nationalist Party survived both these crises because the unity of Afrikaners is to most Nationalists still an overriding consideration.

The United Party did not escape leadership trouble. Mr. Strauss had had the difficult task of succeeding Smuts, whose personality and reputation had enabled him to keep the United Party together. After the 1953 election, dissatisfaction with the new leadership grew, and in 1956 the Party chose Sir de Villiers Graaff in place of Mr. Strauss. In the 1958 election the United Party decided to shed its somewhat embarrassing Labour Party association and to fight the election under its own steam; but even that step could not stem the tide of Afrikaner nationalism and the Nationalists were returned with an increased parliamentary majority of 103 to 53, while the Labour Party was eliminated.

The difficulties inside the United Party did not cease. The more progressive wing was increasingly unhappy about policies that seemed to them designed to catch rural Afrikaner votes rather than to deal with the rapidly developing problems of a multi-racial society. The conservative wing, on the other hand, led by Mr. Douglas Mitchell of Natal, was sensitive to Nationalist propaganda that accused the United Party of being controlled by its 'liberal' wing and of having one policy for the more progressive urban areas and another for the conservative rural constituencies. During the 1959 session of parliament it became evident that the progressives of the Party were growing more restive and the conservatives more impatient, and that a break would occur unless Sir de Villiers Graaff could hold the diverse elements together.

The break occurred at the Party Congress in Bloemfontein in August 1959. The Congress took one step which, in the prevailing South African circumstances, must be considered as progressive: it accepted as policy the restoration of African representation in the Cape Province and its extension to other provinces, such representation to be by Europeans and on separate electoral rolls. But that was the limit of what the conservatives would swallow. Faced with a near-by provincial election, Mr. Mitchell and his followers appear to have gone out of their way to make it difficult for the progressives to remain in the party, and Sir de Villiers Graaff was unable to restrain the conservatives. The final straw was a resolution that if the United Party were returned to power it would honour the undertaking, given in 1936, to buy more land for Native Reserves, but that it would not support the Nationalist Government in buying more land now to be added to the Bantustans which Dr. Verwoerd had envisaged as becoming separate States. Immediately after the Congress a number of United Party M.P.s issued a statement that they could no longer remain in the Party and gave as their reasons the resolution on land purchase for Native Reserves and what they called the 'undertones' that had been in evidence at the Congress. All the resignations did not take place immediately, but within a short time the United Party had lost twelve M.P.s and a few M.P.C.s who proceeded to establish themselves as a Progressive Group under the leadership of Dr. Jan Steytler, M.P. Mr. Harry Oppenheimer, who retired from active political life after the death of his father, publicly resigned from the United Party on the ground that his sympathies were with the Progressives; though he did not immediately join the Progressive Group, he did in effect add the prestige of his name to it. In November 1959 the progressives held a national conference and established the Progressive Party.[1]

During 1959 the Nationalist Party, too, showed signs of internal stress, and one M.P., Mr. J. Basson, was unable to support Dr. Verwoerd's Bantustan policy and was evicted from the Party's parliamentary caucus; but the head committee of the Party in South-West Africa did not immediately support this decision and resolved to give him and the Party time to compose their differences. This they were unable to do, and in October 1959 Mr. Basson was put out of the Party on a majority, not a unanimous, vote of the head committee.

This brief sketch of South African political history since 1910 has been necessary as a background to the present political divisions. Without that background, party policies appear confused and unreal. The time has now come to discuss the different party policies, to try to discover what the reactions of the parties are to the social and economic problems that beset South Africa, and to see to what extent they may differ fundamentally from each other.

The two major political parties in South Africa agree over a wide range of subjects. When they differ, it is frequently a matter of degree rather than of kind, or of a difference of method in arriving at the same result. Policies in such matters as agriculture, industry, mining, and railway development have, for both parties, the same general objectives —to encourage agricultural production and export, frequently at the expense of the South African consumer; to encourage industrial

[1] The programme of the Progressive Party is discussed on p. 157.

expansion by means of tariffs; to tax the mines as much as possible without actually discouraging them; and to use the railway rates to further these aims. Native policy[1] cuts across all these activities, since African labour is a basic factor in them all.

There are four main questions that separate the two parties. The first is the relations between English-speaking and Afrikaans-speaking South Africans; this has been discussed in various parts of this book, and it will be seen later how it affects educational policy. The second and third concern Native policy and the relations between South Africa and Britain and the Commonwealth; and the last question is constitutional.

NATIVE POLICY

One of the ablest and best-informed parliamentarians in South Africa, Mrs. Margaret Ballinger, who is one of the three representatives of Africans in the House of Assembly, once remarked that 'all Union politics are Native Affairs'. It is with an examination of Native policies that we may best begin in order to arrive at an understanding of some of the fundamental differences in party politics.

The necessity for a positive Native policy first began to impress itself on South African statesmen after the 1914-18 War. This is not to say that, long before that, many South Africans, in and out of politics, had not realized the vital nature of the problem nor foreseen the time when policies would have to be framed to meet it; but, before pressure of population and industrialization had brought the question squarely into the centre of political thinking, it had always been possible to regard relations between black and white as susceptible to treatment along the lines of benevolent paternalism—maintaining law and order, Christianizing, kind but firm treatment of the 'child race'. By the 1920's the 'child' was adolescent and showing every sign of growing to lusty manhood, and it was no longer possible to deal with him on an administrative level only, however sound that administration might be. Good government could no longer be regarded as the equivalent of self-government.

At the highest political level it was Hertzog who first turned his attention to this problem. His thinking, as with the vast majority of Europeans in South Africa, was historically and temperamentally grounded in the need to segregate the races. Hitherto a reasonable amount of segregation at the social and economic level had been the general rule—a rule which broke down in industries, in domestic service, and in other places where it proved inconvenient or uneconomic. Now the question of political segregation became

[1] 'Native policy' means policy in regard to Africans. It would be confusing to call it 'African policy'.

prominent. Africans in the Cape Province had been on a common electoral roll since 1853. The educational and property tests that had then limited the number of African voters had less restrictive value after the First World War; the value of money had fallen and literacy increased. If the number was allowed to grow, and if, by example, Africans in the other provinces began to demand the franchise, the chances were that the African voters would in due course outnumber the European. In 1926 Hertzog put forward a comprehensive programme for dealing with the Native question. Africans were to be removed from the electoral roll in the Cape and all Africans were to participate, directly or indirectly, in the election of a representative council; they would be given representation in the Senate; more land for African occupation would be made available.[1]

To carry a policy that deprived Africans at the Cape of their common franchise rights would require, by the terms of the South Africa Act, a two-thirds majority of both houses in a joint session. This Hertzog was unable to achieve since the South African Party opposition, being itself of a divided opinion, refused to support him. The whole of his policy (since he regarded it as one and indivisible) remained in legislative cold storage. The Nationalist Party, however, did not allow the matter to drop. The 1929 election was fought on the issue and was preceded by a document known as the 'Black Manifesto', which warned the country of the dangers of letting the question slide. When Smuts and Hertzog fused their parties, the latter made it a condition that his policy, possibly amended in details, should receive priority treatment. Accordingly, in 1936, the policy was once more before Parliament. In spite of vigorous agitation by liberals, the necessary two-thirds majority was obtained for the Hertzog Bills; but Hertzog had been compelled to compromise by allowing the Cape African franchise to remain, albeit on a separate roll: African voters in the Cape were permitted to elect three European members. Africans throughout the Union elected, by means of chiefs, local councils, and local advisory boards—all acting as electoral colleges—four Senators. An additional $7\frac{1}{4}$ million morgen of land were to be made available for African occupation, and a South African Natives' Trust Fund was established to finance land purchase and to encourage Native agriculture and education. Finally, a Natives' Representative Council was instituted, to consist of twelve elected African representatives, four nominated African representatives, and five European officials, with the Secretary for Native Affairs as chairman.

Although most Europeans hailed these parliamentary Acts as a new

[1] It is important to note, for future reference, that Hertzog regarded the Cape Coloured population as falling on the European side, industrially and politically.

and satisfactory solution, and although Smuts called the Natives' Representative Council a second 'parliament', it was evident to J. H. Hofmeyr and the liberals, in and out of parliament, who supported him that the policy had in fact solved nothing. More land was indeed bought to be added to the Reserves; but adding badly farmed and inadequately capitalized land to more land of the same kind created problems rather than solved them. In any case, the increasing rate of industrialization and the ever-growing demand for African labour made the legislation out of date almost as soon as it was enacted. As for the Natives' Representative Council, it was soon clear that Africans would not long be satisfied with an advisory council whose advice was treated with scant attention. The impotence of the council was demonstrated as soon as it began to advise the removal of the many administrative restrictions that controlled African freedom of movement. The Hertzog policy attempted to reach a permanent solution; but the factors in the situation were all moving so fast that, as his brother said of Louix XVI of France, it was like trying to balance a number of billiard balls. A clever, though not a wise, statesman might juggle with them; but he could not balance them.

The 1939-45 War increased the rate of change in the factors that constitute the Native question—urbanization and industrial development, progressive deterioration of the Reserves, the political awakening of the African. Smuts's government, representing both rural and urban opinion, industrial and farming, liberal and conservative, Afrikaans and English, was pulled in different directions. A small group within the United Party pulled in the direction of more freedom for the Africans, for more education, better housing, more social services. Through the Army Education Services, during the war, many young South Africans had, for the first time in their lives, come to realize some of the disabilities under which Africans lived. Studying these matters in an economically secure position in the Army, they were eager for reforms; and though the eagerness tended to wear off once they returned to the competitive economics of civil life, for a short time they did exercise influence in United Party circles, and found backing from industrialists who welcomed the idea of relaxing colour bars in industry.

Pulling against this force was a stronger force composed of those United Party supporters who, by tradition, by inclination, and by what they considered to be their economic advantage, were fearful of 'going too fast'. They professed to believe in what they called Christian Trusteeship, a vague term that was for ever begging the question of what happened when the wards came of age. Torn between their anxiety to satisfy the rural districts that their supply of labour would be safe and that the government was able to 'look after the Communists', and the needs of the urban areas that were unable to cope with the influx of Africans, the Smuts Government did little besides try vainly to restrict the movement of Africans to the towns. It did, however, set up the Fagan Commission to inquire into the situation. This Commission, one of the most authoritative that has reported on Native affairs, came to the following, among many other conclusions: more than half the African population lived in European areas; an examination of the carrying capacity of the Reserves showed that it was utterly impossible to put the whole Native population into the Reserves; the urbanization of the African in European areas must be accepted, and the process cannot be reversed; it was impossible to 'confine Native labour in South Africa to the migratory type'.[1] The *Fagan Report* bore out what many other commissions and individual authorities had said, most notably the Social and Economic Planning Council under the chairmanship of Dr. van Eck.[2]

Meanwhile the Natives' Representative Council, goaded to despair, refused to co-operate any longer in what had become, to them and to many other people, a political sham, and they took little notice of Smuts's rather vague offer to increase their powers. In one of the three Cape divisions representing Africans, a member of the Communist Party was elected to parliament.

The Nationalist Party inherited the Hertzog policy of segregation, rooted, as it was, in the European fear of being 'swamped'; but, just as they shed Hertzogism in English-Afrikaans relations, so they shed some of his Native policy. Sensing the popular alarm at the developing situation, and realizing that the 'black danger' was a winning election card, they appointed a party committee to work out a policy that could be put before the electorate in the first post-war general election. From this committee came the policy known as apartheid, which means 'separation' or 'segregation'. The word was chosen partly because it had the advantage of being new, and partly because the word 'segregation' was associated with earlier political parties and policies such as Botha's. A minor reason for its choice was that the word 'segregation' was disliked by the Africans.

Apartheid, as a policy, may mean a number of things, from social and residential separation to the establishment of separate African and European states. As an election cry it was extremely useful just because of its vagueness. As a Native policy, it has the weaknesses of its electioneering strength. To many people in 1948 it sounded like a

[1] See *Native Laws Enquiry Commission*, 1948, popularly known as the *Fagan Report* from the name of its Chairman, Mr. Justice Fagan.
[2] See *Social and Economic Planning Council, Sixth Report*.

policy that might solve the African-European question, a question that the United Party did not appear to be doing anything about. The Nationalist Party, supported by Havenga's Afrikaner Party, had the advantage of being homogeneous. It was almost entirely Afrikaans-speaking; its real strength lay in the rural areas; it had been welded, during the war, into a closely knit, cohesive party. It had few of the weaknesses of divided opinion from which the United Party suffered. When, therefore, the Nationalist Party came forward with the policy of apartheid it found considerable response. It pointed to the undoubted danger of allowing things to drift; it played with skill on the fear which most Europeans in South Africa have of an ultimate 'black domination'; and it asserted emphatically that its purpose was not to do the African an injustice but, rather, to give him ampler room for developing his own national identity separately from the European. It rejected the recommendations of the *Fagan Report*. The upshot was that the Nationalist Party won the election.

General election policies are of necessity imprecise; and when Malan's party came to power it found itself embarrassed by the vagueness which had been useful at the election. What, precisely, was apartheid to include? During the early days of the new government separate railway coaches for Europeans were provided on the Cape suburban railway line, and in a great many, though by no means all, post offices separate counters were provided for European and non-European customers. This move was widely claimed as apartheid. But, rather obviously, it was, if anything, an extremely minor part of a policy. It affected chiefly Coloured people, since, in the other provinces, Africans had long been accustomed to separate, though inferior, facilities in these matters. Moreover, it seemed to accept the fact that Africans, Coloured, and European would long continue to live and work in the same areas.

Nor did the next steps which the government took affect the African population as much as they did the Coloured. The Prohibition of Mixed Marriages Act, 1949, prohibited marriages between European and non-European; since, in 1946, there had been 75 such marriages out of 28,000 European marriages,[1] the Act hardly seemed to have been needed. Another Act which claimed in part to aim at apartheid was the Population Registration Act which provides for personal identity cards and for a register on which 'race' is shown. In its draft form, African women and African males under 18 years of age were excluded, which seems to indicate that the government was not mainly concerned with the African population. The intention of the Act, in so far as the question of race was concerned, was

[1] See *Union Year Book No.* 24, 1948.

10

to fix once and for all the 'race' of everyone carrying a card, and was, in fact, another attempt to prevent Coloured people from 'passing'.

In 1950 the Group Areas Act was passed empowering the government to declare any area a group area for Coloured, European, African, or Asian.[1] It was a complicated Act, but its intention was that, in due course, the various 'racial' groups would live in distinct areas, and property in such areas might not be acquired by a member of a different group. Here, again, it was hardly the African whom the government had in mind. The principle of separate areas, nationally and locally, has, as we have seen, long been accepted in South Africa. The Group Areas Act, therefore, added little to the restrictions already borne by Africans, but it powerfully affects the rights of Coloured and Asians. Finally, the Act that places Coloured voters in the Cape on a separate electoral roll and sets up a separate Department of Coloured Affairs does not touch the African, but was designed to limit the influence of Coloured voters.

These measures were all part of the policy of apartheid but they hardly touched the vital question of African-European relations. Between 1951 and 1959, however, a whole series of Acts of Parliament and policy statements have given a clearer picture of what apartheid involves in regard to the African population. Starting with the Bantu Authorities Act of 1951 and culminating in the Promotion of Bantu Self-Government Act of 1959, both of which Acts were described in chapter 5, what emerges is a policy to revive and restore tribalism and to make the Reserves into national homes which, according to Dr. Verwoerd, may eventually become independent states. In European areas, Africans will be regarded as migrants, subject to rigid control in such matters as where they live, how they earn their living, and the amount of freedom of movement they may be granted.

Briefly, the case of the academic apologists for the policy of apartheid is this: the African and the European are two different 'races' and can never live in one political state without producing either injustice to the African or the decline of European power. The European, on the one hand, dare not allow the African his political rights because Western civilization will then be swamped by Bantu civilization. On the other hand, if the African is working in European industries it is unjust not to grant him civil rights. Further, the African, like the Afrikaner, is entitled to develop his own language and culture; in fact, without that development he will never become a really integrated personality. As long as he remains part of the European state he will become an imitation European instead of a good African. In the European state he cannot be allowed equality; he cannot be

[1] In certain areas further subdivisions of Malay and Chinese are provided for.

allowed to attain to positions of trust and power and responsibility, as he could if he were in his own country.

Therefore, the argument continues, the African must have his own homeland, territory that he can call his own and where he can attain to the highest positions of which he is capable. The existing Reserves, augmented by more land to the extent of 7¼ million morgen, must constitute this homeland of the African. When the African leaves his homeland to work for Europeans in their homeland, he does so as a temporary migrant labourer and can expect no civil or political rights. He will, in effect, be visiting European South Africa and will do so in the knowledge that he will return to his own country later. It is admitted that the Reserves must be rehabilitated and that South Africa must accept the responsibility, financial and otherwise, of helping the African to industrialize the Reserves so as to increase their carrying capacity. Also, for some considerable time to come, the Europeans will have to act as trustees over the Reserves since the Africans have not yet reached a stage where they can entirely govern themselves.

In somewhat general terms, that is the basic theory of apartheid. There are other important aspects of the policy. Great stress is laid on mother-tongue instruction and on the encouragement and development of Bantu languages and culture. The restoration of tribal authority and the cultivation of tribal loyalty are essentials. It must be remembered that apartheid is an Afrikaner policy. The Afrikaner knows the important part that his own language and culture played in the preservation of the identity of the Afrikaner people, and he believes that what is true of the Afrikaner is true of the African. As good nationalists, Afrikaners cannot deny to any other nation its right to develop its own identity; but, equally, they cannot allow the African to do this if it is to be at the expense of the Afrikaner people.

To the policy of apartheid as set out here, and as it is being applied legislatively and administratively, there are a number of practical and immediate objections. Earlier chapters have shown to what extent European agriculture, industries, and mining are dependent on African labour, and how much of that labour has already become permanently divorced from its tribal homes in the Reserves. It is accepted as a fact by supporters as well as by opponents of apartheid that to a considerable extent the African has already become integrated into the economy which the Europeans have erected in South Africa. The supporters ask that the process of integration should be stopped and a reverse process gradually introduced. It will take a long time and it is therefore imperative to begin at once.

The theoreticians of apartheid do not appear to have given sufficient consideration to the economics of making the Reserves capable of bearing an increased population. Nor have they faced the consequences that will follow if their policy is logically applied, of black states competing industrially with white. During recent years clothing factories have been set up on the borders of the Reserves where they are, for the moment, free from wage determinations and can thus pay lower wages than obtain in the urban areas. This is in accord with government policy and has already caused unemployment in the clothing industry in Johannesburg and grave concern to industrialists.

The Nationalist Government, responsible for carrying out the policy of apartheid, is more acutely aware of the practical difficulties than the academic apologists. When, in 1950, an important national conference of Dutch Reformed Churches wholeheartedly approved the policy of territorial apartheid and urged the government to put it into force, Malan was compelled to issue a public warning that processes that had taken a long time to mature could not be reversed in a few months. The fact is that no government in South Africa would lightly undertake to put into force a policy that must, if it is to perform what it says, result in a diminished labour supply for farms and industries. The academicians speak about the need to make economic sacrifices in the interests of the principles of apartheid; but practical politicians are not so sure that the electorate will accept these sacrifices. And the clearer the extent of the sacrifice becomes the less prospect of its being acquiesced in does there appear to be. Afrikaners are, to an increasing extent, participating in the establishment of new industries; and there is evidence that they will not easily dispense with African labour.

The dilemma of the Nationalist Party is made clear by the somewhat contradictory public statements on apartheid. In an address given in September 1950 by Dr. Eiselen, who had been appointed Secretary for Native Affairs, against the advice of the Public Service Commission, because of his sympathies with the ideals of apartheid, he said that four major administrative steps are required to create a contented and efficient labour force: a realization of diverse aptitudes of Africans, occupational selection, recognition of continuous and efficient service within each labour category, and building schemes by which bona fide urban Africans may invest savings in home ownership.[1] This policy undoubtedly envisages *local* apartheid, which largely exists already, and makes suggestions for the improvement of urban conditions; but it cannot be said to include the conception of African urban labour as migrant and temporary, since it advocates home ownership for Africans in urban areas.

[1] See *S.A. Outlook*, October 1950.

On the other hand the then Minister for Native Affairs, Dr. Verwoerd, announced four months later that the Cabinet had decided that no African would be allowed to own land outside the Reserves.[1] In addressing the Natives' Representative Council in December 1950, Dr. Verwoerd said that Europeans do not demand overlordship over the whole of South Africa, but only over their own areas. He adumbrated agricultural and industrial development, under European supervision and with European capital, in the Reserves, which would, in time, become self-supporting and self-governing. How long this would take depended largely on the Africans themselves. Dr. Verwoerd did not speak about the majority of Africans, who live in European areas, and the Council adjourned because the Minister refused to allow it to discuss the political aspects of apartheid, though he invited the members to do so with him unofficially as private persons.[2]

There are aspects of the theory of Bantustans that are not clear. Except for Zululand, the Transkei, and the Ciskei, the Reserves are fragmented and few people believe that even these three can become viable States. Unless the Union is to surrender to these homelands far more land, including access to ports, the proposed Bantustans can never be anything else than appendages of South Africa. The prospects of persuading any white electorate to agree to the purchase of more land for this purpose are negligible. Moreover, assuming that one or two Bantustans do achieve independence, would that not merely put South Africa back to the border wars of the nineteenth century? It is inconceivable that Africans would for long remain content with a small fraction of what they regard as their own country. Again, the Tomlinson Commission was emphatic that tribalism and a modern economy are incompatible. How then can the industrial development of the Reserves take place if tribalism is to be revived and strengthened? Finally, more than half the African population lives in what is considered the European part of South Africa, and African leaders are clamouring for political rights now. To call them migrants, and at the same time help to provide them with permanent homes in urban areas, is not going to satisfy either the leaders or their followers for long.

The Nationalist Party has always accused the United Party of having no real Native policy, and of having allowed things to drift until they reached the dangerous state in which they now are and from which only the policy of apartheid will rescue them. Another accusation is that the United Party dog is wagged by its small liberal tail and the Party would, if returned to office, abolish all colour bars

[1] See *Die Burger*, 15 January 1951.
[2] See *Die Burger*, 6 December 1950.

and promote complete equality. There is some justification for the first accusation; none at all for the second. The United Party, by its very nature, lacks the unanimity of opinion that characterizes the Nationalist Party; and there has always been a small liberal wing of the party, associated with the name of the late J. H. Hofmeyr, which, while it does not go as far as to advocate complete equality between European and non-European, is determined that the rights of Coloured and Africans should be defended within the existing situation. On the whole, the United Party accepts the fact that Africans have become integrated into European economic affairs; it would agree with Dr. Eiselen in his diagnosis of what is needed to ensure a contented and efficient labour force. It is prepared to meet social and administrative difficulties as they arise rather than by any clear-cut and comprehensive policy. The basis of this policy is not merely a division of opinion within the United Party; it is also a realization that the situation is fluid and not susceptible of easy solution by cast-iron policies that neglect important economic considerations.

The United Party has consistently opposed that part of apartheid that applies chiefly to the Coloured population and has promised, if returned to power, to restore Cape Coloured voters to the common roll. On the issue of African-European relations there is a considerable area of agreement, or near agreement, with moderate Nationalists. The United Party is in favour of residential and social separation and accepts the principle of the Group Areas Act but wishes to make it less drastic by curbing the powers of the Minister, by promoting voluntary separation, and by paying full compensation where property rights are interfered with. Probably a large majority of the United Party would agree to some form of industrial colour bar but is opposed to rigid legislation on the matter and believes that colour bars should be administered by agreement between workers and employers; the Party is also opposed to job reservation by race. The United Party opposed the Extension of University Education Act largely on the ground that it interfered with university autonomy; but a large number of United Party members would probably agree that mixed universities are not desirable.

The greatest disagreement between the two parties is over the representation of Africans in parliament and the establishment of Bantustans. The Nationalist Party believes that Africans should not be represented in parliament while the United Party believes they should, albeit to a very limited extent, on a separate roll, and by Europeans. In 1957 the United Party put forward a complicated plan for reforming the Senate in such a way as to extend representation to non-Europeans, to protect minority groups, and to entrench white leadership. Both parties believe that the Reserves must be economically rehabilitated, but they disagree on how this is to be done and the United Party is strongly opposed to the establishment of Bantustans which might eventually break up the Union.

Neither the Nationalist Party nor the United Party has put forward a long-term policy that takes cognizance of certain fundamental facts of the interracial situation. The first of these is that the economy of South Africa depends on all its 'races', which have become integrated with it to such an extent that they cannot be separated without damaging that economy beyond repair. Moreover, the situation is not static, but fluid, and any policy that neglects this will certainly not have the support of the Africans, without which no policy will be workable. The real danger in the South African racial situation is that political thought on the part of those who wield political power habitually and traditionally starts off with the fatal handicap of failing to consult the African himself. The African is the big and variable factor in the equation and he must, somehow, be linked to the other factors to make political sense. He is, by shortsighted policy on the part of the Europeans, being driven in on himself to a nationalism that is becoming increasingly anti-white. Most Europeans think either in terms of a 'once-for-all' clear-cut policy or in terms of laissez faire. The racial problem has reached such dimensions that neither policy can hope to succeed.

There is in South Africa a body of liberal opinion that expresses itself on race and on other questions through such bodies as the English-language churches, the South African Institute of Race Relations, and the Civil Rights League at Cape Town. It consists of men and women of all racial groups drawn from the universities, from among teachers, business men and women, and from the churches. It is not a cohesive body, and is difficult to weld into a political party because it is scattered and does not command sufficient votes in one constituency to be able to elect a candidate. It exerts what influence it has by conferences, Press statements, protest meetings, and by briefing members of parliament on proposed legislation. Since the establishment of the Liberal Party in 1953, this opinion has most nearly been represented in the House of Assembly by Mrs. Margaret Ballinger and Mr. Walter Stanford, and in the Senate by Senators Rubin and Ballinger, all of whom were elected by African voters. These parliamentary representatives of Africans are totally opposed to apartheid and have been among its ablest and most trenchant critics. Liberal Party policy advocates the gradual extension of the franchise, on a common roll, leading to the eventual enfranchisement of all South Africans regardless of race; it proposes the abolition of all forms of colour bar and is opposed to any legislation that restricts the free movement of Africans or invades the rights of any section of the population on grounds of colour. Under the Promotion of Bantu Self-Government Act, however, parliamentary representation of Africans ceases in 1960, and the Liberal Party will then no longer be represented in Parliament unless it can capture a European seat, which seems unlikely.

Though it is difficult to judge whether liberalism of this kind is increasing and whether it has any effect on public policy, there certainly are many more liberals in 1959 than there were a generation ago; and liberal views receive considerable publicity in both the English and the Afrikaans Press, the former approving and the latter disapproving. Both major political parties, however, depend so much on the conservative rural vote that neither can afford to pay much attention to such views. The liberals, not deterred by this, continue to express what they believe to be a reasonable policy in the hope that, before it is too late, the electorate will accept it as such.

The advent of the Progressive Party, in the latter half of 1959, indicates that liberalism is on the increase. That Party, though its programme is still in the formative stage, has declared itself against the colour bar and in favour of a common (though not a universal) franchise; it recognizes that there is one nation in South Africa embracing different groups, and that each group is entitled to protection and to share in the government; it proposes constitutional safeguards, in the form of an entrenched Bill of Rights, to guarantee the fundamental human rights and liberties of the individual and of minorities. Both the Liberal Party and the Progressive Party represent liberalism in its various stages; both parties reject the Nationalist Party doctrine of apartheid; and neither Party has any faith in the United Party's ability to deal with race problems in their modern form. The difference between the Liberal Party and the Progressive Party is mainly one of emphasis: while both advocate a common franchise, the Liberals would go faster and further than the Progressives; while neither party shirks the essential political and economic facts in South Africa, the Progressive Party is keenly aware of, and lays great stress on, the need to safeguard the rights of minorities in a mixed society. The Progressive Party is, for the moment, strong in parliament, but it still has to test its strength in the white electorate. In the final analysis, however, the strength of any political party in the Union will be judged by the extent of the support that it can claim from the unenfranchised citizens of the country.

There is no socialist party in South Africa. The small Labour

Party depends for its strength on European trade unions, many of which, as we saw, support a colour bar in industry. The Labour Party has in recent years become much more liberal; but it cannot be called socialist. Since the 1958 general election the Party is no longer represented in parliament.

The Communist Party was declared illegal in 1950, and dissolved itself before the Bill was passed. The Suppression of Communism Act, and its amendment in 1951, gave extremely wide powers to the Minister of Justice, powers against which there is no appeal to the courts. Communists advocated complete and immediate equality for all; but with none of the population groups did their doctrine have any but a limited appeal.

EXTERNAL AFFAIRS

South Africa's foreign affairs may be divided into relations with Britain and the Commonwealth, relations with non-Commonwealth countries, and relations with other states and colonies in southern and central Africa. All of these are influenced, sometimes decisively, by the question of Native policy.

In so far as external relations are a matter of trade, there is not a great deal of difference between the policies of the main parties. Both are anxious to extend South Africa's trade relations by exploring new markets and by negotiating trade treaties with other countries. Individual firms and local authorities do, it is true, sometimes show a preference for buying 'British', or 'non-British', as the case may be; but, in general, sentiment does not play a large part in trade relations. South Africa imports slightly more than half of her requirements from Britain, the British Empire, and the Commonwealth; and the United Kingdom is South Africa's best customer.

It is in political relations, in peace and in war, that differences of outlook occur. The majority of European South Africans, possibly as many as 60 per cent, realize the need for close alliance with Britain and the Commonwealth. Community of interests, of culture, of language, and of traditions are all strongly on the side of a foreign policy whose cornerstone is close relations with Britain. The desire for such relations was shown by the part South Africa played in two world wars, and feelings springing from common experiences in the wars themselves reinforced the policy. There is only a small section of South Africans who have an emotional attachment to England, or who even give much conscious thought to the matter unless it is challenged. But the majority accept the fact that cordial relations with Britain and the Commonwealth are both natural and desirable. There exists a vigorous and growing feeling of national independence and pride, but for the majority of South Africans this is not an anti-British sentiment.

Within the Nationalist Party, on the other hand, there is a strong section of opinion that hopes to see a republic, cut off from the Commonwealth, established in South Africa. Those who hold this opinion maintain that they are not anti-British; that they want a republic because it suits the South African temperament; that association with Britain drags South Africa into war; and that, as long as South Africa is 'tied to Britain', English-speaking South Africans will always regard Britain as the motherland and South Africa only as their second home. Once the republic is established, they say, English-speaking citizens will co-operate more readily with Afrikaners because they can no longer regard England as having first claim on their loyalty.[1]

There is little substance in these arguments. In spite of a nostalgic and sentimental attachment to the idea of a republic, there is no proof that the republican form of government is more suited to the South African temperament than is a constitutional monarchy. As for her attitude in time of war, the position of South Africa astride the Cape route has made neutrality impossible ever since the Napoleonic Wars. The mere possession of Cape Town does not put her in a position to dictate terms to any Great Power, and since she must perforce choose her allies, she will obviously choose that Power that is likely to be able to maintain South African trade routes during war. Invaluable as the Cape route is to Britain, its protection against another Power is no less important to South Africa. The Naval Base at Simonstown was, by agreement, handed over by Britain to South Africa in 1957; but whoever may own it, the existence of the Base is vital both to Britain and to the Union.

There is, historically at any rate, more substance in the argument that political and cultural bonds exist between English-speaking South Africans and England. South Africa's first cultural and political ties were with Holland, but the political ties were cut in 1806, and the cultural ties, though maintained for many generations, languished and were gradually supplanted by those of British origin. For more than a hundred years the majority of Europeans living in what is now the Union were closely linked, economically, socially, and politically,

[1] Malan (then Prime Minister) was reported in *Die Burger* of 23 May 1951 as follows: 'We shall be free from a divided loyalty only when we have a republic.' This view was reiterated by Dr. Verwoerd in January 1959 when, speaking in the House of Assembly on the republican issue, he said: 'I go further and say that the republic will bring peace in South Africa, not only peace between us but also peace as regards the suspicion being spread abroad.' *Hansard* (1959) Col. 57.

with Great Britain. Those Afrikaners who, by temperament and political history, were antagonistic to Britain were unable to look to an overseas country for moral or cultural support. In this way Afrikaans nationalism was born and grew up in a context where to be an Afrikaner meant to be opposed to Britain. Twelve years after the Boer War Britain was at war with Germany, and Afrikaner nationalism, being anti-British, tended to be pro-German. English-speaking South Africans, and those Afrikaners who followed Botha and Smuts, quite naturally looked to Britain for physical support and spiritual comfort.

These habits of thought persisted. During the Second World War those members of the Nationalist Party who did not positively hope that Germany would win did, at any rate, regard the anticipated break-up of the British Empire with equanimity; at all events, they prepared for the coming republic. Followers of Smuts, English- and Afrikaans-speaking South Africans, looked all the more eagerly to Britain to stand between them and conquest by Nazi Germany. Thus the gulf between those who 'looked to England' and those who did not, widened. The more the Afrikaner in the Nationalist Party spoke about a republic, the more strongly did non-Nationalists feel the need of close ties with Britain. This was the more so since, during the war years, various Nationalist Party groups and individuals defined the republican constitution as one that was authoritarian in character, and had, moreover, no room for 'un-Afrikaans' elements. Such a republic held no attractions for non-Nationalists. Moreover, many non-Nationalists who might, in 1948, have been indifferent on the question of a republic have become increasingly antagonistic to a republic established and dominated by an Afrikaner nationalism that has shown few signs of having purged itself of authoritarian leanings.

There is, therefore, some justification for Nationalists who say that English-speaking South Africans look to England for their salvation. It is, however, a saying that can easily be misinterpreted. The generation that used to refer to England as 'home' has, for practical purposes, passed away. Britain does not interfere in South African affairs, nor is there any justification for suggesting that, consciously or subconsciously, English-speaking South Africans rely on Britain to 'take their part' in South Africa. But the fact remains that many South Africans have close cultural and linguistic associations with Britain, that they admire, and have copied, many British institutions, and that Britain stands, in general, for an interpretation of Western civilization that fits most closely with their own ideas. Furthermore, the two countries are bound by economic interests. The establishment of a republic in South Africa would not break these affiliations so long as Britain stands for those ideas that are acceptable to most South Africans.

The Nationalist Party is not unanimous on the republican issue. Possibly half the party favours a republic provided that a large majority of the voters support it and, probably, provided it remains within the Commonwealth. The remaining half consists of the two extremes—those who are not republican, and those who want a republic soon and outside the Commonwealth. The constitution of the Nationalist Party of 1951 (when the Nationalist and Afrikaner parties united) contained a clause maintaining that a republican form of government, outside the Commonwealth, was best suited to South Africa. In 1957 this clause was changed to make the republic and association with the Commonwealth separate issues—a change which may indicate that there are a number of Nationalists who might vote for the republic provided they are assured that it will be within the Commonwealth. The Party has all along maintained that a republic would not be brought about except by the 'broad will of the people' as ascertained by a special plebiscite; but there has been difference in interpretation on what this means. The most recent interpretation is that of the prime minister who said that he would consider a simple majority sufficient 'provided the government of the day is convinced that it can establish a stable republic'.[1] It is doubtful whether the majority of voters would today support a republic; and if it did, the opposition would be so fierce and bitter that it would not be a stable republic. Meanwhile, the government has not allayed fears by removing some of the symbols of South Africa's association with the Crown: the British national anthem is no longer played (with the South African) at official ceremonies, and the Defence Force is not allowed to take part in unofficial ceremonies where it is played; the Union Jack is no longer flown on public buildings with the South African flag; the crown has been removed from Defence Force insignia and military uniforms have been redesigned to make them look less British; even the O.H.M.S. on official envelopes has been done away with.

Though it is impossible to speak with any degree of accuracy about the views of the non-European population regarding a republic, it is tolerably certain that the vast mass of them are opposed to the idea. The Coloured people of the Cape associate their political rights with Britain, for it was under British rule that they attained the franchise on equal terms with Europeans. That equality was removed by parliament in 1956, and it was by a parliament in which the Afrikaans-speaking Nationalist Party was in power. Africans in the Cape

[1] *Hansard* (1959) Col. 58.

Province, too, associate their political rights with Great Britain, and the loss of those rights with Hertzog and, more recently, with the Nationalist Party. In the other provinces most Africans have always, whether justifiably or not, tended to think of the Afrikaner as a worse 'oppressor' than the British. Present-day British colonial policy, too, appears to thinking Africans as more hopeful for the future than the policies of Union governments. There seems little doubt, therefore, that Coloured and African opinion would be overwhelmingly opposed to a South African republic, particularly if it were to be outside the Commonwealth.[1]

So far we have discussed South Africa's relations with Great Britain. With regard to the rest of the Commonwealth, the Nationalist Party's attitude is, broadly, either sceptical or hostile. It does not feel that there are any special advantages in belonging to a Commonwealth of such diverse peoples—advantages, that is, that could not be as well obtained by direct dealings between South Africa and Australia or Canada. Although the word 'British' has been dropped, it is still felt that the Commonwealth is British, and that South Africa, as a member, may become involved in undesirable international policies through that connexion. When certain Commonwealth nations sided against South Africa at U.N.O. over the Asian question, Nationalist newspapers asked whether there really was a Commonwealth. Further, when the Secretary of State for Colonies, early in 1951, expressed the hope that the Gold Coast would in time become a member of the Commonwealth, the Nationalists were up in arms. If the Commonwealth really exists, they asked, who gives Great Britain the right to invite additional members? Nevertheless, when Ghana became independent in 1957 the South African Government was represented by a high official at the inaugural ceremonies.

[1] Since the foregoing paragraphs were written a Bill has been introduced to create machinery for a referendum on the republican issue. Voters will be asked a straight question on whether they favour the institution of a republic; voting will be by constituency but only white voters will take part; South-West Africa, excluded in the first announcement of a referendum, will participate. No date was set for the referendum, but Dr. Verwoerd stated that it would not be before 31 May 1960, when the Union celebrates its fiftieth anniversary, and that two to three months' notice would be given. The Prime Minister also stated that he would regard a simple majority of one vote as a mandate to proceed with the constitutional change necessary to make South Africa a republic. Although the Bill does not ask for a decision on whether South Africa should remain in the Commonwealth, the government has promised to indicate what its policy in this regard is. The Referendum Bill has made the question of a republic a live political issue, and the indications are that there will be a fierce campaign in which many arguments will be advanced for or against a republic, in or out of the Commonwealth. One argument alone would seem to be conclusive: to arrive at such momentous decisions without consulting the non-white citizens of South Africa would be, in present-day Africa, a hazardous, not to say foolhardy, policy.

The United Party, on the other hand, regards the Commonwealth as a positive achievement, as something which gives South Africa greater security. True, the United Party finds that relations with India and Pakistan are not easy; but it is prepared to put up with such difficulties for the sake of the other advantages and because it likes the idea of a Commonwealth associtiaon.

In actual practice, there is no difference in peacetime between the policies of the two parties in regard to their day-to-day relations with other Commonwealth countries. The differences that have been discussed are those of general attitude; and it is only in time of war that practical differences may flow from these attitudes. In the two world wars, as we have seen, the Nationalists were opposed to South Africa's participation. If Britain and the Commonwealth were to become involved in a third world war against Communist countries there is little doubt that, for the first time in her history, the European population of South Africa would be united over foreign policy. Whatever government was in power, South Africa would go to war against Communism. It is probable that the enthusiasm of the Europeans for a war against Communism would not be shared by the non-Europeans. This does not mean that Communism has any particular hold on the non-European population. It means rather that they might not regard as an unmitigated evil conquest by a creed that acknowledges no colour bar.

South Africa has trade and diplomatic relations with a number of non-Commonwealth countries, either at the consular or at the ambassadorial level. Two countries are mentioned here only for the sake of rounding off the picture and not because they reveal any marked differences between the two parties. In the post-war atmosphere of the 1950's it was to be expected that South Africa, with a large non-white population, would be sensitive about Communism, and when it came to power in 1948 the Nationalist Party set about dealing vigorously with the danger that, it was convinced, threatened South Africa from this source. The Suppression of Communism Act of 1951 made the propagation of Communism illegal and gave the Minister of Justice powers to 'deem' any person a Communist and subsequently to 'name' him and prohibit him from attending meetings or belonging to specified organizations; against these powers there was no effective legal remedy. Under pressure from the Afrikaans churches and other bodies this Act was in due course followed by the closing down of the U.S.S.R. Consulate. It may be added that this has not stopped trade between South Africa and the U.S.S.R.

In the post-war world the United States of America became as interested as the U.S.S.R. in Africa, and it was natural that a great deal of this interest should have been centred on South Africa where the advent and actions of the Nationalist Government were attracting world-wide attention. Encouraged and largely financed by the State Department in Washington, the Carnegie Corporation of New York, and the Ford Foundation, a steady two-way traffic was developed in journalists, editors, professors, professional and business men, and government officials. The Americans came to study the situation on the spot, and South Africans went to find out what lessons might be learnt from American practice. The South African Government has been somewhat embarrassed by this intense interest in its apartheid policies, particularly when an American television company sent a camera team to make what turned out to be an unflattering film of apartheid in practice. On two occasions ministers rather petulantly referred to 'dollar imperialism in Africa' and to the support given by an American foundation to so critical a body as the South African Institute of Race Relations. On the whole, however, the government is not anxious to alienate the sympathies of so economically and politically powerful a State, and the exchange of personnel has continued though, to some extent, American interest has shifted its emphasis to Central and West Africa.

Until the end of the Second World War South Africa's relations with other territories in southern and central Africa were economic rather than political. Johannesburg is the centre of an economic empire, and the Union draws most of its labour for the mines, and a good proportion of its labour for industries, from outside its borders. Further, the Union has valuable trading relations with other African territories and is intent on developing these markets. With the exception of German East Africa and South-West Africa in the First World War, relations between South Africa and other African territories have always been peaceful. Belgium was, in two world wars, an ally; and Portugal was an ally in the first, and neutral in the second; the remaining territories are British or French.

Cecil Rhodes dreamt of a united South Africa that would include Southern Rhodesia; and when union was being debated, at the National Convention of 1908, Southern Rhodesia was represented by observers. The most serious attempt to unite her with South Africa took place in 1923 when Smuts toured the country and tried to persuade Rhodesians to throw in their lot with South Africa. They were, however, afraid of an Afrikaner majority, and refused. In the last years of the Second World War Smuts talked a good deal about pan-Africanism; but it is doubtful whether he had any specific policy in mind beyond the need for closer co-operation in the exploitation of natural resources, the development of transport, and in fighting pests such as locusts. Smuts, like others, was impressed by the smallness of the European population in southern Africa.

New factors are beginning to weigh in South Africa's political relations with territories to the north of her borders. In the first place, there is an increasing immigration of South Africans into the two Rhodesias. These two territories are expanding rapidly and there is a demand for technicians, for railwaymen, and for civil servants. Land is cheaper there than in the Union, and young South Africans find the conditions for settlement attractive. Many of these South African immigrants are Afrikaners, and the beginnings of a language problem have already made their appearance. In 1950, Afrikaners in Southern Rhodesia were sufficiently numerous to have their own newspaper, and they petitioned the Rhodesian Government for Afrikaans-medium primary schools. The government refused, and the Nationalist Press in South Africa took strong exception to the refusal. Even in Kenya the language question has arisen. In 1951 a party of Afrikaans children from Kenya toured the Union to raise money for the establishment of a private school, and they were received cordially in official and unofficial circles. The reaction of the Nationalist Party Press to this question of Afrikaners who have trekked to other British territories seems to indicate that, in due course, the Union Government may be under pressure to interfere on behalf of the emigrants.

The second political factor that is assuming increasing importance is the question of the part that Africa may have to play in another war. From the points of view of strategic position, of European manpower, and of ability to manufacture war materials, South Africa must be regarded as the dominant single state south of the Sahara; and it is obvious that she will play an important part in the co-ordination of military plans. There are, however, difficulties in the way of effective co-operation. South Africans in general, and the Nationalist Party more particularly, are opposed to the use of armed non-European troops. During the First World War Coloured troops were armed, and fought well, while Africans were used as a labour force only. In the last war, Coloured troops were used chiefly as transport drivers; they were, nevertheless, mostly armed when on active service. Africans were not used as fighting troops and this caused great dissatisfaction among them and hindered recruiting. It may well be that, in another war, Africans in the Union will be reluctant to volunteer in sufficient numbers unless they are armed, and this may have repercussions on the African populations of other territories.

The third and most important factor that affects South Africa's external relations is the astonishing speed with which political events in the rest of Africa have marched since 1950. It is too early to attempt to analyse with any degree of accuracy the reasons why, within a decade, territory after territory in Africa achieved independence. Immediately after the Second World War, most people with a knowledge of Africa knew that fresh and more progressive colonial policies would be adopted in Africa and that such policies would, in the fullness of time, lead to responsible government. Few would have believed that, within ten years' time, more than half the population of Africa would be politically independent, and that the white governments of the territories occupied by the rest would be faced with urgent and immediate problems of extending political power to their African subjects. Changes in the political climate of Europe and the world, the wooing of Africa by the two greatest Powers, and the simultaneous bursting into flower of African nationalism are among the main general causes of the revolution that has taken place. But whatever the causes, the result is indisputable: it is no longer a question of *whether* political rights and power will be extended to Africans; it is only a question of *when* and *how* this will happen.

The full import of these startling events was not at first realized by the white population of South Africa. The first reaction of the Nationalist Party Press to the independence of Ghana was to accuse Britain of a policy of scuttle and of leaving the white man in Africa to his fate. This was followed by a strongly expressed belief that the experiment in self-government could not possibly succeed because Africans were not ready for it; but when it became clear that this belief was not necessarily well founded, and that other territories were soon to follow Ghana's example, the uneasy realization began to dawn that the Union would have to come to terms with this situation. The Nationalist Press and ministers then began to take the realistic line of recognizing and welcoming any new States and of offering, in advance, to co-operate with them in solving common African problems; at the same time, great stress was laid on the need to respect South Africa's right to deal with her interracial problems in her own way—that of apartheid. There were debates and discussions on whether to exchange diplomatic representation with the new States and on the social difficulties of having black diplomats in South Africa; there was even talk of erecting a multi-racial hotel to house distinguished non-white representatives. Both the Nationalist Party and the United Party have, however, been extremely cautious about these matters and have left it to individuals to make the bolder suggestions that could, if necessary, be disowned officially. The debates and discussions continue, and an increasingly urgent tone is being injected into them by the speed of events outside South Africa's borders.

11

There are two aspects of South Africa's relations with the emerging States of Africa that require discussion. In the first place, there is a community of outlook among the majority of Europeans who have made their home in Africa and who have entrenched themselves economically and politically in Southern Rhodesia and the Union, and to a lesser extent in other territories. They have in common a powerful incentive to protect their vested interests by retaining and increasing their political hold on the countries they inhabit; they regard themselves, as indeed they are, as small communities surrounded by an alien civilization; and they are convinced that no mother-country government can really understand the problem of dealing with Africans. There are minorities in all these territories who do not share these views and who look forward to a common citizenship regardless of race; but the majority will not lightly surrender their privileged position. The largest body of Europeans lives in South Africa, and many of those beyond her borders have, for the time being, grave suspicion of the Afrikaner nationalism that is in control in the Union. Nevertheless, the urge to stand together in face of a threat to vested interests, to have a common policy towards the African, may well become stronger as African freedom grows, and Europeans outside the Union may begin to look to her for leadership.

The second aspect is the reverse of the first: Africans in the Union look with growing pride and admiration at the new independent African States, and contact between African leaders in those States and in the Union is becoming closer. It has become popular for African leaders outside the Union to talk about liberating their brothers in the south; more seriously, a powerful trade union in Ghana and the African National Congress in Tanganyika have spoken of boycotting South African products. South African governments may, for a time, be able to regard such threats lightly or use them as a pretext for banning African leaders and organizations; but their significance cannot be overlooked by anyone, black or white, who thinks of Africa as home and for whom a ganging up of black against white spells disaster. The supreme test of statesmanship in Africa, and of South African foreign policy, lies in the ability to ward off that disaster.

CONSTITUTIONAL QUESTIONS

The fourth question that divides the two major parties is constitutional. It is not merely a question of whether South Africa should be a republic, in or out of the Commonwealth, but whether she should be governed on the lines of a parliamentary democracy in which respect for constitutional conventions plays a considerable part.

By the time the Union was constituted South Africa had had experience of two kinds of popular government. In the Cape there was parliamentary government which was based on the British model and which inherited and developed the traditions of British parliamentary democracy. The Transvaal, on the other hand, had a republican constitution that was unstable and subject to such continual stresses that constitutional traditions had no chance to mature. Constitutionalism in the Cape connoted adherence to the spirit of parliamentary democracy as well as to the letter of the written constitution; in the Transvaal the practice of constitutionalism was empirical. Natal had followed the British model, and the Free State was closer in spirit to the Cape than it was to the Transvaal.

Broadly speaking, the United Party adheres to the British conception of constitutional government, and the Nationalist Party shows a tendency to hark back to the republican constitution of the Transvaal. Many Nationalists have expressed strong opinions against what Malan called 'British parliamentary democracy', and have maintained that it is not suited to the Afrikaner temperament or to South African conditions. The first of these contentions has no substance. The histories of the Cape Parliament, and of the Union Parliament since 1910, show that Afrikaans-speaking South Africans have been foremost among parliamentarians and the staunchest upholders of constitutional conventions. The second contention, that British parliamentary democracy is unsuited to South African conditions, is based on doubtful premises. Soon after Germany and Italy had popularized the idea of the one-party state, it became customary in Nationalist Party circles to maintain that the Boer Republics were one-party states and that that system was more suited to the Afrikaner temperament. The cry, therefore, became: Back to the Boer Republics. As the Council of the Dutch Reformed Churches has pointed out, however, the theory that the Boer Republics were one-party states is an illusion.[1] In the *Volksraad* there were, as yet, no clearly defined parties, but that was because there was general agreement on the simple fundamental issues that faced its members. Towards the end of the nineteenth century there were clear signs that parties were beginning to

[1] See *Fundamental Principles of Calvinist Christian Political Science*, quoted in chapter 9.

emerge, and presidential elections were usually contests between two groups.

Another argument against British parliamentary democracy is that it does not work where there is a non-homogeneous population. The system may work, say the critics, where there are a common language and a common cultural background. But, in South Africa, there is no such bond between Europeans and non-Europeans, and even between the two main European groups there is a lack of common background. This argument, too, is of doubtful validity. Cape statesmen of pre-Union days were practically unanimous in maintaining that a common voters' roll of citizens of all colours and based on civilization tests was practicable, and they fought hard to have that well-tried system adopted in the South Africa Act. The history of South Africa from 1948 to 1959 has shown that the mere existence of a parliament is in itself no guarantee of individual liberty; but that is not because the population is non-homogeneous but because parliament is elected by one-fifth of the population. There is indeed a danger in a non-homogeneous society that a majority, or even a well-organized minority, may use the control of the parliamentary machine for its own purposes and, in the process, deprive other groups of rights and liberties. The remedy for that lies in a more rigid constitution in which individual and group rights and liberties are entrenched, and this is the remedy that the newly formed Progressive Party strongly advocates.

Where the Nationalist Party differs from other parties is that many of its members are less firmly attached to the constitutional principles and conventions of parliamentary democracy. Like those who worked the nineteenth-century Transvaal constitution, they tend to be empirical and to justify constitutional changes whose main object is the advancement of the interests of a racial group or of a political party. This tendency was evinced in the passage of the Separate Representation of Voters Act which has already been described. In the debate on that Bill the United Party declared its intention, if the Bill was passed, of testing its validity in the courts, and Malan replied that if the courts found against the government he would have to consider action similar to that taken by President Kruger when he dismissed his Chief Justice for pronouncing against the validity of a resolution of the *Volksraad*.[1] The subsequent history of the Separate Representation of Voters Act, as well as other legislation introduced by the Nationalist Government, shows a curious mixture of respect for the letter of constitutional forms and a disregard for their spirit. Moreover, the tendency to give far-reaching and arbitrary powers to ministers, though not unique to South Africa or to the Nationalist

[1] See Walker, *A History of South Africa*, pp. 464–6, 472.

Government, has been pushed to lengths which argue, at the least, an impatience with the legal and legislative safeguards that a parliamentary system is presumed to provide.[1]

Parliamentary democracy assumes an independent judiciary whose status all parties are concerned to uphold; only thus can individual freedom be safeguarded against arbitrary government. In 1952, when the Appellate Division of the Supreme Court declared the Separate Representation of Voters Act invalid, ministers permitted themselves and their followers to refer in public to the judges as 'paid officials' who should be brought under control; and in 1959 the Minister of Justice introduced a Supreme Court Bill which contained a provision empowering the Governor-General to suspend a judge for 'misconduct', subject to the subsequent approval of parliament. Under the South Africa Act, a judge may not be removed except by the Governor-General on an address from both Houses of Parliament, and the proposed Bill would, virtually, have made judicial tenure subject to the executive. There was so much criticism of this proposal that it was dropped; but the fact that the proposal could have been brought forward at all augurs a lack of steadfastness of belief in the importance of an independent judiciary.

It is important to determine whether this attitude towards constitutional conventions is inherent in Nationalist Party policy or whether it has grown up in justification of acts which its opponents have stigmatized as unconstitutional. Nationalists are divided on this as they are on republicanism or the Commonwealth. Many have a deep respect for constitutional forms and were concerned when their own government appeared to be disregarding them; some resigned from the Party because of this disregard. Nevertheless, it is possible to discern a link between what might be called Krugerism and the dominant group in modern Afrikaner nationalism: in both are to be found an impatience with opposition and criticism, a conviction that Afrikaners are the real 'people' (die volk) of South Africa, and a determination to retain political control in Afrikaner hands even if that involves flouting constitutional procedures. Whatever the truth, the issue is one of paramount importance to South Africa, for on its resolution will depend whether the Union will continue to be governed according to the principles of parliamentary democracy which came from Britain and were nourished and developed in the Cape Parliament.

A discussion of political parties and policies would be incomplete unless it mentioned political pressure groups, those extra-parliamentary

---

[1] For a carefully documented account of the extent to which the rule of law has been eroded see Brookes and Macaulay, Civil Liberty in South Africa.

forces that attempt to influence legislation and administration. There are many such, and counterparts to most of them are to be found in all countries. Agricultural unions, chambers of commerce and of industries—both English and Afrikaans—the Chamber of Mines, and the trade unions, all use their organizations to obtain favourable legislation and administration and, thus, to further their economic interests. In the same general category are English and Afrikaans teachers' associations, the Public Service Association, and the various professional associations. There are also a number of disinterested organizations that use their influence for the advancement of specific or general social aims. Such are the various child welfare organizations, the English and Afrikaans women's councils, the churches, and the South African Institute of Race Relations, which has acquired a considerable reputation as a body that makes an objective study of interracial affairs and is concerned to influence public opinion and parliament by the presentation of facts. On the borderline between political and cultural organizations are a large number of Afrikaans societies which exist to promote Afrikaans culture. Owing to the close connexion between the Afrikaans language and nationalism, these societies exercise a direct influence on political thought, and the *Federasie van Afrikaanse Kultuurverenigings* may not unfairly be regarded as a powerful unofficial ally of the Nationalist Party.

There are a few organizations that require further description because of the influence they have had on party politics. The War Veterans' Torch Commando came into being in May 1951 as a spontaneous movement of ex-servicemen and women who opposed what they regarded as unconstitutional actions by the Nationalist Party Government, such as the alteration of the South Africa Act without observing the constitutional terms laid down in the Act, and the removal of free access to the courts under the anti-Communist legislation. Led by 'Sailor' Malan, the Torch Commando's declared object was to evict the Nationalist Government, by constitutional means, because it considered that the government was tampering with the freedom for which the ex-servicemen fought. The movement spread rapidly and attracted to its ranks a large number of men and women who were not normally active in politics. It was not confined to ex-servicemen, though only they might hold executive positions and, thus, control policy.

The Nationalist Party and its Press took the Torch Commando seriously as a new political force. From Malan downwards, the Commando was accused, alternatively, of being an adjunct of the United Party and of usurping the functions of that Party; of being Communist-inspired and of being financed by the United South

Africa Trust Fund, a capitalist foundation; of being a new political party and of being subversive of parliamentary institutions. In actual fact, the Torch Commando was none of these things. It was a manifestation of the frustration of men and women who suddenly realized that they were being governed by a political party that had sympathized with the enemy during the war. Few of the members of the Torch Commando had political ambitions and they regarded their activities as called for by exceptional circumstances; they had no common policy except to evict the government at a general election. In the 1953 election they threw all their energies and enthusiasm on the side of the opponents of the Nationalist Party which was, nevertheless, returned with an increased majority; and, its initial momentum spent, the Torch Commando dissolved, some of its more active members joining the United Party or the newly formed Liberal or Federal parties.

The Women's Defence of the Constitution League, more generally known as the Black Sash, was founded in 1955 to rouse public opinion over the government's proposal to enlarge the Senate and, thus, to secure the necessary two-thirds majority for taking Coloured voters off the common roll. The women who founded the movement, and those who joined it in large numbers, regarded the Senate Bill as an attempt to circumvent the constitution as embodied in the South Africa Act—hence the full name of the League. The movement chose as its emblem a black rose, and in all public appearances connected with the work of the League, women wore a black sash—hence the popular name. The movement rose and spread with startling rapidity, like the Torch Commando; but unlike the Torch Commando it developed objectives that were not purely negative and it was able to maintain an effective organization after the initial momentum had died down.

The methods chosen by the Black Sash to rouse public opinion were the normal ones of public meetings, protest marches, and mass petitions; but two new methods were tried and proved effective. The first was to maintain a vigil round parliament and, in other towns, at public buildings. During a vigil, women in black sashes stood with bowed heads as a sign of mourning to mark the passing of Acts of Parliament that appeared to them to disregard the constitution or attack the rights and liberties of individuals or groups. The second method was known as 'haunting' and took the form of standing in two silent rows through the middle of which any minister, in his official capacity, would have to pass as he entered or left railway stations, airports, or public buildings. It was an impressive sight to see women from all walks of life maintaining a vigil, and the Black Sash gained the respect and sympathy of the public at large. As for 'haunting', there is evidence that ministers felt the effects of being stared at by silent women to such an extent that they became secretive about their movements; one or two ministers attempted to treat the whole thing lightly by making facetious remarks, but the women accepted that as proof of the efficacy of their demonstration.

The new methods of attracting attention to public affairs owed much of their success to novelty and surprise, and now that these have worn off, haunting and vigils are practised less frequently. The Black Sash continues to act as a protest organization and, in addition, has developed a practical programme of assisting Africans who may have become entangled in one of the many administrative meshes of the pass laws, of drawing public attention to infringements of civil and human liberty, and of educating its own members and the public generally on public issues by means of a monthly periodical and by organizing brains' trusts at which all points of view are expressed.[1]

The South African Bureau of Racial Affairs, usually called Sabra, was founded some years ago by Afrikaners who support the policy of apartheid, and it has had considerable influence on Nationalist Party thinking. It draws its support largely from the Afrikaans-speaking universities and from the Afrikaans churches, and its annual conferences attract much attention because Sabra provides intellectual support for government policies in race matters. Unlike the older South African Institute of Race Relations, Sabra is open to white membership only; but, though its policy is basically one of apartheid, it by no means rejects contact between white and non-white. On the contrary, Sabra has emphasized that cultural and social contact, at a responsible level, is essential if non-whites are ever to be persuaded that territorial separation is a sound policy, and that, unless they are persuaded, apartheid will never be possible. Though Sabra has had close contact with the Nationalist Party Government, that contact has become less cordial for two reasons: the government has paid scant attention to the recommendations of the Tomlinson Commission Report which Sabra believes to provide the only economically sound basis for apartheid; and the present Prime Minister, Dr. Verwoerd, has openly expressed his disagreement with Sabra's insistence on discussions with African leaders. In 1959 several prominent members of Sabra resigned from the Nationalist Party because they felt that it was not carrying out either the letter or the spirit of apartheid as Sabra understood and expounded that policy.

[1] For the early history of the movement see *The Black Sash*, by Mirabel Rogers. Present activities are mirrored in a monthly periodical called *The Black Sash*.

The *Afrikaner Broederbond* is a secret society, although the names of a few of its more prominent members, including cabinet ministers, are publicly known. Because of continued accusations that the Broederbond was a secret power behind the throne, the Dutch Reformed Church Council decided, in 1949, to investigate the matter. The committee of investigation reported in 1951 and its conclusions were published in that year.[1] This report says that the Broederbond came into being in 1918, at a time when there was great confusion in Afrikaner ranks, as an attempt on the part of a few people to end the division among Afrikaners. The objects, as set forth in the constitution, are to establish unity among all those who desire to promote the welfare of the Afrikaners; to arouse a national self-consciousness among Afrikaners; and to promote the interests of the Afrikaner nation. Membership is open to those who are Afrikaans-speaking Protestants of good character and who regard South Africa as their only fatherland. It is a cardinal principle of the Bond, says the report, that the names of its members and all its proceedings are strictly confidential, though any member has the right to make his own membership public. It was explained to the committee of inquiry that this secrecy was a matter of efficiency, just as cabinet discussions are secret until they come before the public.

The committee of inquiry of the Dutch Reformed churches says that it was assured that politics are not allowed in the Broederbond and that matters affecting the moral, intellectual, social, and political progress of the nation are discussed on a non-party-political basis. Among the many subjects to which the Broederbond devoted attention were the Native question, immigration, usury, mother-tongue instruction, and libraries. The committee of inquiry came to the conclusion that the Broederbond was sound and salutary, that it did not wish to harm anyone, but merely aimed at serving the best interests of the *Afrikanernasie* (the Afrikaner nation).

That this report of the Dutch Reformed churches has not satisfied those who regard the secret activities of the Afrikaner Broederbond as dangerous is due partly to the belief that some ministers of the Afrikaans churches are members of the Bond and that the committee of inquiry can, therefore, not be regarded as impartial. Further, the committee had to depend on information supplied by the Broederbond itself and, since it is a secret society, it is to be presumed that the Bond did not necessarily reveal all its secrets. Critics of the Broederbond recall that, in 1935, General Hertzog, then Prime Minister, publicly castigated the Bond in these words:

[1] See *Agenda vir die Twee-en-Twintigste Vergadering van die Raad van die Kerke*, 1951, pp. 49–52.

They are sworn not to entertain any co-operation with the English-speaking population and thereby they stand in direct racial conflict with our fellow English Afrikaners, and are striving by way of domination on the part of the Afrikaans-speaking section to put their foot on the neck of English-speaking South Africa. . . . The Broederbond has become a grave menace to the rest and peace of our social community, even where it operates in the economic-cultural sphere.[1]

Towards the end of the 1939-45 War General Smuts yielded to pressure in his own party and banned membership of the Broederbond to public servants. Those public servants who were known to be members were given the option of resigning either from the Bond or from the public service, and, in justifying this measure, Smuts referred to the Broederbond as 'a dangerous, cunning, political, Fascist organization'. Since these denunciations by Hertzog and Smuts most opponents of the Broederbond have looked upon it as an organization that worked in secret to promote its aims by influencing public appointments to key positions and by exercising a hidden control on the policies of the Nationalist Party.

It is, of course, impossible to arrive at the truth without a rigorous public inquiry. If the Broederbond is, as the Nationalist Party and Press maintain, merely another Sons of England, no great exception can be taken to it. If, on the other hand, it does exercise the secret and all-pervading political influence that its opponents allege, it obviously constitutes a serious threat to parliamentary democracy.

The vast majority of non-whites in South Africa have no vote. Nevertheless, non-white political organizations are assuming increasing importance as extra-parliamentary bodies of great potential strength. There are a number of these organizations and they have never succeeded in establishing one national body to represent non-white opinion. This is not surprising, for, just as European public opinion is divided on racial questions, non-white opinion is divided on how to achieve what all non-white leaders want: to share political power with the whites. At one extreme are those who argue that their aim will never be achieved by co-operation with Europeans and that their only hope is to strengthen their own organizations to the point where their demands will be irresistible. At the other extreme are those who believe that such action will breed a non-white nationalism and that a more hopeful approach is to seek co-operation with white liberal organizations. The strongest bodies are the African National Congress and the South African Indian Congress, and in practice both follow a policy between the two extremes: while strengthening their own

[1] Quoted in *The Friend*, 21 May 1951.

organizations and using their own methods to exert political pressure, they co-operate on an *ad hoc* basis with such groups as the Black Sash, the Liberal Party, and the Civil Rights League, and they are prepared to take part in discussions with Sabra. It is important to notice that no responsible non-white leader has advocated evicting the Europeans. So acute an observer as Prof. Gwendolen Carter has noted that non-European leaders in the Union are not revolutionary and that, in contrast with other parts of Africa, they 'seek changes within the existing system, not its overthrow'. 'They want', she says, 'a share in political power, not to oust the Europeans. They want a fuller return for their contribution to the economy, not to change its character. They want to become more Western, not less.'[1]

NOTE

The speech of the British Prime Minister, Mr. Macmillan, to both houses of the Union Parliament, on 3 February 1960, is relevant to the discussion on pp. 158–67 above. Mr. Macmillan was widely interpreted as having served friendly but firm notice to South Africa that her racial policies were not acceptable to the West, and that, if the West had to choose between the friendship of two hundred million blacks and a few million whites, the whites would be 'thrown to the wolves'. The conclusion drawn from this by the Nationalist Party Press was that the whites should unite to defend their right to a separate and independent existence. The Opposition Press, and the non-white leaders, drew a different conclusion: that South Africa should modify her racial policies. Mr. Macmillan's speech, coming from such a source and so urbanely expressed, had a profound impact on South Africa. It is too early to speak with confidence, but it is possible that the speech may have shaken the strong belief in the validity of apartheid. If so, it will have assisted the process of loosening the rigid ties that characterize party-political divisions—a process that had begun before Mr. Macmillan's visit.

[1] Gwendolen M. Carter, *The Politics of Inequality*.

8

Education

ORGANIZED EDUCATION IN SOUTH AFRICA, AS IN THE REST OF SOUTHERN Africa, is entirely a product of Europe. What African or Coloured educationists there are, are themselves the product of an educational system that has its roots in Western culture, that has been planned and instituted and largely paid for and controlled by Europeans. Europe found southern Africa inhabited by heathen tribes, barbarians whose progress in the scale of civilization had been slow; a people whose lives were dominated by witchcraft and superstition. When they came to settle in South Africa, men and women of European stock brought with them the spiritual and intellectual equipment of Western civilization. Either by accident or, for the greater part, of set purpose, they transmitted this equipment to the heathen with whom they came into contact, and, in doing so, they began to set free the spirit and the mind of Africa. This process is continuing.

Few Africans today would deny this debt to European civilization. In transmitting Western civilization to Africa the Europeans have made many mistakes—mistakes that sprang from an impatient desire to speed up the process of civilization as well as from greed and selfishness, mistakes due to over-zealousness as well as indifference. But for better or worse, European education has left the indelible impress of Western civilization on South Africa. Many Europeans in South Africa are today alarmed at the rate of progress of African education, and their alarm is a measure of the extent to which Western ideas have taken hold of Africa. To those who believe in the fundamental values of Western culture there is no real cause for alarm.

Until the last quarter of the nineteenth century it was common for European and Coloured children in the Cape Colony to attend the same school for the first few years of their education. More than half the schools in 1860 were state-aided mission schools, which were attended by European and Coloured children, and in 1883 almost 6,000 of the 38,000 children in mission schools were European. It gradually became the practice, however, to separate European and Coloured schools in the Cape and in Natal. In the Transvaal and Free State Republics there was strict separation between black and white, though Coloured children who were not too pronouncedly dark were to be found in European schools.

Until industrialization began to draw them to the towns, the vast majority of Africans lived in their own tribal areas, which had been conquered by the Europeans. The different governments regarded mission education as a valuable instrument in pacifying these conquered territories and gave grants to the missions for this purpose. By the time that the four colonies united, therefore, it was well-established practice that European and non-European education were administered separately and that the former should be completely financed by the state while the latter should be conducted through state-aided mission societies. It is convenient, therefore, to discuss the European and non-European educational systems separately.

EUROPEAN EDUCATION

Primary and secondary education and teacher training other than that given in universities are controlled by the provincial councils. In each province there is an education department in charge of a Director, called a Superintendent-General in the Cape. Although the directors and the school inspectors are regarded as Union civil servants they are controlled by the provincial authorities. The education departments are responsible for the establishment and maintenance of schools, and they conduct their own school examinations and prescribe their own syllabuses; the school-leaving or matriculation examination is subject to the supervisory control of a Joint Matriculation Board on which the universities are represented. Education is financed to the extent of about 50 per cent by the Union Government, the balance coming from provincial taxes; with minor exceptions it is compulsory and free for all Europeans. There are, in round numbers, 620,000 scholars, 25,000 teachers, and 2,800 schools. In addition to these state schools there are about 260 private schools, most of them run by the Anglican, Roman Catholic, and Methodist churches, with about 45,000 pupils. Some of these private schools are state-aided and all must be registered and open to inspection by the education departments. The largest of them are independent of government aid and are among the oldest and best-known schools in South Africa, enjoying a reputation akin to the great public schools of Britain on which, with local adaptations, they are modelled.

The primary school ranges from standard I to standard V. Below the primary school are sub-standards A and B; above it are the secondary standards VI to X, which is the school-leaving or matriculation standard. Each sub-standard and standard implies a year's schooling, and ages range from almost 9 years in standard I to 17 plus in standard X. About 20 per cent of all children are in secondary schools.

In all the large towns, and in small towns that have acquired a reputation as educational centres, boys and girls are in separate schools;

but in all the smaller centres and in the large number of farm schools co-education is the rule. Separate education is, in fact, the accepted principle except where sparsity of population makes it too expensive. Many secondary schools, and a few primary schools, have boarding departments, usually known as hostels.

An important feature of primary and secondary education, except in Natal, is that each school has a school committee elected by the parents.[1] The committee selects and appoints teachers, subject to the approval of the education department, and has limited powers of control over the school. The practice of having school committees is an old one in South Africa, and arises from the belief that the parents should have some control over the education of their children. Given a principal and a committee who are in sympathy the system may have many advantages. The committee strengthens the hands of the principal and staff; it helps to create local interest in the school; and it serves as a useful link between the school and the impersonal education department. But the system is not without its faults and its dangers. Party politics loom large in South Africa, and many committees are today elected on a party-political basis. When that happens either there is friction between staff and committee, or, what is worse, the staff accepts decisions that are based on considerations other than educational. In neither case are the best interests of the school served.

There is another danger inherent in the system. In a great many of the country districts one of the three Dutch Reformed churches is the strongest religious body. The minister of that Church is an important man in local affairs and is frequently chairman of the school committee. His influence in the matter of appointments is considerable, and the result is that staff appointments are frequently and increasingly made on religious and denominational as well as on party-political grounds. In the larger urban centres, where the authority of the Church is less than that of the business and professional world, political rather than religious considerations are a determining factor. Moreover, applicants for teaching posts are required to submit testimonials from a minister, often the chairman of their previous school committee, and many less liberal ministers demand strict religious conformity before giving them.

The result of all this is that a great many teachers must, for bread-and-butter reasons, be careful of the opinions they express, whatever opinions they may hold. A teacher who openly expressed so-called 'liberal' views on race relations would find a large number of country schools closed to him. On the other hand, it is improbable that one

---

[1] There are also, except in Natal, elected school boards for districts. These have administrative rather than educational functions.

who held pronounced Nationalist Party views would be appointed in an English-speaking urban centre, however good his qualifications, except, possibly, to teach Afrikaans. There is, therefore, a strong temptation to conform to a particular religion for the sake of a job.

This lack of intellectual and religious freedom on the part of teachers must affect adversely the standard of professional work. When considerations other than those of character, professional qualification, and intellectual integrity obtrude themselves in the appointment of teachers, the schools are bound to suffer. An editorial in the official organ of the Afrikaans-speaking teachers in the Transvaal drew attention to the 'unpleasant wire-pulling which occurs in various places among Churchmen when a teacher is to be selected for a post by a parent body such as a school board or school committee'. The editorial pointed out that all three Afrikaans churches were Calvinist and that they should co-operate to ensure that education was Christian and National. 'No school in the Transvaal', said the article, 'serves the members of one Church only; therefore, no Church has the right to demand the services of one of its members as a teacher.'[1] Coming from Afrikaans teachers, the strong warning contained in this editorial is indicative of the extent to which denominational considerations may count in the selection of teachers. It also suggests that teachers who do not belong to one of the three Afrikaans churches are unlikely to be appointed in strongly Afrikaans centres.

One of the thorniest problems in South African education is that of language, a problem that has become thoroughly mixed up with party politics. Just after the Boer War, in the early years of the century, teachers were largely English-speaking men and women who had been imported from Britain. Many of them were fine teachers to whom South African education owes a great debt. Not many of them, however, learnt to speak Dutch or Afrikaans, with the result that Afrikaans-speaking children were taught through the medium of a language which was not their mother tongue, though many of them did have some knowledge of English. We have seen how the rise of nationalism coincided with the rapid growth of the Afrikaans language. It was to be expected that the demand for mother-tongue instruction would be raised with insistence by Afrikaners. It was a reasonable demand; but there were three difficulties that had to be overcome. The first was the lack of trained Afrikaans-speaking teachers. That difficulty was soon overcome. The second difficulty was, and is, one of finance. During the first two decades of the twentieth century, urban areas were predominantly English-speaking, and it was beyond the resources of the State to pay for two sets of teachers. Even when

[1] *Die Onderwysblad*, November 1951.

teachers were efficiently bilingual, it would still have required increased staff to provide complete mother-tongue instruction.

The third difficulty, which still exists, is that many Afrikaans-speaking parents preferred to send their children to English-speaking schools so that they should become proficient in the language which had so much social and economic prestige. The Nationalist Party, realizing the close relationship between language and nationalism, then began to agitate for unilingual schools and for compulsory mother-tongue instruction, at least in the primary schools. In the Free State and the Transvaal it became compulsory for a child to receive primary school education through his mother tongue, no matter what the wishes of the parents were. For the time being, the choice of medium in secondary classes was left to parents or to the dictates of circumstances.

By 1940 there were two main types of secondary school. The majority were either parallel medium schools or dual medium schools. In the first, parallel classes were provided in English and in Afrikaans; in the second, some subjects were taught through English and some through Afrikaans. The second type of school was the single medium school, where the second language was taught as a subject, but where all other subjects were taught through the mother tongue. This second type was economically possible only in those centres where the school population was large enough to warrant two separate schools; but it remained the object of Afrikaner nationalism to make single medium schools the general rule.

As a reaction against the insistence on single medium schools there arose a strong movement in favour of dual medium or parallel medium schools. The arguments for and against the single medium school are partly educational and partly political. The arguments for parallel medium schools are that in such schools boys and girls from both language groups meet one another, learn one another's language naturally, and learn to respect one another's cultural traditions. It is socially and politically necessary for South Africans to be completely bilingual; and the only way of achieving that is to have bilingual instruction at school. The principle of mother-tongue instruction in primary schools is admitted as sound; but if South African children are kept in separate schools, the gap between Afrikaner and English will never be bridged. Single medium schools make for cultural isolation, and in them the standard of bilingualism deteriorates.[1]

[1] Whatever the reason, it is generally believed that the standard of bilingualism is falling. The Public Service Commission has, for some years, drawn attention to this. In its Report for 1950, the Commission says that of the total candidates appointed in 1949 only 21·8 per cent 'can be regarded as reasonably bilingual'. See 29th Annual Report of Public Service Commission, U.G.23/1951. Subsequent reports tell the same story.

English-Afrikaner differences are perpetuated, while parallel medium schools make for tolerance in racial matters. Finally, neither English nor Afrikaans is a completely *'foreign'* language to any white South African and, therefore, the principle of mother-tongue instruction is not really violated by parallel medium schools.

Against these arguments, those who favour single medium schools maintain that children who are not educated entirely through Afrikaans as their mother tongue never really become genuine Afrikaners; and it is supremely important, they argue, to keep alive the Afrikaner nation. The Afrikaner has a right and a duty to his own language and traditions, and the atmosphere of parallel medium schools is not favourable to these, and if he relinquishes his language he will soon become anglicized. Bilingualism, they maintain, with some justice, is usually interpreted to mean that the Afrikaner must speak English, not that the English must speak Afrikaans. Why therefore, should the Afrikaner be penalized for not being proficient in English?

How thoroughly this question has become a party-political one is illustrated by the dominant part it continues to play in provincial elections. In the 1943 election in the Transvaal, for example, the United Party won the election and began to introduce dual medium instruction. Staffing difficulties hindered progress and, in 1948, the Nationalist Party won the election and reversed the policy. In that province mother-tongue instruction is now compulsory in all State and private schools.[2] The lengths to which the Transvaal administration is prepared to go in insisting on single medium schools is shown by the case of the Hendrik van der Bijl school at Vanderbijlpark. This was a parallel medium school about which the parents were happy and where, according to all accounts, the pupils of both language groups got on very well with one another. In 1956 the Administrator disestablished the school with the intention of making it an Afrikaans-medium school and providing elsewhere for the English-speaking children. A practically unanimous petition by the parents to leave the school alone was rejected, whereupon the parents applied to the Supreme Court to restrain the Administrator and Executive Council on the ground that the wishes of the parents had been ignored. The parents won their case, but in 1957 the Education Ordinance was amended to give the Administrator power to decide the language medium of any school.

In Natal, in May 1951, a Nationalist Party member petitioned the

[2] The right of parents to send their children to a private denominational school where the medium was not the mother tongue of the children was tested in the courts. The Supreme Court of the Transvaal decided, by a two to one majority, that the parents did have this right: but the decision was reversed, by a three to two majority, in the Appeal Court (June 1951).

Provincial Council to take away the right of parents to decide through which medium they wanted their children instructed. The petition was decisively rejected, but the agitation has continued. Mother tongue as a medium is compulsory in the Orange Free State and, in the Cape Province, till standard VIII, and the department's inspectors, not the parents, decide what the mother tongue is. The right of parents to send their children to private schools, and thus to decide on the medium through which they want them educated, has not been taken away in these two provinces as it has in the Transvaal.

Related to this question of language is what is called Christian National Education, usually referred to as C.N.E. Immediately after the Boer War the Dutch Reformed churches saw the need for rehabilitating the shattered Boer morale. Ministers of the Afrikaans churches took the lead in demanding from the British administration the right to establish Church schools subsidized by the state, as had been the case in republican days—schools in which Afrikaner children would receive religious instruction according to the tenets of the Calvinist churches. The agitation for C.N.E. schools was not successful and, as the Dutch churches played a prominent part in school committees, and were thus able to influence policy, the need for such schools became less pronounced, and undenominational schools financed by the state became the accepted rule. But the agitation never quite died down, and was stimulated by the fact that the Roman Catholic and Anglican churches had their own private denominational schools which attracted many Afrikaans children.

In the 1940's, when the struggle over language medium became acute, the agitation for C.N.E. was revived. It was led by the most conservative of the Dutch Reformed churches, the *Gereformeerde Kerk*, whose headquarters and whose inspiration was the University of Potchefstroom in the Transvaal. A group of university professors and Nationalist Party politicians (including two who subsequently became cabinet ministers) prepared a programme for Christian National Education in which they went very much further in their demands than the supporters of C.N.E. after the Boer War had done. Under the influence of ultra-Calvinist churchmen, extreme fundamentalist doctrines were put forward as principles on which to base education. The theory of evolution was condemned as opposed to predestination; history and geography were to be taught as divinely inspired in the narrowest sense of the word—God had given to each people a country and a task, and it was the Afrikaner task to rule South Africa, and no one had the right to question what was divinely ordained. Teachers who were not prepared to subscribe to these doctrines would not be appointed.

The publication of the programme in 1948 aroused a storm of protest from teachers, from university staffs, and from the general public. An Education League was formed to combat C.N.E. and to defend liberty of conscience in the teaching profession. While English-speaking teachers' associations condemned the proposals, Afrikaans-speaking associations declared themselves in favour of C.N.E. A number of prominent Afrikaners publicly opposed the programme; but many, while privately disapproving, were not prepared to go against the stream of Afrikaner nationalist opinion. So strong is the influence of the Dutch Reformed churches that, in the country districts, few teachers would brave church disapproval by opposing C.N.E.

In 1948 the Nationalist Party, having newly come to power, was not sufficiently sure of itself to pursue a policy of Christian National Education vigorously. The men who had prepared the programme, however, were for the most part men of considerable standing in the community: two became cabinet ministers in 1948; one subsequently became Superintendent-General of Education in the Cape Province; two were university professors; and three were ministers of religion. It must be assumed that men of such standing would not lightly set aside a programme they had taken many years to produce. Indeed, the history of South Africa between 1948 and 1959 is evidence that, as the Nationalist Party proceeded from strength to strength, C.N.E. as an official policy gained ground. In the Transvaal and Orange Free State it has become the official policy; in the Cape Province it is all but officially laid down; only in Natal has the provincial council refused to accept it.

There are other aspects of the C.N.E. programme, as published in 1948, that have been applied. The use of the mother tongue as a medium of instruction in the primary school, in the early years of a child's life, is a reasonable educational principle though there is plenty of evidence that, in a bilingual country, its educational importance has been grossly exaggerated. What is less reasonable in a bilingual country, however, is the application of that principle in the secondary school, in the teeth of parental opposition. Yet that is what has happened in three provinces since 1948, and it follows closely the C.N.E. programme which states, 'We will have nothing to do with a mixture of languages, of culture, of religion, of race'. This conception runs through much of the legislation concerning university education and African and Coloured education, as will be seen presently.

The programme of Christian National Education is, then, a reality in South Africa. It should be clearly realized that in that programme the word 'Christian' is explicitly equated with the Calvinist creed, and the word 'National' is implicitly equated with Afrikaner nationalism. So close has the association of C.N.E. been with Afrikaner nationalism that, in its South African context, C.N.E. means Calvinist Nationalist Education. No real Afrikaner nationalist would wish to deny this. Indeed, it is a source of pride that the church, the language, and the political party are three mutually supporting pillars of Afrikaans culture.

Two questions remain to be discussed: officially sponsored though the C.N.E. programme is, to what extent is it in fact carried out in schools, and, in any event, what are the effects? It seems improbable, on the face of it, that many teachers would in practice teach the kind of fundamentalist history and geography advocated by the programme. The idea that divine providence has allocated to each 'nation' its geographical place on earth, and has given it a divine mission, is not one that ordinarily commends itself to educated men and women, particularly in a country where the known facts of history and geography seem so singularly to fail to endorse those theories. Nevertheless, the history of the world, more especially perhaps since the 1930's, is a warning not to underestimate the capacity of men and women to reconcile the irreconcilable. As recently as 1959 the Transvaal Education Department placed on its list of approved books a series of history text-books based on the theory that the world was created some eight thousand years ago. In that province, too, a conference of teachers held in 1959 to discuss methods of guiding and advising pupils was told by an inspector of schools not to worry too much about psychological theories but to base their advice on sound Christian National principles. Under this kind of pressure there is, of course, an incentive to conform for fear of losing one's job or of missing promotion.

It is impossible to be specific either about the extent to which C.N.E. is being applied or about the effects. It seems clear that one of two things is happening, and is bound to happen if the upholders of C.N.E. push their programme too hard: either the teachers are teaching according to C.N.E. principles from conviction, or they are finding it expedient to combine outward conformity with inward scepticism. Neither of these results can be anything but unhappy. More than 80 per cent of the towns of South Africa have populations too small to support two separate schools, and in three of the four provinces the small town school is predominantly Afrikaans-speaking. It is in these three provinces that the provincial authorities accept the principles of C.N.E., and it is already evident that the pupils in those schools are being more and more isolated from the main currents of European thought. Unless the process is halted the chief sufferers from C.N.E.

are going to be the Afrikaners themselves. In August of 1959 the campaign for the provincial election got under way and the Nationalist Party Congress of Natal took the opportunity of castigating its opponents for tying the Nationalist Party to the 1948 document. The leader of the party in Natal protested that the 1948 programme was not the Nationalist Party policy. It would be a happy augury if this announcement could be taken to mean that supporters of C.N.E. had seen the danger signals. It is to be feared, however, that it was an electioneering move to pacify Natal voters whose antipathy to C.N.E. is well known and whose provincial executive was just then engaged in a struggle with the Union Government over the appointment to high office in the Natal Education Department of an Afrikaner of known C.N.E. sympathies. The announcement may have had a second purpose: the Nationalist Party has, from time to time, toyed with the idea of making school education a national rather than a provincial matter, and early in August the Prime Minister once more mentioned this—rather more positively than previously. Reaction throughout the country was immediate and strong, and, on the eve of provincial elections, the Nationalist Party organization must have thought it advisable to calm the undoubted fears of a very large number of voters that a national education policy would inevitably mean a Christian National Education policy.

Primary school teachers are trained in normal colleges and training colleges run by the education departments. Training for secondary school-teaching takes place at the universities as a post-graduate course. Neither the Afrikaans training colleges nor the universities have escaped the political atmosphere that pervades South Africa. Nationalism, closely associated with the exclusive use of the Afrikaans language, invaded these institutions as it did the schools, with similar results.

The social status of teachers has, during half a century, suffered a change. In the early years of the twentieth century the schoolmaster, particularly in the rural areas, had a social position comparable to that of the Scots dominie. Together with the minister, he represented learning and culture, and despite his small income he was looked up to by all. He was referred to, affectionately and with respect, as 'meester' (master), and his advice was sought by the community in which he served. With the spread of education and the growth of a more sophisticated urban civilization, the rest of the community caught up with the minister and the schoolmaster, and their status and influence have, relatively, declined. Teachers still enjoy much of the prestige that attaches to their office, but it is today the exceptional headmaster who commands widespread respect and affection.

Teachers are not allowed to take active part in party politics. A teacher who wishes to stand for parliament or for a provincial council must resign his post and lose pension and other benefits. In the Transvaal he may be given six months' leave without pay and without loss of privileges to fight an election. He may be allowed, in exceptional circumstances, to take part in local government and to become a town councillor, but the permission is rarely granted.

European teachers in all the provinces have professional associations. Except in the Orange Free State, these are divided into English- and Afrikaans-speaking associations, which have their annual conferences separately. The executive councils of the two teachers' associations in the Cape meet each other from time to time, and the two associations co-operate when it comes to a question of agitating for better service conditions. On all academic matters, however, they deliberate separately and, on such matters as Christian National Education, they have arrived at diametrically opposed conclusions. African, Indian and Coloured teachers have their own organizations, separate from each other and from the European associations. There is, thus, no one body in South Africa that represents all those who are engaged in teaching.

AFRICAN EDUCATION

The problems of African education have exercised many minds in Africa, and in South Africa they have done so for longer than elsewhere. Even when regarded in isolation the problems of educational content and medium of instruction are difficult. When they are considered in the social environment of a multi-racial society, they become formidable. It is not merely a question of what and how to teach, but of what the evolving African society asks, and of what the European society will be prepared to pay. The early missionaries naturally assumed that education was education, and that the quickest way of christianizing and civilizing the African was to open schools where European education in a European language was made available. Later generations doubted the wisdom of a policy that seemed to run counter to all the psychological theories of education. The belief grew that greater emphasis should be laid on the mother tongue; that school education for Africans had become too bookish and not sufficiently 'practical'; and that greater attention should be paid to the cultural background of the African. The early missionary took it for granted that the cure for barbarism was European civilization. Later, men began to ask by what right Europeans foisted their civilization on to the African. Would it not turn him into a bad imitation of a European instead of a good African?

In the Cape Colony and in Natal the policy of aiding mission schools was begun in the middle of the nineteenth century. In the Transvaal and Free State republics there was no state aid for mission schools, and it was only after the Boer War that the system was introduced there. By the time of Union, in 1910, the system was general. African education was financed and controlled by the provinces; but, as with European education, the provinces soon found that the cost of education was beyond their resources. In 1922 the central government took over the financial responsibility for aiding African education, while leaving the control to the provincial authorities. In that year the government contributed a block grant of £340,000 to African education, and this sum was to be a fixed annual grant. It was inadequate for the existing needs, let alone the needs of expansion, and in 1925 a proportion of the Native poll-tax was added to the block grant. The ever-increasing demands of African education led successive governments to increase the proportion of the Native poll-tax to be allocated to education until, in 1943, four-fifths of the tax (about £900,000) went to African education. Then in 1945, government acceded to the wishes of those who had for years been asking that African education should not be made dependent of the amount of direct taxation the African could pay. From that year until 1953, funds for aiding African education were drawn entirely from general revenue.

The story of financing of African education is interesting because it illustrates changes in European public opinion. There was a time when educating Natives was strongly disapproved of—it gave the Africans 'ideas beyond their station' and unfitted them to do manual labour. Money derived from European taxation should certainly not be spent on such an object; if the African wanted education he should' pay for it himself. Very gradually, however, public opinion changed. In the beginning, small annual grants were made to mission societies for schools. As the demands grew, the grants expanded; but the principle that Africans should pay for their own educational facilities was adhered to, and the Native poll-tax was used to finance African education. Then, as late as 1945, the principle that African education should depend on what the African could pay was abandoned, and the state accepted financial responsibility for aiding African education. As we shall see presently, the Bantu Education Act of 1953 brought about radical changes in the organization and financing of Bantu education and in the relationship between the state and the mission societies that had until then had a major control.

While African public opinion asks for European education, European public opinion is divided on what education for Africans should mean.

The division is not entirely on English-Afrikaans lines; but it is true that the Dutch Reformed Church missions and Afrikaner educationists are, on the whole, in favour of a specifically 'African' type of education, and that the other missions tend to regard differences between European and African education as temporary and negligible. There are historical reasons for this. Dating from the early nineteenth century, the missionaries, who were then for the most part English-speaking, were cordially disliked by the Afrikaans farmers. They said that the missionaries treated the blacks as equals and 'spoilt' them—a view by no means held only by the Afrikaans-speaking settlers, as any missionaries in the Rhodesias and Nyasaland and elsewhere could testify. They said, moreover, that the missionaries 'blackened' the name of the Afrikaner. When the Dutch Reformed churches entered the mission field they did so with a different outlook from that of the English-speaking societies. As a Christian mission, the Dutch Reformed Church has a good record in Africa, as far north as Nigeria; but while in its missionary endeavours it by no means neglected education, it was not enthusiastic for academic education on European lines.

This difference between the Afrikaner churches and the English-speaking churches has been accentuated in recent years by the growth of Afrikaans nationalism and its insistence on the doctrine of apartheid. Although there is still a great deal of opposition among Afrikaners to any but an elementary and rather severely practical education for Africans, the Afrikaans churches realize that formal education cannot be withheld from the African. Since, however, the doctrine of apartheid postulates the perpetual overlordship of the Europeans, educational theory based on that doctrine must differentiate sharply between European and African education. This leads Nationalist theorists to stress mother-tongue instruction and to insist that tribal traditions must be the foundation on which African education is built.

It is improbable that tribal traditions can survive the impact of Western economy and culture, and it is, therefore, difficult to see how an educational system can be constructed on what is, at best, a shifting foundation. The conclusion seems inescapable that the Africans will adapt themselves to European standards, and increasingly demand European education.

In the matter of the various Bantu languages that are mother tongues to Africans, it is not so easy to see what is likely to happen. Bantu languages are living, and, since missionaries and scholars reduced them to writing, they have a growing literature. But, unless Africans are going to develop a new civilization, which is based on Europe and is yet African, it is fairly evident that they will become absorbed into the stronger Western civilization. It does not seem likely that

Africans will develop a distinctive form of Western civilization, though they will undoubtedly help to enrich the existing form. It is probable, therefore, that the English and Afrikaans languages will remain the chief means of communication of a society embracing Western culture, and that all Africans will, in due course, acquire one or both of these languages. The various Bantu languages may for long remain the everyday language of Africans among themselves; but, unless one assumes the disappearance, gradual or sudden, of the European population, the two European languages have a survival value far greater than that of any Bantu language in South Africa.

It is against this background that the Bantu Education Act of 1953 and the present state of African education must be seen. The Act transferred control of African education from the provincial education departments to the Department of Native Affairs of the Union Government, and in 1958 a new department of state, the Bantu Education Department, with its own Minister, took charge of all African education. Until 1954 about 90 per cent of all schools were state-aided mission schools under the control of more than forty mission bodies, and in that year these bodies were given the option of handing their schools over to the government or of retaining control under a diminishing state subsidy; all teacher-training institutions were either to be handed over or closed down; and all schools for Africans, whether privately run or state-aided, had to be registered. This placed the missions in a difficult position. Most of them believed that the time was not ripe to relinquish control of African education and thus, in effect, to remove from it the religious influences that had played such an important part in moulding it. Moreover, many of the institutions founded by the early missionaries had, by 1954, gained well-merited reputations beyond the borders of South Africa and had developed traditions of which they and their past students were justifiably proud. Two such only need be mentioned: Lovedale in the eastern province of the Cape, and Adams in Natal; but there were many more. On the other hand, apart from the buildings and equipment, for which the government offered compensation, practically all the money to run these institutions was, by 1954, coming from the state, and mission institutions could not face the great financial demands that would be made if state subsidies were diminished and finally ended. It was a cruel dilemma. The Roman Catholic Church and the Seventh Day Adventists refused to relinquish control of their schools, and the former set about establishing a million-pound fund against the day when subsidies would end. With the exception of the Anglican diocese of Johannesburg, where the well-known St. Peter's school was situated, all other mission bodies handed over control to the state, though at least two well-known teacher-training institutions closed down rather than surrender control.

The Department of Bantu Education next set about organizing the great number of schools it had taken over and reconstituting the form and content of African education. In 1953 there were 5,769 schools of which only 309 were government schools; by 1958 there were 6,591 schools of which 4,563 were government, 1,561 were aided schools on farms, mines and factories, and 467 were Roman Catholic schools. In 1958 there were, in round numbers, about 24,000 teachers and 1,250,000 pupils in primary and secondary schools, this number representing just over half the number of African children of school-going age. Of the pupils at school, 72 per cent were in the lower primary school (sub-standard A to standard II) and 23 per cent in the higher primary (standard III to standard VI); the remainder were in secondary schools, teacher-training classes, or vocational classes. The annual expenditure on African education had been, from 1945 to 1953, a charge on general revenue, but the Bantu Education Act reverted to the old system of a fixed annual amount from general revenue plus a proportion of the poll-tax, which is a tax paid by Africans only. In 1959 the total expenditure was £9,500,000, of which £6,500,000 was the fixed grant from general revenue.

The department has introduced other new features into the organization of African education. By far the most important of these is the attempt to secure the active participation of Africans themselves in the management of schools by setting up school committees and school boards, as in European education but with one vital difference: European school boards and committees are elected, while their African equivalents are nominated by chiefs and headmen and their continuation in office is subject to the approval of the minister or his deputy. It was a criticism of mission-controlled education that it did not give Africans sufficient training in managing their affairs, and in setting out to correct this the department laid great stress on the restoration of tribal authority;[1] but the tribal authorities set up by the Bantu Authorities Act are themselves rigidly controlled by the Department of Bantu Administration and Development, and there is a real danger that with this double control on their activities the school boards and committees may become instruments for carrying out departmental policy rather than organs of local self-government.

The form and content of African education has been considerably altered by the great stress laid on Bantu languages, by the introduction into the syllabus of a second official language, and by the separation of the certificate examinations from those written by Europeans. It was

[1] See Report of the Department of Native Affairs, 1954–1957, p. 17.

formerly the custom that, in the lower primary school, the African child learnt his own language and one of the two official languages of the Union; both languages are now compulsory. During the first four years the vernacular was used as the medium of instruction and, there-after, one of the two official languages; the vernacular is now compulsory as the medium of instruction throughout the primary school and the policy is to make it so in the secondary school as well. This policy involved creating technical terms for which the Bantu languages had no words and of producing the necessary text-books, a task which the various language boards of the Department of Bantu Education performed with energy and skill.

Much criticism has been levelled at the Bantu Education Act, some, though not all, of it ill-informed. Sooner or later African education would have had to be taken over by the State, and whenever that happened there would almost certainly be opposition from the bodies that had previously controlled it. The government underestimated the strength of the opposition, and in its hurry to complete the operation was impatient of criticism. In extenuation it must be said that the operation was gigantic. The small staff of officials who had previously been responsible for supervising African education was called upon at short notice to create the machinery for a job a hundred times larger and more complex; and this had to be done in an atmosphere of suspicion and in the face of opposition from white and black alike. That errors of judgement and delays should have occurred was inevitable. Nevertheless, the Department of Bantu Education has a few achievements to its credit. More schools have been built and many more children are at school than formerly; more educated Africans have been able to find employment as clerks and secretaries of school boards, and the policy has been introduced of making higher posts, such as sub-inspector, open to Africans; finally, whatever criticism there may be about school boards and committees, it is obviously sound policy to associate the African community as closely as possible with the education of its children. To list these achievements is not to share in the belief that a modern education system can be built on tribalism or to deny that grievous mistakes have been made. Rather, it is to welcome the achievements in the belief that when tribalism has disappeared a more durable system of education can be built.

COLOURED AND ASIAN EDUCATION

In Natal, where the large majority of the Asian population lives, there are separate schools for Indians; in the Transvaal there are a few separate Indian schools and, for the rest, Indian and Coloured attend the same schools, as they do in the Cape Province. In the Orange Free State there is no Indian population, and Coloured pupils attend separate schools. In 1958 there were 265,000 Coloured children at school, of whom 230,000 were in the Cape Province; and there were 112,000 Asian children at school, of whom 94,000 were in Natal. In the Transvaal all Coloured schools are fully financed by the province; in the Orange Free State more than half the schools are fully financed by the province and the rest are aided; in Natal and the Cape Province the large majority of Coloured or Asian schools are aided and the rest are fully financed by the province. Most of the aided schools in the Cape Province are mission schools. The annual expenditure on Coloured and Asian education is in the neighbourhood of £9,500,000.

With slight differences, Coloured children follow the same primary and secondary school syllabuses as European children do. The languages, the culture, and the general outlook of the Coloured population are European, so that the problems of Coloured education are not those of African education. In such matters as equipment, salaries and state expenditure per child, Coloured education stands about half-way between European and African education. Coloured teachers are, as a class, very conscious of the social distinction between European and Coloured. Many of them are well educated, with the same academic and professional qualifications as European teachers, but they receive smaller salaries and have to teach under far more difficult conditions. They are, not unnaturally, embittered and resentful of a social system that closes so many doors to them and to their children.

Although the Cape Province does not spend as much money on Coloured as on European education, it has always regarded Coloured schools as an integral part of the Cape education system. The theory of apartheid, however, demands a complete separation between European and Coloured education, and in 1957 a Nationalist Party majority in the Cape Provincial Council voted in favour of Coloured education being taken over by the Union Government where it would, presumably, be placed under the Department of Coloured Affairs. It is probable that this step will be taken, though Coloured people on the whole are very much opposed to it. Their argument is that Coloured people are part and parcel of Western civilization and that, while there might be some excuse for separating African from European education, there is none whatever for isolating Coloured education. It is an argument with which many Europeans, including Nationalists, would agree.

UNIVERSITY EDUCATION

Until the early 1920's the majority of the teaching staff of South African universities came from overseas, chiefly from Britain, and, to a lesser extent, from Holland and Germany. Till then, too, it was the ambition of South African students to complete their university education at an overseas university. Those who wished to become medical doctors were compelled to go overseas, and the rugby football teams of Guy's Hospital, of Edinburgh, of Trinity College, Dublin, and of other universities drew great strength from their South African students. It was not, however, only British rugby that benefited by this happy arrangement. South Africa was, and is, a thinly populated country; it was, and is, of the utmost importance that she should keep intellectual contact with her cultural motherlands in Europe. The constant stream of students travelling to Europe to study medicine, law, engineering, the humanities, and the arts, and the returning stream of qualified men and women, immensely enriched the intellectual life of South Africa.

It was, no doubt, necessary for South Africa to develop her own university institutions so that her students should no longer have to travel 6,000 miles to qualify in foreign countries; and it was inevitable that those universities should, gradually, be staffed by South Africans. But the country has lost something in the process. One of the most necessary and difficult things in South Africa's multi-racial society is for the representatives of Western civilization to maintain high intellectual and moral standards. In performing that task, European South Africa was immensely strengthened by the influx of men and women trained in European universities where high standards are traditional. The best of the 'imported' professors and lecturers became South Africans without losing contact with Europe. They brought to their task a breadth of learning and a standard of intellectual integrity that has left a deep mark on South African life. The stream of importations has, fortunately, not quite dried up. Also, the tradition of studying in Europe still lives, and many of the university professors and lecturers have had a period of overseas study. South Africa will, however, have to guard against the dangers of attempting to live on her own intellectual fat. A virile nationalism has its virtues; but its greatest danger is in its intellectual isolation.

The University of the Cape of Good Hope was the first statutory university authority in South Africa. Established in 1873, it was nothing more than an examining body; the actual university training was, at that time, carried on at the Victoria College at Stellenbosch and at the South African College in Cape Town. It was at those institutions that men like Smuts, Hertzog, Rose Innes, and Schreiner took degrees before going to England or Holland to complete their training. The two Boer Republics had no university institutions, and their young men went to Cape Town and Stellenbosch. By 1918, university colleges had been established at other centres, and, in that year, Stellenbosch and the University of Cape Town became full universities, while the University of South Africa, successor to the old University of the Cape of Good Hope, consisted of constituent colleges at Grahamstown (Rhodes University College), Bloemfontein (Grey University College), Pietermaritzburg (Natal University College), Pretoria (Transvaal University College), Johannesburg, Wellington (Huguenot University College) and Potchefstroom (Potchefstroom University College for Christian Higher Education).

One by one the university colleges achieved full university status. In 1922, the college at Johannesburg became the University of the Witwatersrand; in 1930, the college at Pretoria became the Pretoria University; in 1949 the University of Natal was constituted, and by 1951 Rhodes University at Grahamstown, the University of the Orange Free State at Bloemfontein, and the Potchefstroom University had been constituted. Huguenot University College ceased to exist, and the University of South Africa has remained as an examining body and to cater for the large number of external students who cannot attend a university. There are, thus, eight residential universities and the University of South Africa.

Not all the universities are able to offer full courses. Only at Cape Town, Witwatersrand, Pretoria, Natal and Stellenbosch, for example, can medical students qualify. Theology may be studied at Stellenbosch, Pretoria, Grahamstown and Potchefstroom. At all the universities the normal arts and science courses may be taken for a degree. The universities do not conduct their own entrance examinations but accept the provincial examinations and those of the Joint Matriculation Board for this purpose and are content to exercise a control over the syllabuses prescribed for these. Of recent years there has been considerable complaint that the standard required for provincial examinations is too low and that students enter the universities at an immature stage, with the result that a good deal of the work at the universities is merely a continuation of school teaching. There has been talk of instituting a preliminary year of training at the universities, but the difficulties of expense have, so far, defeated this project.

University education is financed from two main sources: State grants and fees. Of the £4,845,000 university revenue in 1958, about 63 per cent came from government grants, about 32 per cent from fees, and the balance from endowments and donations. The universities are, thus, dependent on government support and on numbers of students. Further, government support depends partly on the number of full-time students at each university, and partly on the extent of private donations. There can be little doubt that this dependence has a deleterious effect on the freedom of the universities. In the first place, universities are forced to compete for students. It is not unknown for universities to advertise extensively and to appoint special canvassers to travel the country to recruit students. In order to make the universities more attractive, courses are included that are more suitable for technical institutions—courses in domestic science and in physical culture—and academic standards tend to be lowered so as to avoid too many failures.

There is another way in which dependence on numbers undermines university freedom. The Dutch Reformed churches have a powerful influence on schools and on parents in the *platteland* or rural areas. The Afrikaans universities, which depend largely on the rural areas for their students, have thus to be particularly careful not to offend those churches; and the close connexion between the churches and the Nationalist Party places a further restriction on university freedom. University appointments, expressions of opinion by university professors and lecturers, and even student social activities, are all matters in which those universities that depend on the support of the Dutch Reformed churches have to be 'careful'. English-speaking universities, in their turn, are subject to pressures from commercial, industrial, and mining interests; but these pressures are less pervading than the religious and political pressures, and they can be, and are, more easily defied.

Until 1950 every Act of Parliament for the establishment of university colleges and universities contained a so-called 'conscience clause' which provides that no religious test may be applied to students or staff in making appointments. This clause has always been jealously guarded by university staffs and by those who are concerned to maintain independence of thought in the universities. In 1950, when the old Potchefstroom University College for Christian Higher Education achieved university status, the Act omitted the usual conscience clause in so far as it affected the staff and substituted a clause forbidding the application of dogmatic tests in the admission of students.

Taken by itself, there could be little objection to the application of a religious test at an institution that, professedly, exists to promote Christian higher education. The main objection is that public funds should finance such an institution. However, the omission of the 'conscience clause' in this one instance cannot be taken by itself. There exists an organized move to abolish the clause altogether, a move supported by Afrikaans teachers' associations, by the Dutch Reformed churches, by some, though by no means all, of the staffs of Afrikaans universities, and by the promoters of Christian National Education. Unofficially, religious tests are already frequently applied in the appointment of teachers; and even in the Afrikaans universities, membership of one of the Dutch Reformed churches and strong Nationalist sympathies are sometimes powerful recommendations. It is improbable that the deletion of the 'conscience clause' will be made compulsory; it is more likely to be optional. Nevertheless, men and women in all universities would strenuously oppose such a move as an attack on academic freedom.

Though, as will presently become apparent, grievous harm has been done to the freedom of universities by direct legislative inter-ference, there is little evidence that government aid to universities has, so far, been used to interfere with their freedom. The Minister of Education has charge of university education, all appointments are subject to his approval, and no new post may be established without approval from him and from the Treasury. Universities have always been severely hampered for lack of funds and the *per capita* grants from government are inadequate for their growing needs; but the grants have been given impartially.

In 1916 there was established at Fort Hare, in the eastern province of the Cape, the South African Native College. It was founded and supported partly by missionary and private funds and partly by govern-ment aid which, increasing year by year, assumed an ever larger proportion of the College's total revenue. Of the total revenue in 1957 of £110,000, about four-fifths was from government funds. Although the college was intended to provide university education for Africans, Asian and Coloured were admitted, and of the total enrolment of 438 in 1958, just under 100 were Asian or Coloured, in about equal numbers. The staff was originally entirely European, but by 1958, 12 of the 46 members of the academic staff were Africans; the principal has always been a European, but in recent years the vice-principal, who frequently acted for the principal, has been Prof. Z. K. Matthews, one of the most intellectually distinguished Africans in the Union. Another African of great distinction who served the college for many years was Prof. Jabavu who died in 1959.

Under the Education Act of 1923 the college was incorporated as an institution for higher education and students were prepared for degrees of the University of South Africa, and in 1951 it became affiliated to Rhodes University and changed its name to Fort Hare University College. The college has thus always prepared its students for university degrees common to the rest of South Africa and has wisely eschewed the idea of separate examinations that could be stigmatized as inferior. Until a few years ago, when government prohibited the admission of students from outside the Union, African students at Fort Hare came from many parts of Africa, and Fort Hare graduates are today to be found occupying responsible positions in South Africa, the High Commission Territories, the Central African Federation, Portuguese East Africa, Kenya, Tanganyika, and Uganda.

Until 1959 there was no legal colour bar in the various Acts establishing universities. Nevertheless, there were only two universities at which non-Europeans were admitted to the same lectures as Europeans: these were the so-called 'open' universities of Cape Town and Witwatersrand; at a third, the University of Natal, there were three constituent colleges—one at Pietermaritzburg for Europeans, one for Europeans at Durban, and one (which included a medical school) for non-Europeans at Durban. In none of these university institutions did non-European students live in the same residences as European students, and they were excluded, by general practice and tacit agreement, from many student social (as distinct from academic) activities. No non-European student would, for example, be chosen to represent the university in any of the athletic sports. In Cape Town and Witwatersrand non-European students could be, and normally were, elected to the Students' Representative Council. No distinction of colour was made at graduation ceremonies at Witwatersrand and Cape Town; in Natal, such distinction was made until a few years ago when the combined pressure of staff, students, and convocation, together with a boycott of the ceremony by non-white students, brought about a change of policy. Outside of actual university functions there had been increasing social contact between white and non-white at the open universities.

In 1958 there were 4,408 European students and 552 non-European students at the University of Cape Town; at Witwatersrand the figures were 4,757 and 258; in Natal there were 592 non-European students; and at Fort Hare 438. In all, then, 1,840 non-white students were enrolled at these four universities and a large number were enrolled as external students of the University of South Africa. In no other universities were non-European students allowed.

There are great differences of opinion on the whole question of university education for non-Europeans. Among thoughtful and responsible South Africans, of all shades of opinion, it is agreed that facilities for university education for non-Europeans must be provided. The only question is what form these facilities should take. The majority of Afrikaners—though by no means all—say that the two

13

groups must have entirely separate facilities. To do anything else is to go contrary to all the traditions and beliefs of South Africa and is in the interest neither of the Europeans nor of the non-Europeans. The majority of English-speaking South Africans—but, again, by no means all—would agree to mixed universities as at Cape Town and Witwatersrand. It may be doubted, however, whether they would continue to agree if the number of non-Europeans increased rapidly. At the moment, the proportion of non-Europeans to Europeans is negligible. If the proportion increased, opinions might change.

Those who favour the compromise of Natal argue that a small group of non-Europeans among European students means that the non-Europeans are always in an abnormal situation. Either they are merely tolerated, when they are not ostracized, or else they are treated on a somewhat emotional basis. In neither case are they really treated on their merits, simply as human beings. In such circumstances they miss the opportunity of developing powers of leadership which a university should provide. If they are in a separate institution, as in Natal, they form a coherent 'natural' group, and are not subjected to the emotional stresses of life in a mixed university where they are excluded from many social activities.

Finally, a considerable and increasing minority of English-speaking and Afrikaans-speaking people not only agree to mixed universities, as at Cape Town, but actively favour them. Where, they ask, can educated people from all racial groups meet if not at a university? It is, they maintain, essential that the future leaders of the different population groups should mix on equal terms, and the universities should provide facilities for this. Non-Europeans in segregated universities may not suffer social strains, but they suffer the worse strain of frustration. They themselves prefer to go to a mixed university whatever the social disabilities may be.

Soon after the Nationalist Party came to power in 1948 it became apparent that an attack would be made on the open universities to compel them to conform to the pattern of apartheid. For a time, the Minister of Education resisted the pressure from party congresses to take active steps; at two such congresses he maintained that, while he personally was opposed to mixed universities, he was loath to do anything that might infringe the autonomy of universities. By 1955 the pressure had become too strong and in the following year it was announced that a Separate Universities Education Bill would be introduced in parliament in 1957. Before the Bill was published the open universities began actively organizing opposition. The Universities of Cape Town and Witwatersrand set up a joint Academic Freedom Committee which was responsible for drawing up a full

statement that would inform the public on the issues involved.[1]
After the Bill was published, in March 1957, these activities were
intensified and were backed by strong public reaction against a measure
that proposed to prohibit the open universities from admitting
non-white students, to place the University College of Fort Hare
under the Department of Native Affairs, and to separate the non-
European medical school from the University of Natal and place it
under the Department of Education, Arts and Science. Protest meetings
were held, petitions were drawn up and presented, deputations
visited the Minister; solemn processions of students and academic
staffs, in academic dress and led by their respective chancellors, marched
through the streets of Cape Town, Johannesburg, Durban, Pietermaritzburg, Grahamstown, and the little town of Alice near which
Fort Hare is situated. Statements were issued by convocations, by
groups of prominent citizens, and by a number of national organizations; mass meetings of students at the English-language universities
issued protests against the Bill, and at the Afrikaans-speaking universities resolutions strongly favouring the Bill were passed by students.
At Cape Town the students lined the main roads carrying placards
proclaiming their ideals of open minds in open universities, and
women of the Black Sash stood in vigilance outside parliament in
Cape Town and outside public buildings in other centres. Private
and public appeals were made to the academic staffs of the Afrikaans
universities, as colleagues, in the belief that they would realize that a
threat to the academic freedom of some universities was a threat to all.
There are, at the Afrikaans universities, men and women who value
academic freedom, and there is evidence that they used their influence
as individuals to dissuade the government; but with a few exceptions
they would never associate themselves publicly or concertedly in
opposition to government proposals. Nor, in the long run, was their
influence sufficient to restrain the government from depriving the
open universities—and, therefore, all South African universities—
of their freedom to decide who should be admitted to their fellowship.

The Separate Universities Education Bill was, because of a
technicality, sent to a Select Committee which became, when the
session ended, a Commission of Enquiry. In giving evidence before
the Commission, individual members of Afrikaans universities did
indeed oppose the proposed interference with the open universities
and attacked the proposed new university institutions for non-whites
on the ground that the regulations controlling these, as published in
the Bill, would deprive those institutions of all real autonomy or

[1] This was published as a book, *The Open Universities in South Africa*, and widely
distributed both in South Africa and to universities overseas.

academic freedom. As the Bill finally emerged and was passed in 1959, it was renamed the Extension of University Education Bill and, under that title, became law.

Fort Hare was dealt with in a separate Act which, briefly, brought to an end the existence of that college as an independent university institution and placed it under the control of the Minister of Bantu Education. Fort Hare is unlikely to retain its name or its identity, and the Minister of Bantu Education has announced that, since it is intended to serve the Xhosa people, it is wrongly sited and will probably be moved. The Extension of University Education Act provides for the establishment of three more university colleges, one in Natal for the Zulu, one in the Transvaal for the Sotho, and one in the Cape for the Coloured. Students at these tribal university institutions will be prepared for examinations conducted by the University of South Africa. The regulations laid down for the management and control of these institutions are such that it is difficult to believe that they can maintain any pretence to independent intellectual activity. All appointments of staff, senate, and council are under ministerial control; since there will not be enough non-whites to fill the academic posts, whites will be appointed, but white and non-white are to be segregated and are not to share a common room or sit on the same senate or council, as was customary at Fort Hare; there are to be two separate senates and councils for each institution, it being envisaged that the black senate and council will eventually take charge. Stringent regulations are laid down for the conduct of staff and students by which they are, among other things, forbidden to take any part whatsoever in politics or to criticize government policy or the conduct of any government department; and the Minister has far-reaching powers of dismissal.[1]

The final passage of the Bill was accompanied by renewed protests and demonstrations. The parliamentary opposition parties combined to fight the Bill at every stage, including the first reading, and it was only by all-night sittings and the application of the guillotine that the government was able to secure the passage of the Bill before

[1] Within three months of the passing of the Act the Minister of Bantu Education dismissed eight European members of the staff at Fort Hare. In doing so he stated that he would not hesitate to dismiss any member of staff who 'sabotaged' apartheid, but he did not specify in what manner the eight members had been guilty of this. At the same time, the Department of Bantu Education made it clear to African members of staff that political activities, such as membership of the African National Congress, were contrary to regulations. Rather than accept such limitations on their academic freedom, several African professors resigned, thus forfeiting all pension rights. One of those who resigned was Professor Z. K. Matthews, the first graduate of Fort Hare, who had taught at the College for twenty-four years and had two to go before retiring.

the end of the session. On the night when the Bill was finally passed, members of the Black Sash stood in silent all-night vigil at the entrances to Parliament. After the Bill had become law, the universities of Cape Town and Witwatersrand held solemn official ceremonies to mark the passing of their autonomy and to dedicate themselves to the task of recovering it; and they have decided to have annual ceremonies in order to keep alive the idea of university autonomy and to restate their belief in academic freedom.

Until 1959 South Africa was, perhaps unconsciously, experimenting in different solutions to the problem of university education in a mixed society. These experiments were of immense social importance to Africa, for on their results would depend in no small measure the extent to which European and non-European in Africa would be able to co-operate. That they will have to co-operate is certain, but whether the co-operation will be fruitful or not will depend on the extent to which European South Africa can provide effective and constructive university education for non-Europeans. It was all to the good, there-fore, that different experiments were being carried on, and to put a stop to them was a short-sighted policy which cannot but cause serious worsening of relations.

The attitudes of students to national and racial questions are of importance. There are, as we have seen, English and Afrikaans universities. The former are Cape Town, Witwatersrand, Natal, and Rhodes; the latter are Stellenbosch, Pretoria, Bloemfontein, and Potchefstroom, though there are English-speaking students at Stellen-bosch and Afrikaans-speaking students at Cape Town; but, since language, politics and religion are all connected in South Africa, it is generally true to say that the Afrikaner universities are nationalist and are supported by the Dutch Reformed churches. The English-speaking universities are much more cosmopolitan, and, the Afrikaner would say, irreligious and 'liberal'.

In 1924 a National Union of South African Students (commonly known as Nusas) was established and all university centres were members. By 1932, however, it had split and the main body of Afrikaans students hived off to form the *Afrikaans-Nasionale Studente-bond*, usually known as A.N.S. The split was political and cultural. Nusas was felt to be too liberal and unnationalistic and, as it had shed the more conservative Afrikaner element, Nusas became increasingly liberal in its political tendencies. As we saw in chapter 7, the period of 1932-48 was one during which the Nationalist Party was divided. These divisions were reflected in the Afrikaans universities, and A.N.S. went through a lean period. In 1948 a new body was formed, the *Afrikaanse Studentebond*, known as A.S.B.

Nusas and A.S.B. have made various attempts to find a common basis for student co-operation in inter-university matters. Both bodies organize student tours to Europe; both organize inter-university student activities in South Africa. But all attempts at co-operation have failed, largely because of the fundamental difference between the two bodies on the question of non-European students. While Nusas admits non-Europeans, A.S.B. refuses to do so. The A.S.B. declares that it is prepared to have conferences with non-European students provided that they come from a separate university institution, and are neither represented by, nor represent, European students.

There are, of course, other points of difference. Nusas decisively rejects the ideas of Christian National Education, while A.S.B. officially, at any rate, supports these principles. Then, too, A.S.B. speaks in terms of Afrikaans culture, which it defines in a manner that excludes English-speaking South Africans, while Nusas claims that it speaks in terms of a broader South African culture. All in all, therefore, the division between the English and the Afrikaans university students is fairly complete. As with the single medium schools, so the single medium universities have tended to perpetuate divisions between the two European groups in South Africa.

There is one more aspect of universities in South Africa that must be mentioned, and that is research. Facilities for research are far too limited. In most of the universities, but particularly in the smaller ones, the professors and lecturers are so busy teaching that there is no time for independent research. Some of the universities have extra-mural or part-time students, who earn a living and can attend classes after working hours only, and the extra teaching load on the staff that this involves further reduces the free time that might be devoted to research. Instead of making more money, and thus time, available to the universities, governments have concentrated on establishing research laboratories which have, for the most part, no direct connexion with any university. The South African Council for Scientific and Industrial Research and the National Council for Social Research are government bodies. The universities are, indeed, represented on these councils, which make grants for individual pieces of research. But research tends to become divorced from the universities and controlled by government departments. If this tendency is not checked it will deprive the universities of the services of those who must have unfettered research facilities and will seek them elsewhere if the universities cannot provide them.

9

Religion

ALMOST HALF THE AFRICAN POPULATION OF SOUTH AFRICA IS CLASSED
as 'heathen'. The word connotes barbarism, lack of contact with the
ways of civilization, and the practice of witchcraft. In previous
census returns 'heathen' were classified as 'others and indefinite', a
loose description which probably covers all the grades between
complete heathenism and mere religious indifference. But it is
significant that, out of a total population of over $14\frac{1}{2}$ million people,
close on 4 million are, officially at any rate, classed as having no
religious affiliation with any Christian community. It illustrates,
once more, the lack of homogeneity in the South African population,
and what a long road civilization still has to travel in South Africa.

Since Christian missions play such a large part in the history of
non-European education it is instructive to compare the relative
strengths of the major Christian communities. The figures reveal
that there are almost twice as many Europeans in the Afrikaans
churches as in the other Protestant churches put together. On the other
hand, there are nine times as many Africans, and almost twice as many
Coloured, in the other Protestant churches as there are in the Afrikaans
churches. These facts are significant as showing the great influence
of the Afrikaans churches on European social and political life, and
the predominant influence on non-European education of the English-
speaking churches—which, combined, have played a far bigger part
in missionary work than the Afrikaans churches.

It must not be assumed that the Afrikaners have been lacking in
missionary enthusiasm. There are two explanations of the comparatively smaller part they have played in mission work. In the first
place, the English-speaking churches originated in Britain, and in
nineteenth-century Britain there was an enthusiasm for foreign
missions that created a fund of good will and of money on which these
churches could draw. The Afrikaans churches had no such outside
reserves at their disposal and were entirely dependent on their own
financial resources. These financial resources were meagre. The
nineteenth-century Afrikaner was seldom wealthy. He was the
agricultural pioneer with land but little cash, and it is only since the
1920's that there have been Afrikaners who could make large donations
to their churches. Money for missions came from people who had
little money themselves, and many a Dutch Reformed Church parson
and his wife have collected pennies from people who, in Britain,

would be considered extremely poor; these pennies went to support a missionary or an evangelist in Nigeria, in Nyasaland, in China, or in the local African location. The Afrikaans churches have certainly played their part in establishing Christianity in Africa, and they are taking an increasing share of the common burden.

There are a large number of African separatist churches, and their number as well as the numbers of adherents fluctuate considerably, since most of the churches have little stability. They are established for a great variety of reasons, such as personal jealousies and ambitions, the temptation to make what seems to be a comparatively easy living, and dissatisfaction with the too irksome discipline of the white-controlled parent church. In some cases there are more than personal and petty motives and one may discern two more important elements: the desire to adapt the Christian religion to primitive beliefs, and an awaking nationalism that wants a separate and independent organization. The first of these is often indistinguishable from dissatisfaction with church discipline and is unlikely to make much headway; the second is, in prevailing social and political circumstances, likely to attract increasing numbers of Africans who feel frustrated.

The Roman Catholic Church in South Africa is organized under the Apostolic Delegation of Southern Africa. The English-speaking Protestant churches, deriving from Britain, are today all separate from any control by the parent churches overseas and are governed by their own synods or conferences or assemblies. After considerable controversy during the 1850's and 1860's a constitution was drawn up for the Church of the Province of South Africa, which is governed by a provincial synod under the presidency of the Archbishop of Cape Town, and is the legally recognized representative of the Anglican Communion in South Africa.

There are three Dutch Reformed churches in South Africa, and these must be described in some detail. The smallest is the *Gereformeerde Kerk van Suid-Afrika*, which has 112,000[1] adherents. It was established in 1859 as a breakaway from the main Dutch Reformed Church in the Cape Colony. It is more rigidly Calvinist than the main church and has its headquarters at Potchefstroom, where it controls the university and trains its own ministers. It has no moderator or permanent executive, and the control of the church rests mainly with the individual congregations. Although the *Gereformeerde Kerk* has a small membership, it has exercised a considerable influence on theological thought and on education, largely because it has produced, at Potchefstroom, a succession of able and vigorous ministers.

[1] These and subsequent figures are from the most recent census, that of 1951, and are in round numbers. *Official Year Book No. 28.*

The *Nederduits Hervormde Kerk* was the first state church of the Transvaal Republic in 1858. The parent church at the Cape had been slow in following up the Trekkers who had left the Cape and established the two northern republics. The Transvaal, being farthest away from the Cape, established its own church and looked to Holland rather than to the Cape for its ministers and for its spiritual guidance. When, in 1866, the church from the Cape did establish itself in the Transvaal, a number of members of the *Hervormde Kerk* joined the new church. The *Hervormde Kerk* remained as a separate institution not differing greatly from the parent church, and it has today about 184,000 adherents, most of whom are in the Transvaal.

By far the largest church is the *Nederduits Gereformeerde Kerk* (usually abbreviated to N.G.K.), which has 1,108,000 European adherents, or almost half the total European population. When people refer to the 'Dutch' church in South Africa it is chiefly the N.G.K. that they have in mind.

While a federal council advises on and co-ordinates church work, the churches in each of the four provinces are independent self-governing bodies. Thus, the N.G.K. of the Cape Province has its synod, which meets annually and is presided over by an elected Moderator. The unit of organization is the congregation, in which church matters are regulated by a representative church council of elders and deacons presided over by the minister. Ministers are 'called' by the church council and, in accordance with an old custom, if the voting for two candidates is equal, lots are cast. Several congregations form a presbytery, which functions as a link between the church councils and the synod. Both in its separate congregations and as an organized church the N.G.K. does a great deal of social welfare and mission work, which is co-ordinated by such bodies as the Federal Mission council and the Federal Poor Relief Council.

In religious dogma the N.G.K. is Calvinist and stems direct from the seventeenth-century parent church in Holland. The doctrine of predestination is a cardinal belief, and many of the church's social attitudes on such matters as dancing, card-playing, and the sabbath are strongly Calvinist. In 1951 various members of the Orange Free State Synod deplored the fact that, at the University of the Orange Free State, students were allowed to give dances; and in the same year the church at Kimberley protested strongly because a local rugby football team, touring in Rhodesia, was to play one match on a Sunday. South African rugby teams playing in France insist, to the bewilderment of the French, on Sunday observance. The church is strong enough to be able to insist on a certain outward conformity in these matters, but a large number of its members, particularly in the big urban centres, no longer conform even outwardly. To many of them Sunday is their only day for recreation.

Candidates for the ministry in the N.G.K. are trained at the Theological Seminary at Stellenbosch or at the University of Pretoria. Coloured ministers are trained at a separate institution at Wellington, and Africans are trained at the Stofberg-Gedenkskool in the Orange Free State.[1] On the completion of the course a few European ministers go overseas, either to Europe or to the United States, for further study; more frequently, however, they go straight to work, usually as temporary assistant to an experienced minister, from where they are called to a congregation of their own.

Traditionally and by the very nature of the positions they occupied, ministers of the N.G.K. played a prominent part in the history and development of the Afrikaner people. During the nineteenth century it was the ministers of the Afrikaans churches who organized congregations and built churches and schools. When the Boer War broke out ministers in the Republics went on commando, usually as ministers, but, in one case at least, in a prominent combatant role.[2] And the sympathies of ministers in the Cape and Natal were largely with the Boer forces. Lord Milner regarded what he called the 'Predikants' with equal detestation and suspicion as dangerous opponents of his policy.

After the Boer War the ministers took the lead in restoring the shattered morale of the Afrikaner. Most of them loyally accepted the terms of peace and worked hard to promote good understanding between Boer and Briton. Some of them voluntarily reduced their salaries because their congregations were too poor to pay them. With self-sacrificing devotion, they rebuilt churches and established schools, and turned the thoughts of their people from the bitter defeat of the past to a more hopeful future. In doing so they helped to awaken the spirit of Afrikaner nationalism, which, when political conditions became favourable, turned aside from its original course and developed into a strong political movement which they were powerless to control. The First World War, and the rebellion in South Africa, split the Afrikaner and his church, and a new generation of ministers, strongly imbued with nationalism, partly followed and partly led the new political movement.[3]

We saw in Chapter 7 how rapidly Afrikaaner nationalism

[1] In terms of the Group Areas Act this institution was in a 'white' area and has been moved to a Reserve in the Transvaal.
[2] The late General Roux, who, after the Boer War, returned to his congregation.
[3] Dr. D. F. Malan, for example, was a N.G.K. minister until 1915, when he entered politics as a Nationalist.

developed during the period between the two world wars and how close its association with the growth of the Afrikaans language was. The Afrikaans churches were deeply involved in these twin developments. There are numbers of ministers and church adherents who have never been politically associated with the Nationalist Party; but they are in a minority. Whether passively or actively, the majority of those who control the Afrikaans churches are supporters of the Nationalist Party, to whose policies the churches lend all the considerable weight of their moral influence. During the 1939-45 War, for example, it was extremely difficult to find Afrikaans chaplains for the Forces, despite the fact that about 60 per cent of the troops were Afrikaans-speaking, because the Nationalist Party was opposed to South Africa's participation in the war.

{Relations between the Afrikaans churches and other Christian communities have suffered because of the cleavage between Afrikaners and English-speaking South Africans.] There was a time, in the 'twenties of this century, when co-operation between all the Protestant churches was cordial. In many centres a Ministers' Fraternal met regularly, inter-church meetings discussed common problems and took combined action, and the interdenominational Christian Council was well supported by Afrikaans ministers.[The language used at such meetings was always English because most of the ministers from English-speaking churches could not understand Afrikaans. This fact, combined with the increasing emphasis on nationalism, gradually destroyed the spirit of co-operation, and the Afrikaans churches began to isolate themselves from the English-speaking Christian communities. Today a few Afrikaans ministers still co-operate actively with those of other denominations, and they work together amicably enough on official educational and welfare boards; but nothing like continuous inter-church co-operation between the actual churches now exists. Many ministers on both sides feel that this state of affairs is unfortunate; but political forces are strong, and the Afrikaans churches would find it extremely difficult to go against the current of nationalism of which they have for so long been an integral part.

In 1953 the Federal Missionary Council of the Dutch Reformed churches convened a three-day conference of European Protestant church leaders of all denominations to discuss common missionary problems. It was a notable achievement to bring together men of such widely differing ideas, but the conference revealed just how wide the differences were on the question of relations with non-Europeans. Since that time there have been private meetings and unofficial discussions between leaders of the different churches; but political events since 1953 have increased, rather than reduced, the differences.

Relations between the Protestant churches and the Roman Catholic Church have never been cordial, since the latter does not usually co-operate with non-Catholic churches. On the part of the Afrikaans churches there has always been a marked enmity towards the Roman Catholics. There are various reasons for this. Being staunch Calvinists, the Afrikaner churchmen have an ingrained fear and distrust of Roman Catholicism, and, as nationalists, they fear any organization that has a foreign governing body. The Roman Catholic Church appears to have plenty of money and has set up many excellent schools which have, rightly or wrongly, acquired a reputation as good 'finishing' schools, and of being able to 'get pupils through their examinations'. Some Afrikaners send their children to these schools, despite the warnings of the Afrikaans churches who fear that the children will become Romanized and denationalized. Under an ordinance in the Transvaal[1] it is no longer legal in that province for parents who are Afrikaans-speaking to send their children to a church school where the medium of instruction is English.

Antagonism on the part of the Afrikaans churches to Roman Catholicism is openly expressed in many ways. Sermons are preached annually on Reformation Sunday on the 'dangers of Rome'. When Mr. te Water, then South Africa's Ambassador Extraordinary, paid an official visit to the Pope in 1949, there were strong protests from synods and from Nationalist Party congresses. Finally, at a provincial congress of the Nationalist Party in 1949 it was proposed to exclude Roman Catholics from holding office in the Nationalist Party, but the proposal was withdrawn under pressure from the party executive.

It is in the theory and, to a lesser extent, the practice of race relations that the greatest differences exist between the Afrikaans churches and other Protestant communities. Previous chapters of this book have attempted to explain the origins and development of race attitudes and policies in South Africa. The Afrikaans churches are part of the fabric of the Afrikaner people, and the opinions of these churches are both form and are formed by the attitudes and policies of the majority of the Afrikaner people. Though there are, no doubt, individual exceptions, the Afrikaans churches believe in separate congregations for the different racial groups. They maintain that while it is the function of the European church, by missionary effort, to help the Africans to establish their own separate church, non-Europeans must not have membership or control in the affairs of the parent church.

[1] See p. 182.
[2] An editorial in *Die Kerkbode*, official organ of the N.G.K., of 29 September 1951 said: 'It [the Roman Church] wants to catch the Afrikaner in its meshwork of propaganda and to lead him to new points of view. . . . Rome is seeking more and more authority in every sphere of life.'

In this way only will each develop a mature Christian community. This argument, sincerely advanced by men who have devoted their lives to the spiritual welfare of the non-European, is not to be lightly set aside. It affirms the essential equality in the eyes of God of all men, but maintains that for spiritual as well as for practical reasons people of different races should worship God, each in their own church.

The English-speaking churches believe that while it may be practically expedient for white and black to worship in separate churches, they are all members of the same community and should share in the government of the church. In practice there are a small number of Anglican churches where Europeans and non-Europeans worship together, but the great majority of congregations have separate churches. When it comes to synodical meetings, European and non-European ministers and elders deliberate together. In the Afrikaans churches such meetings are always separate, one for the European church, and one for the mission church, where, however, European missionaries and non-European ministers sit together. The English-speaking communities regard the non-European churches as an extension of the European; the Afrikaans churches regard them, rather, as separate mission churches that will one day be independent. Though the approach differs, all churches are concerned to bring Christianity to the non-European.

It is in political, non-church matters that there is even more far-reaching difference of opinion · between the two groups. The Afrikaans churches have all expressed themselves strongly in favour of the Nationalist Party's policy of apartheid, while the English-speaking churches have, equally strongly, opposed that policy. At a meeting of the Federal Mission Council of the N.G.K. the policy of territorial and political separation was supported and the government was urged to put it into practice as soon as possible.[1] So strongly worded was the resolution that the then Prime Minister, Malan, felt impelled to issue a warning that apartheid could not be applied in a hurry.

At its 22nd Annual Meeting, the Federal Council of the N.G.K. considered the whole question of the relations between church and state. After affirming the right of the church, warranted in history and in the Scriptures, to express its opinion on political matters, the statement issued by the Council goes on to analyse and describe the origin and functions of the State.[2] Fundamental to all its Calvinist thought is the doctrine of Divine creation, the fall and redemption.

[1] Die Naturellevraagstuk, April 1950.
[2] This document was published as Annexure C of the Council's Agenda and was approved by the Council, May 1951.

Further, the state has been created by God, and exists independently of its citizens; its authority over the individual is ordained by God, and what distinguishes it from other divine creations is that it possesses a monopoly of might, of 'the power of the sword'. It is the duty of the state to organize this power internally and externally, by means of a police force and an army.

In every state God is the fountain of authority and power, irrespective of whether rulers and subjects acknowledge it. The Christian state acknowledges God's sovereignty while the non-Christian acknowledges merely the sovereignty of the people or of those in authority. Strongly opposed to this Calvinist conception are the humanistic theories of individualism and universalism which regard the state as something created by man for his own use. These ideas are decisively rejected by the Council. God instituted the state to counteract the worst effects of the fall of man, and no Christian may regard the state merely as a necessary evil, as Liberalism does. It is the duty of the state, thus instituted, to hold the balance between its subjects. But it has no right to interfere in non-state matters, and cannot dictate in religious matters.

Although the state is created by God, the form which it may take is the work of man. This accounts for the great diversity of forms. Historically, the establishment of most states was natural and unconscious just because it was divinely ordained. The small number of states that were consciously 'established' owe their origin to men who were, formerly, subjects of natural states.

As regards the relations between subject and ruler, the authority of man over man is not a human invention, but a gracious gift of God to a fallen generation. The authority of the state over the individual is derived from God; it must be exercised according to God's will; it is not unlimited; it cannot be replaced by another authority; and it is indivisible. Consequently, the humanistic conceptions of titular, legal, political, or popular sovereignty have no validity; further, there can be no division of power between legislature, executive and judiciary. The state has the authority and the duty to integrate harmoniously the various interests of its subjects. This doctrine is opposed both to liberal democracy and to totalitarianism. Under the former, for example, workers are compelled to form trade unions to defend their rights, often to the detriment of society as a whole; had government done its duty properly, there would have been no need for trade unions. Totalitarian states, on the other hand, go too far and seek to legislate on matters such as science and religion as well as on those in their own legitimate sphere.

The divinely ordained authority of the state has definite territorial limits. These are part of God's plan, and attempts to wipe them out are of the devil. The humanistic ideal of a world-state must be rejected as contrary to Scripture and an attempt to achieve world peace outside the Kingdom of Heaven.

The state must ensure civic freedom by not interefering in private matters, except that it must protect the individual against exploitation and wrong-doers even if, in so doing, it has to interfere temporarily with individual liberty. Political freedom consists in the right to a voice in political matters, without which no one is politically free; but it does not entitle citizens to a voice in matters relating to the church or the school or the factory. In primitive communities and in dictatorships the only freedom granted to citizens is the right of access to authority to acquaint it with their wants; the only way they can get rid of a government is by assassination or a *coup d'état*. A Christian people may not be satisfied with anything less than the right to replace a government that is not acting in accordance with God's will.

Applying this theory to South African conditions, the statement of the N.G.K. Federal Council continues: the greatest problem lies in the ideas of the revolutionary democratic school of Rousseau. According to those ideas all men are equal and, therefore, every individual is a sovereign and a lawgiver; all, white and black, must participate in the making of laws. The mass of individuals then become the source of State authority; the government becomes the servant of the people instead of the authority over them, it receives its mandate from the people, and is unseated as soon as it no longer serves the wishes and the needs of the people. This is nothing more nor less that the myth of sovereignty opposed to God. To the Christian, on the other hand, the franchise is a means of grace that must be used with the greatest care and responsibility to God. The Christian does not regard the franchise as qualifying him to make laws, which is a function of the State;[1] the vote, for the Christian, is always a symbol of God's sovereignty and every vote cast must reflect the will of God. Thus being enfranchised gives the voter the right to apply a religious test to authority.

In the light of this belief, says the statement, various points in relation to the African become clear. Those who do not have the franchise are by no means slaves or suppressed people. They still have civic rights and are protected by government. The franchise is a treasure which should belong only to those who are of age politically and are able to use it responsibly before God. The African does not fulfil these requirements, and, therefore, will not be able to use this

---

[1] This seems to contradict an earlier statement that 'the Christian citizen knows just as well as the government what is politically right and wrong'.

right correctly. Since the franchise implies having a say in the establishment of government, and since government is clothed with such sacred responsibility, it is obvious that not everyone should automatically have the vote. Not only undeveloped groups, but all those who are openly in rebellion against God, such as the Communists, should not be given it. In a Christian state, therefore, the necessary qualification is not only that a man should be of age, but that he should be a Christian.

Political parties are necessary in a state, and no Christian people will tolerate the dictatorship of a clique or of one party, as happened in Germany and Russia. But this is not the only reason why the Christian cannot do without political parties. Where political life is threatened by doctrines born of unbelief—'powerful in Liberalism, much stronger in Democracy, and most dangerous in Communism' —it is without doubt the duty of Christians to try to become the strongest political factor in the country and to establish a Christian government.

The question is raised whether the holders of all forms of political thought should have the right to organize in political parties. In the existing democracies, says the statement, not only has everyone who is of age the vote, but the holders of all forms of political thought have the right to organize and, if they are strong enough, achieve power.[1] This is the cancer at the root of modern democracy, because right and truth are made dependent on a mere majority of votes. The Christian citizen may not rest content with this. Only the Christian political faith is valid, and no anti-Christian philosophy should be given the right to form political parties. This applies particularly to Communism; but a Christian people ought to go even further and ought not to allow the right of organization to any group who aim at a dictatorship.

Finally, the actual form of the state is a matter of secondary importance, because a Christian people will organize a Christian State in God's good time; and for each people there will be a particular form of state. It is obvious, then, that there is such a state for the Afrikaner people. While leaving the details of this to Christian citizens, the church declares that any form of government born of unbelief must be rejected as displeasing to God. This applies not only to Communism and National Socialism, but also to 'revolutionary democracy' with its belief in the sovereignty of the people.

This statement by the N.G.K. Federal Council has been set out in some detail because it is an important document. The statement is

[1] This statement of the churches was drawn up before the Communist Party was made illegal by Act of Parliament.

entitled *Fundamental Principles of Calvinist Christian Political Science*. It was approved as its official policy by the highest council in the N.G.K. and was sent to all members of parliament and cabinet ministers. The N.G.K. plays a major role in the life of South Africa because of its influence over Afrikaans-speaking South Africans, at least two-thirds of whom support the Nationalist Party now in power. We must therefore, analyse further these principles of Calvinist political science and estimate their effect on South Africa.

Speaking of sixteenth-century Calvinism at Geneva, Professor R. H. Tawney says: 'It was a creed which sought, not merely to purify the individual, but to reconstruct Church and State, to renew society by penetrating every department of life, public as well as private, with the influence of religion.'[1] And again: 'He . . . taught them to feel that they were a Chosen People, made them conscious of their great destiny in the Providential plan and resolute to realize it.'[2] There is much in the history of the Afrikaans Calvinist churches to which these two quotations are applicable. Calvinism is a determinist creed which consorts naturally with conceptions of racial superiority and of national separateness. The religious beliefs of the Afrikaners thus powerfully reinforce the tendencies to isolation which arise from the history of the Afrikaner people and from the fact of their having a distinctive language. Luther's religious beliefs took shape in a peasant society; Calvin's beliefs were formulated in a middle-class commercial society. It is, perhaps, not fanciful to suggest that the statement of the N.G.K. could not have been made while the Afrikaner was still an agriculturist with strong individualist tendencies; the statement became possible only after he had entered the world of business in a modern urban society. If there is truth in that, then Calvinist political doctrines are likely to become increasingly influential.

Historically, Calvinism is revolutionary or authoritarian, depending on whether it represents a minority or a majority in the state. It was revolutionary in England, and authoritarian in Geneva and in Scotland. Now, in South Africa, Calvinism represents both a minority and a majority. In relation to the whole population, adherents of Calvinist churches form a minority; but in relation to the total European population they are in a small majority, and, for the present at any rate, it is the European population that is politically and economically dominant. Within the European group, therefore, there is a tendency for Calvinist political beliefs to become authoritarian. In the statement of those political beliefs which we described above there is constant

[1] R. H. Tawney, *Religion and the Rise of Capitalism*, p. 102.
[2] Tawney, op. cit., p. 112.

opposition to the idea of the sovereign will of the people. This is repudiated as liberal and democratic error, born of humanism and utterly opposed to true Calvinist doctrine. It is true that the statement repudiates totalitarianism of the German or Russian model. But it explicitly enunciates the doctrine of the authoritarian state. R. H. Tawney says: 'In the struggle between liberty and authority, Calvinism sacrificed liberty, not with reluctance, but with enthusiasm.'[1] The statement of the Federal Council of the N.G.K. is entirely Calvinist in this respect.

Whether the Afrikaans churches will succeed or fail in establishing a theocracy in South Africa depends on many things. This statement of political beliefs must be taken as representing the official views of the N.G.K., but it may be doubted whether all the adherents of the church accept all the doctrines there enunciated. Even so staunch a Calvinist as the late Prime Minister, D. F. Malan, stated publicly that the sovereign power in South Africa is the will of the people, and there are many other Afrikaners who would not agree with a political theory that contradicted that democratic principle. Nevertheless, the Afrikaans churches are politically powerful, and authoritarianism is an insidious doctrine, particularly in a multi-racial society where it promises an easy solution to so many problems.

Since 1951 there have been signs that the struggle between liberty and authority will not necessarily end in the establishment of a Calvinist theocracy in South Africa. Afrikaner nationalism has been in power since 1948 and has had the support of the Afrikaans churches through thick and thin. Apartheid, vague though it was in the beginning, seemed to be a Christian way of preserving the Afrikaner 'nation' without doing any harm to other 'nations'. But as the legislative fruits of Afrikaner nationalism and of apartheid began to be plucked, a few Afrikaner churchmen began to wonder whether something had not gone wrong somewhere. When the English-language churches were moved to protest against the toll of human suffering involved in such measures as the Group Areas Act, Nationalist politicians could pass those protests off as the manifestations of an anti-Afrikaans complex; Father Michael Scott and Father Trevor Huddleston could be written off as the modern equivalents of the nineteenth-century missionaries who 'blackened the name' of the Afrikaner. Officially, the Afrikaans churches remained silent rather than hamper an Afrikaner government; in many cases they gave active support. Nevertheless, two prominent church leaders spoke out clearly against what they believed to be bad theology and worse Christianity. Prof. B. B. Keet of the Theological Seminary at

[1] See Tawney, op. cit., p. 131.

Stellenbosch and Dr. Ben Marais of the Theological Seminary in Pretoria did not join in public protest; but they did what was at that time more important: they wrote to the official Afrikaans church organs and spoke at church conferences; to the members of their own churches they exposed the hollowness of the argument that apartheid is supported by the Bible.[1]

Criticism did not come only from inside South Africa, where it could be discounted as born of anti-Afrikaans sentiment. Race questions are not confined to South Africa, but they are sharply defined in that country, and this sharp definition has attracted world-wide attention. Ministers of Afrikaans churches who attended international gatherings, such as the World Council of Churches, found themselves constantly on the defensive, put there by Christian colleagues who could not be accused of lack of sympathy. Moreover, churchmen from other countries visited South Africa and were greatly perturbed by what they found. Dr. Visser 't Hooft, General Secretary of the World Council of Churches, visited South Africa in 1952. As a Hollander he had every tie of sympathy with the Afrikaans churches—language, religion, history—and in writing about his visit he expressed all this sympathy and begged churchmen not to judge the Afrikaans churches harshly. Yet even he was constrained to say that the danger in South Africa was not that the churches interfered in politics but that 'owing to the historical co-operation between church and nation, the church is far too much inclined to support uncritically the decisions and policies of the Afrikaner political bodies'.[2] Dr. 't Hooft was followed by others, notably by J. J. Buskes jr., a minister from Amsterdam, who visited South Africa in 1955 on behalf of the International Fellowship of Reconciliation. His report, while once more expressing sympathy for the Afrikaner churches in their predicament, is a scathing attack on the government's policy of apartheid.[3]

Criticism coming from such sources cannot be lightly dismissed. Nor is it only criticism from abroad that impinges on the Afrikaner churches. The missionary work of the Afrikaans churches has been intensified of recent years, and Afrikaans missionaries are finding that a good deal of the Nationalist Government's legislation is hindering their work. The South African Bureau of Racial Affairs, an Afrikaner body wholeheartedly supported by the Afrikaans churches, has since

---

[1] See *Whither South Africa?*, by B. B. Keet, and *The Colour Crisis and the West*, by B. J. Marais. Both books were first published in Afrikaans and written for Afrikaners.

[2] Quoted from Gwendolen M. Carter, *The Politics of Inequality*.

[3] J. J. Buskes jr., *Zuid-Afrika's Apartheidsbeleid: Onaanvaarbaar*. (In translation: South Africa's Policy of Apartheid: Impracticable.)

1957 found itself openly at odds with the government and it, too, is finding its work hampered by too close a connexion with the government in power. Thus, criticism of apartheid as it affects the Christian churches is beginning to be heard *inside* the Afrikaans churches. Moreover, it is not criticism alone that comes from abroad. In the matter of race relations, fresh winds are blowing from Europe and America bearing messages of the more positive approach that the churches are making in interracial living—messages that do not merely tell of how to prevent people from quarrelling by keeping them apart, but of the experiences of the Christian churches in keeping people together.

One last point must be mentioned in connexion with the relations between the Afrikaans- and the English-language churches. Afrikaner politicians have been accustomed to castigate the English-language churches for preaching against apartheid while practising it in their own churches. This has compelled the churches to take stock of their position, only to find that there is truth in the accusation. The South African pattern that has developed for all churches has been one of social separation, and in so far as the African members of the different churches are concerned, this is often a matter of practical expediency dictated by language differences and geographical separation. That is not, however, an argument that applies to the Coloured population, particularly in the Cape Province where the question of separation in churches is most acute. Yet, in the Cape, many English-language churches do practise separation in church attendance, though not in synodical meetings. The attacks on the English-language churches and the visible results of apartheid have induced the churches to take an increasingly strong stand against racial separation in churches. The present Archbishop of Cape Town, Dr. Joost de Blank, has made it abundantly clear that he will not allow separation in any churches under his control. And when, in 1956, a clause in the Native Laws Amendment Bill threatened freedom of worship by making it unlawful for Africans to attend European churches, Dr. de Blank's predecessor, Archbishop Clayton, in what proved to be a few hours before his death, signed a letter to the prime minister on behalf of the Anglican bishops saying that while they recognized the gravity of disobeying the law of the land, they felt bound to state that 'if the Bill were to become law in its present form we should ourselves be unable to obey it or to counsel our clergy and people to do so'. All the English-language churches took similar action, and the Afrikaans churches, though not associating themselves with the protests, sent a deputation to the government.

There is, therefore, increasing pressure on the Afrikaans churches from three sources: from within its own ranks, from the ranks of the Christian Church in South Africa, and from world Christendom. It is difficult to believe that the Afrikaans churches will for ever cut themselves off from Christian fellowship in their own country and in the world; but only when they cease to be the handmaiden of Afrikaner nationalism, in or out of power, will they once more be able to enjoy that fellowship.

No description of the part played by religion in the history and politics of South Africa can omit the Jews. There are about 108,000 Jews in the Union, and the Jewish contribution to the economic and cultural life of South Africa has been considerable. From the early days of settlement, when Jewish pedlars wandered about the country with a pack-horse or a donkey cart, Jewish traders have been foremost in commerce. When diamonds and gold were discovered, individual Jews helped to develop these industries and, subsequently, to start secondary industries and to expand trade and commerce. But the contribution of Jews to South African life is not confined to economics. In the encouragement of the arts, in helping to establish universities, and in the spread of enlightenment, Jews have always been prominent. While clinging tenaciously to their religion and in that respect isolating themselves from the rest of the community, they have, nevertheless, thoroughly identified themselves with South African life. A great many are Zionists, but they manage to combine Zionism with a genuine patriotism for their own country and thus to demonstrate that the oft-maligned 'divided loyalty' may be no bad thing.

South Africa did not escape the evils of Hitlerian anti-Semitism. But until Hitler began to poison the mind of Western Europe, anti-Semitism was never either sustained or virulent. The writer recalls growing up in a typical Orange Free State village where the mysteries of the synagogue and the queer and apparently arbitrary Jewish holidays were a source of wonder to Gentile children; but they were no cause for enmity or for social distinctions. In recent years, however, social discrimination against Jews has become more common. Headmasters of popular schools are prone, while careful to deny any anti-Semitic feelings, to limit the number of Jewish entrants; and appointments to public posts are frequently decided by whether the applicant is a Jew or not. Discrimination against Jews is so common in many clubs that most Jews would not apply for membership and thus place themselves in the embarrassing position of being blackballed.

Social discrimination against Jews is far more common, and more humiliating, among English-speaking than among Afrikaans-speaking South Africans. The Afrikaner has never been a thorough-going anti-Semite. There have been periods when 'the Jew' has been used as a bogy in Nationalist political propaganda; but the Afrikaner has always respected the Jews and their religion and has, indeed, had a kind of fellow-feeling for them. Until comparatively recent years the Afrikaners were not prominent in commerce, while the Jews were. So were the English-speaking South Africans, and the result was that commercial rivalry with the Jews induced anti-Semitism.

During the second and third decades of the twentieth century, when nationalism was developing fast, so-called 'Jewish' capital was a convenient scapegoat and bogy on to which to fasten responsibility for economic ills and with which to frighten the electorate. The Nationalist Party Press made great play with 'Hoggenheimer', the symbol of Jewish capitalism, who was depicted in political cartoons as an obese Semite smoking a cigar and looking prosperous. This mythical creature was presumed to be the financial power behind the Botha-Smuts Party; he represented the mine magnates who pulled the strings to which the political puppets danced. The propaganda paid good dividends and, when no longer required, was put into cold storage. It was recently revived in order to discredit the United South Africa Trust Fund. This fund was started by Mr. Harry Oppenheimer, then an M.P., and a number of business men with the expressed aim of furthering good relations between the two main European groups in South Africa. The trustees of the Fund were all supporters of the United Party, and the Nationalist Party Press revived 'Hoggenheimer' in cartoons to show that the United Party is controlled by big business dominated by Jews.

It would be surprising if Jews were not opposed to the Nationalist Party. Just before, and during, the 1939-45 War that party gave many signs of underwriting Hitler's race theories: the Transvaal Nationalist Party excluded Jews from membership, a prohibition that was removed only in 1951 when the Afrikaner and Nationalist parties united. Moreover, many of the younger professional Jewish men and women were stirred to action by legislation passed since the Nationalist Party came to power in 1948—legislation that seemed to them to bear a strong resemblance to the racial laws in Hitler's Germany. The Jewish Board of Deputies, which regulates Jewish affairs in South Africa, issues statements from time to time to the effect that, as a Board, it is neutral in politics. Indeed, as a Board, it has not joined the controlling bodies of other religions in protesting against such laws as the Group Areas Act. The Nationalist Party Press has, however, always been lukewarm about accepting these statements of neutrality because most Jews are in fact, openly or less publicly, supporters of parties opposed to the Nationalist Party. Moreover, it is normal for nationalism to regard those who are not for it as against it.

10

The Union's Colonies

A GLANCE AT THE MAP WILL SHOW FOUR TERRITORIES, BORDERING ON the Union of South Africa and either partially or completely surrounded by it, whose history and future are intimately connected with it. Their total area is one and a quarter times as large as that of the Union, but their total population is only one-ninth the size of South Africa's and consists for the greater part of non-Europeans. These territories are South-West Africa and the three High Commission territories of Basutoland, Swaziland, and the Bechuanaland Protectorate.

SOUTH-WEST AFRICA

Settlement in South-West Africa was begun in 1883 by Germans under a charter from the German Imperial Government. By treaties with African and Hottentot chiefs, the country became a German Protectorate, which at that time meant that other nations recognized Germany's right to exploit the country when she was in a position to do so. In 1892 the German Government took over the country and colonization began in earnest. Germans were settled on the land, harbours were built at Lüderitz and Swakopmund (near Walvis Bay), and railways and roads were constructed.

German history in South-West Africa followed a pattern that was common in nineteenth-century colonization of Africa: treaties with chiefs who did not understand what they were agreeing to, followed by rebellion and 'pacification'. German administration, neither worse nor better than that of other colonizing powers in this respect, caused constant discontent. In 1904 a major rebellion of African and Hottentot tribes broke out which took three years to crush and ended only with the near destruction of the Herero. In 1915 South-West Africa was conquered by South African forces in a brief campaign, and the Peace Conference of Versailles decided that the territory should be a C Mandate administered by the Union Government as an integral portion of its own territory. In 1925 a Legislative Assembly of twelve elected and six nominated members was set up. The franchise and membership of the Assembly were open to Europeans only, and the Assembly was given powers to make ordinances subject to the approval of the Union Government. A long list of subjects such as Native affairs, mines, justice, posts and telegraphs, railways and harbours, defence, customs, currency, and banking, was reserved to the Union Parliament.

With the rise to power of Hitler, agitation for the return of former German colonies became vigorous both in Germany and in South-West Africa. So flagrant was pro-Nazi propaganda among the Germans living there that the Union Government appointed a commission of inquiry in 1936. The report of this commission revealed the existence of Nazi cells, Labour Front Groups, Hitler Youth Cadres, and Winter Help Centres, not only in South-West Africa, but in the Union, and the government, acting on the report, declared Nazi organizations illegal. When war broke out in 1939, many of the German inhabitants of South-West Africa were interned.

Between the two world wars South Africa was responsible to the League of Nations for her administration of South-West Africa, and she had to report annually to the Permanent Mandates Commission of the League. The Mandates Commission was severely critical of the way in which the government had exercised its mandate, and its reports contain constant references to 'complete stagnation' of social work, to the inadequacy of provision for health and education, to the general policy of discrimination on the grounds of colour, and to the 'apparent assumption by the white population that "Natives exist chiefly for the purpose of labour for the whites"'. From the annual reports of the Mandatory and from those of the proceedings of the Permanent Mandates Commission itself it is evident that the Union Government was far more concerned with the interests of the 30,000 European inhabitants than with those of the 300,000 non-Europeans. The government maintained law and order, but despite continuous encouragement by the Mandates Commission it was reluctant to initiate any positive welfare or educational projects or to spend money on the development of the Reserves. As late as 1938, the Chairman of the Mandates Commission said bluntly that in South-West Africa it appeared that taxpayers benefited from public expenditure in proportion to their contribution to revenue, contrary to the practice in most civilized communities. Previous chapters of this book will have made it clear that the South African Government was, in fact, applying to South-West Africa principles that obtained in the Union. Article 2 of the Mandate declared that the Mandatory 'shall promote to the utmost the material and moral well-being and social progress of the inhabitants of the territory subject to the mandate', and, judging by the reports of the Commission, the Union Government failed to comply with this article.

By 1945 a large majority of Europeans in the Union and in South-West Africa was in favour of full incorporation of the territory. When, therefore, the question of Mandates was debated at the San Francisco Conference of the United Nations, the South African delegation told the Conference that South-West Africa had been administered for twenty-five years as an integral part of the Union, that there was no prospect of its ever becoming a separate state, and that the Mandate should be terminated and the territory incorporated as part of the Union. In November 1946 Smuts, then Prime Minister, appeared before the Trusteeship Committee of the United Nations and asked for permission to incorporate South-West Africa. He maintained that the territory was already firmly integrated with the Union and that the uncertainty about incorporation was retarding its development, and he added that the wishes of the inhabitants had been consulted and were found to be overwhelmingly in favour of incorporation. During the long and bitter debate that followed this request, South Africa's Native policy was severely criticized and the deficiencies of her previous administration of South-West Africa were quoted as proof that she was unfit to have uncontrolled authority over the non-European inhabitants of the territory. South Africa's request was rejected and the General Assembly of the United Nations adopted a resolution inviting her to place the territory under the trusteeship system. This South Africa refused to do, though Smuts kept the door open for negotiation by continuing to send reports on the territory to the Trusteeship Committee.

In 1947 the General Assembly of the United Nations maintained its previous attitude and called upon the Union Government to propose a trusteeship agreement. The acrimonious debates at U.N.O., during which South Africa was bitterly attacked, did much to consolidate European opinion in the Union and in South-West Africa in favour of incorporation at all costs. The Nationalist Party blamed Smuts for having raised the question at U.N.O. and maintained that South Africa was no longer legally bound by the Mandate system since the League of Nations was defunct. The Nationalist Party under Malan came to power in 1948, and, in the next year, agreed to have the matter submitted to the International Court of Justice for an opinion. This was given in 1950, but it offered no way of settling the dispute between South Africa and the United Nations. Malan, meanwhile, decided to incorporate South-West Africa whatever international opinion might be, and in 1949 introduced a Bill to do this. The United Party did not oppose the Bill, except in a few details, because it knew that the European voters of South-West Africa were almost unanimously in favour of incorporation.

The South-West Africa Affairs Amendment Act, 1949, provides for the representation in the Union Parliament of the European inhabitants of the territory, who elect six members to the House of Assembly. The territory is represented in the Union Senate by two senators,

chosen by an electoral college consisting of the six members of the
Union House of Assembly and the eighteen members of the South-
West Africa Legislative Assembly, and one senator nominated by the
government and selected mainly on the ground of his acquaintance
with the reasonable wants of the coloured races of South-West Africa.
This representation is heavily weighted in favour of the territory,
which has a European population of only 69,000, and each elected
member, therefore, represents a constituency which is about one-third
the size of a Union constituency. The two major political parties in
the Union have branches in South-West Africa, and at the first election
in 1950 the Nationalist Party gained all six seats, thus giving much-
needed parliamentary support to Malan.

In local affairs an administrator and an elected Legislative Assembly
govern South-West Africa in much the same way that administrators
and provincial councils govern the four provinces of the Union.
Article 34 of the 1949 Act provides that any reference to a province
in the Union shall be construed as including South-West Africa. To
all intents and purposes, therefore, the territory has become a fifth
province of the Union, except for the important difference that, by
agreement entered into before incorporation and embodied in the
1949 Act, South-West Africa is not subject to taxation by the Union
Parliament. This provision, which has been dubbed representation
without taxation, was introduced to allay the fears of the European
inhabitants of the territory, which is economically weak and heavily
in debt to the Union.

South-West Africa is not, for the present at any rate, of any
economic value to the Union. It has never paid its way and is heavily
indebted to the Union, to whom it must look for further borrowing.
The reasons, however, why South Africa was so determined to
incorporate a territory that has been an economic drag rather than an
asset are not far to seek. The first in point of time is the strategic one.
After the 1914-18 War the South African Government of Botha and
Smuts favoured outright annexation almost entirely on the grounds
that South Africa could not afford to allow Germany to occupy a
territory from which the Union might so easily be attacked, and whose
harbours might prove a threat to the Cape route. The temper of the
time, however, was opposed to outright annexation of ex-enemy
colonies and the government had to be content with a mandate.

The second reason is that, once South Africa had begun to administer
the territory, South African citizens settled in South-West Africa in
sufficient numbers to warrant local self-government and to create
ties of sentiment as well as of administration between what became,
in effect, a mother-country and her colony. Both major political

parties in South Africa came to regard the mandated territory as South African. The Nationalist Party was, for a time, slightly embarrassed by the situation because it had opposed the Treaty of Versailles as unjust and found it awkward to explain why Germany should have all her colonies back except South-West Africa. It resorted to the argument that the wishes of the inhabitants must be taken into account, and in 1938 Malan said that the Nationalist Party was not prepared to surrender the territory but wished to settle the matter in a friendly way with Germany.

Finally, there was considerable force in the arguments put before U.N.O. by Smuts and others that South-West Africa was firmly integrated with the Union, that it was improbable that the mandatory principle of developing the country to a state of independence could be carried out, and that, in the circumstances, it was reasonable to incorporate it.

None of these arguments for incorporation takes account of the interests or the wishes of the non-European inhabitants. It is improbable that they would be better off under a trusteeship agreement. Even a casual reading of the reports of the Permanent Mandates Commission till 1938 shows that international supervision made little difference to the policy of the sovereign mandatory state. The obligation to submit an annual report to international scrutiny may have had a slight beneficial effect; but the economic backwardness of a territory and the pressure of its European inhabitants are far more potent policy-makers than distant international opinion unbacked by sanctions. Further evidence of this is to be found in the history of South-West Africa since its incorporation by the Union. Year after year there are attempts in the Trusteeship Council or in the General Assembly to bring South-West Africa within the cognizance of the United Nations, and these attempts are successfully countered by South Africa's contention that this is a matter of internal policy. In 1957 the General Assembly set up a Good Offices Committee to explore, with South Africa, the possibilities of giving South-West Africa an international status, and the Committee recommended the partition of the territory, the southern portion to be annexed by the Union and the northern portion (where most of the Africans live) to be administered by her under a trusteeship agreement. South Africa proposed, as an alternative, an agreement with France, Britain, and the United States of America; she was, in other words, not prepared to recognize the jurisdiction of the United Nations. The Trusteeship Committee and the General Assembly turned down both these proposals and asked the Good Offices Committee to continue its efforts. It is improbable that those efforts will be successful since white votes in South-West

Africa are more significant to any South African government than are adverse comments at U.N.O.

Although the arguments advanced for incorporation take no account of the wishes of the non-European inhabitants, they were consulted before South Africa applied to U.N.O. to be allowed to incorporate the territory. In his statement to the Trusteeship Committee in 1946 Smuts said that the wishes of the European inhabitants had been expressed in the Press and by a unanimous resolution of the Legislative Assembly, while those of the non-Europeans had been ascertained by consultation with tribal units. The detailed results of this consultation showed that 208,000 were in favour of incorporation, 33,000 were against, and 56,000 could not be consulted. These figures can hardly be taken seriously, since the wishes of officially recognized chiefs are not an accurate guide in a country where tribal authority has been so much weakened by the breaking up of the tribes. Moreover, the total estimated non-European population at that time was 322,000, and in arriving at the figures quoted by Smuts the Native Affairs officials must have included a large proportion of children, since there could hardly have been more than 160,000 non-European adults in the territory.

The host of problems that arise in the Union of South Africa from the co-existence of a minority of European and a majority of non-European inhabitants exists in South-West Africa too, though not in such an acute form. There are poverty-stricken Reserves that cannot support themselves and whose chief export is their manpower, and urban areas where conditions of housing, health, and education are far behind those in the Union, themselves admittedly inadequate. There are, too, the same dependence on untrained and inefficient African labour and the same policy of maintaining the position of the European population on the insecure foundation of colour-bar practice, and legislation that discriminates against non-Europeans. Finally, we find the same breakdown of tribalism in face of Western economy and the same tardiness on the part of Europeans and of non-Europeans to recognize this and to adjust themselves to these changing circumstances. South-West Africa has, in fact, become part of the Union, and whatever virtues or vices there may be in the policies adopted in the Union, these are likely to be found in the Union's recent territorial acquisition.

THE HIGH COMMISSION TERRITORIES

The territories of Basutoland, Swaziland, and the Bechuanaland Protectorate are known as the High Commission territories because they are administered by Her Majesty's High Commissioner in South

Africa, whose post falls, not under the Colonial Office, but under the Commonwealth Relations Office. This chapter is concerned with the relations between the Union and her neighbouring territories rather than with a detailed description of those territories. A few general remarks must, therefore, suffice to illuminate the background to those relations and to explain why the Union has asked for, and Great Britain has refused, the transfer of the High Commission territories.

Basutoland has been under British control since 1868 when its chief, Moshesh, a man of great ability, fearing conquest by the Free State Republic, successfully applied to the British Government for protection. According to the 1956 census it has a population of 639,000 Sotho, and 1,926 Europeans who are officials, missionaries, or traders and who may not own land. It is estimated that, in addition, 150,000 Sotho are absent from the territory as migrant workers in the Union, which means that more than half the adult males find work outside the territory. Basutoland is administered by a Resident Commissioner assisted by district commissioners and a technical staff, and tribal institutions are recognized and play an active part in central and local government. By an agreement between the Basutoland National Council and the Secretary of State for Commonwealth relations, reached in 1959, Basutoland has a new constitution which provides for a Legislative Council, to be known as the Basuto National Council, of eighty members, half of whom are elected by district councils which are themselves predominantly elected. An Executive Council consists of four senior officials (including the Resident Commissioner) and four unofficial members chosen from the Basuto National Council; the Resident Commissioner, as chairman, enjoys both a deliberative and a casting vote. The Basuto National Council has power to legislate for all persons in respect of all matters except external affairs, defence, internal security, currency, public loans, customs, excise, copyright and patents, posts and telegraphs, telephones, broadcasting, and the public service. In these matters the Council acts as a consultative body only. The first elections were held in January 1960 and resulted in a victory for the Basutoland Congress Party; some 50 per cent of those entitled to vote went to the polls.

Basutoland has a climate eminently suitable for agriculture and for stock-farming, but it is not a wealthy agricultural country. Chiefs apportion fields for ploughing, while grazing land is common, but the system of communal farming is not efficient. Further, about 50 per cent of able-bodied adult males are, at any given time, absent in the Union earning a cash wage at the mines or on farms, and this is both a result and a cause of the low agricultural yield. The administration, with the aid of the Colonial Development and Welfare Fund, has done much to promote better farming methods and to combat soil erosion, but a great deal remains to be done before Basutoland can be self-supporting and her imports balance her exports. In 1955 imports amounted to £3,200,000 and exports to £1,800,000, the latter consisting mainly of wool, mohair, cattle, beans, and wheat. It is probable that when the scheme to dam the Orange River, which rises in Basutoland, is completed, more intensive cultivation will become possible; but as long as the drain of manpower to the Union labour market continues the economy of Basutoland is bound to suffer.

Swaziland is the smallest of the three territories, and its control was for many years a matter of dispute between Britain and the Transvaal Republic. In 1894 Britain recognized the Transvaal's right to protect Swaziland, and at the conclusion of the Boer War the territory was administered by the Governor of the Transvaal until, in 1906, it was transferred to the High Commissioner. There are 234,000 Swazi, 6,000 Europeans, and 1,400 Coloured inhabitants of Swaziland. Like Basutoland, the territory is administered by a Resident Commissioner under the direction of the High Commissioner; the paramount chief and his council of chiefs and leading men do not, however, have as much power as the Basuto National Council does. Unlike Basutoland, too, nearly half the area of Swaziland is owned by Europeans, and it is not a purely African state in which a small number of Europeans are living to serve the needs of the territory. The Europeans have established rights and property and they elect an Advisory Council of ten members to advise the Resident Commissioner on European affairs.

Swaziland is well watered and fertile, but the eastern lowveld region is unhealthy because of the heat and malaria. The middle and highveld regions are excellent agricultural and stock-farming areas, but, like Basutoland and for similar reasons, Swaziland is not a wealthy country. It is, however, better off than Basutoland. In 1955 imports amounted to £2,000,000 and exports to £3,300,000, of which asbestos accounted for £2,300,000; and big afforestation schemes, with the possibilities of paper mills, hold out bright prospects.

The Bechuanaland Protectorate came under British control in 1896. The eastern border of Bechuanaland marches with the western border of the Transvaal, and a study of the map will show why the territory played such an important part in Rhodes's plans. He called it the 'neck in the bottle', the Suez Canal to the north, and it was vital to his schemes of expansion northwards that it should be in British hands and not in those of Germany or of the Transvaal. There had been continuous friction between the Transvaal and the Bechuana tribes, and in 1885 Khama and two other chiefs applied to Britain for protection, which, after some delay, was granted. In 1895 southern Bechuanaland was annexed to the Cape Colony, and, a year later, northern Bechuanaland came under direct Imperial control as the Bechuanaland Protectorate. In exchange for British protection, the Bechuana chiefs had to surrender part of their tribal lands for a railway to Rhodesia and for European settlement.

The territory of the Bechuanaland Protectorate is about three times the size of Great Britain and has a population of 300,000 people, of whom 3,000 are European. Large portions of it are desert or semi-desert areas where nomadic Bushmen and Makalahari manage to exist in a never-ending struggle against drought; but the eastern portion, though subject to severe droughts, is good ranching country with an average rainfall of about 18 inches a year. Administration is on the same lines as in Basutoland and has the usual apparatus of indirect rule—tribal authorities, councils, and treasuries; but where Basutoland and Swaziland are each inhabited by a single tribe, the Bechuanaland Protectorate has separate tribal reserves for its eight different tribes, one of which is the Bamangwato, who leapt into prominence because of the dispute between Seretse Khama, Tshekedi Khama, and the British Government. An African Advisory Council, consisting of thirty-five members who are either chiefs, sub-chiefs, or nominees of chiefs, is the counterpart in Bechuanaland of the Basuto National Council. There is also a European Advisory Council elected by the Europeans; and a Joint Advisory Council, consisting of eight members from each, meets twice a year under the presidency of the Resident Commissioner. In 1955 imports were £2,460,000 and exports £2,820,000, consisting mainly of meat.

The three High Commission territories have much in common. In legal and civil administration they conform to the general pattern of indirect rule, and there is a genuine effort to associate Africans with both local and central government. Within the territories Africans do not have to carry passes, and they are free from most of the restrictions that are in force in the Union. Within the limits of their revenue, the administrations of the territories are concerned to promote the social and economic interests of the Africans, and they spend a higher proportion of the revenue on African education, health, and social welfare than is the case in the Union. Further, the Colonial Development and Welfare Fund provides some of the capital required for development schemes such as boreholes in the Bechuanaland Protectorate.

Another characteristic of the territories is their close economic and administrative relation with, and dependence on, the Union. Posts and telegraphs, currency and banking, and customs tariffs are all operated by the Union Government; South Africa is the principal source of their imports and the principal market for their exports and labour; many pupils and students from the territories receive higher training at Union institutions and enter for their examinations; South African newspapers circulate in the territories; and, generally, there is constant contact between the inhabitants of the territories and of the Union. Apart from the important fact that the territories are British possessions while South Africa is an independent state, the territories might quite accurately be described as Native Reserves of the Union. Whether they remain British or become South African, the ruling power will have to face the same problems that are, in the Union, created by the existence of Native Reserves.

At the time when the union of the four South African colonies was being discussed, British and South African statesmen realized this close connexion between the territories and the rest of South Africa and visualized a time when they might be handed over to the Union. A schedule to the South Africa Act, 1909, provided in detail for such a transfer, which might take place on addresses from both Houses of the Union Parliament to the King-in-Council, and, though the request in this official form has not yet been made, the matter has from time to time been publicly raised. Hertzog was the first Prime Minister to raise the matter formally with Britain. He approached J. H. Thomas, the then Secretary of State, in 1935, at the rather unpropitious time when Union Native policy was hardening. British public opinion was, on the whole, unfavourable to handing over the territories, and M.P.s in the House of Commons extracted promises from the government that it would not grant transfer without consulting the wishes of the inhabitants. In 1938 the matter was taken a step further when the British Government agreed to the establishment of a Standing Joint Advisory Conference to consist of officials of the Union and of the territories and, it was suggested, to facilitate ultimate transfer.

The Second World War effectively put the question into cold storage, where it remained until the Nationalist Party came to power in 1948. Malan raised the question tentatively in 1949, and much more definitely at an official dinner in 1951 to Mr. Gordon Walker, Secretary of State for Commonwealth Relations. There were discussions between the United Kingdom and South Africa in 1952; and in 1956, at the Commonwealth Prime Ministers' Conference, Mr. Strydom and Mr. Louw reiterated South Africa's desire to have the territories transferred to her. Since this question is likely to become of increasing urgency, and deeply concerns Great Britain, the High Commission territories, and the Union of South Africa, it is worth discussing in some detail.

It is not easy to establish with any degree of precision why South Africa wants the territories. They are not self-supporting, and require considerable investment of capital to make them so. What economic advantages the Union might expect to acquire by transfer are, in fact, already enjoyed by her in the shape of labour supply and markets, and Britain would hardly agree to terms which gave her additional advantages, such as making land in the territories available for European occupation. The territories are so closely bound to the Union's economy that, from their point of view, there are good reasons for throwing in their lot with South Africa. But if the Africans are to be left in undisturbed possession of their tribal lands, there does not seem to be any immediate or long-term economic inducement for the Union to take responsibility for what will be, in effect, three additional Native Reserves.

Such reasons as have been advanced for South Africa's taking over the territories are extremely vague. It is said that 'geographical conditions' favour transfer, and there is talk of 'rounding off our territories'. In the speech referred to above, Malan spoke about the intolerable situation of having these territories 'in the heart of our country'. These topographical arguments come from a close study of the map and are part of the imperialism to which nationalism is always prone, but they are in themselves not a very convincing argument.

It is possible that the desire to change the map of southern Africa has an historical basis. Had Great Britain not taken Basutoland and Bechuanaland under her protection, it is highly probable that these two territories would have come, as Swaziland had done, under the control of the two Boer republics. The history of European settlement in Africa shows that, sooner or later, African tribal land was bound to pass into the control of the better-equipped European, whether he was British, Afrikaans, German, or Portuguese, and it is a fair assumption that Moshesh and Khama would not have been able to maintain their independence. Great Britain, therefore, may be regarded as having prevented the Boers from acquiring the territories, and, just as the descendants of the Boers want to regain the republican independence which they lost in the Boer War, so they want to acquire what, but for Britain, would have been part of their country. While most South Africans have a vague desire to 'own' the High Commission territories, it is not without significance that the most ardent protagonist of transfer is the Nationalist Party, which regards itself as heir to the Boer republican tradition.

There is another reason why the Nationalist Party has taken the lead in asking for the territories and has become increasingly urgent in its request. South African Native policy in general, and more particularly the Nationalist Party policy, is in strong contrast to British Native policy in the territories and in other colonial possessions. This contrast is seen in such matters as pass laws, industrial and political colour bars, and in the amount of attention given to education and to social welfare. There is an idea prevalent in South Africa that the Union spends much more on educational and social services for Africans than do the British territories in southern Africa. The actual amount per head spent is more, but when these figures are taken in conjunction with those for revenue and for national income, the difference in proportion becomes apparent. Thus, South Africa spends £1 18s. 3d. per head on services for Africans, while Southern Rhodesia spends £1 9s., and Basutoland 13s., but these figures represent 8·8, 16·5 and 35·0 per cent of revenue respectively, while South Africa's figure is 2 per cent of her national income and Southern Rhodesia's is 4 per cent of hers.[1] These figures, then, show a proportionately larger expenditure on education and social welfare in the British territories than in the Union, and when, in addition, recent trends in British colonial policy are borne in mind, it is evident that the Union and Great Britain view Native policy from very different angles. Moreover, there is no room in the same country for both policies, and many South Africans regard British policy as a positive danger to European security in Africa. The natural conclusion is that the more areas there are under South African control, the more secure will the position of the white man be. The reactions of the Nationalist Press to the marriage of Seretse Khama to a European and to constitutional developments on the West Coast show how strong are the fears of those to whom the perpetual European control of Africa is a fundamental political tenet.

There is one further argument for transferring the territories that has come into prominence since 1955. The Tomlinson Commission investigated the Native Reserves in the Union as a possible homeland for Africans and found that when all the land promised in 1936 had been added, the Reserves would constitute about 13 per cent of the

[1] The figures for expenditure are taken from *A Survey of Race Relations*, 1949–50, published by the South African Institute of Race Relations. The figure for Southern Rhodesia's national income is taken from Cmd. 8,233, *Central African Territories Report of Conference on Closer Association*, 1951. Though more recent comparable figures are not available, there is no reason to believe that the relative proportions have altered.

area of the Union. If the High Commission territories were included in the term South Africa, however, and if they could be added to the existing Reserves, the percentage would amount to something like 45. Moreover, the addition of the territories would make it possible to reshuffle boundaries in such a way as to reduce the fragmentation of the present Reserves. Some of the maps in the Tomlinson Report indicate clearly that the Commission did, in fact, rely on the transfer of the territories to enable South Africa to carry out the Bantustan policy. In speaking on the question in 1959, the Prime Minister, Dr. Verwoerd, tied up Bantustans and transfer more closely by saying that the Africans in the territories need not fear that transfer would involve a loss of their land because, he said, South Africa had just embarked on the Bantustan policy of giving the Bantu in her own areas increasing control.[1] This whole argument seems to amount to saying two things at the same time: that South Africa cannot establish Bantustans unless she has the territories; and, the inhabitants of the territories need not fear South Africa since she is following the enlightened policy of establishing Bantustans.

The transfer of the High Commission territories to South African control would involve a number of matters. The Schedule to the South Africa Act provides that, if the territories are transferred, they shall be governed by proclamation of the Governor-General-in-Council and shall be administered by the prime minister with the aid of a commission. Each territory is to be administered separately and is to have its own budget, and no land may be alienated from the Native tribes. The King may disallow any proclamation, and any Bill to alter the provisions of the Schedule shall be reserved for the signification of His Majesty's pleasure. These provisions were made in 1909, before the Statute of Westminster and the Status of the Union Act had removed any control that the British Parliament may have had over South Africa. In 1951 the Union Parliament disregarded the provisions of the South Africa Act relating to the Coloured franchise, and there seems to be no reason why it should not, if it so chose, disregard the provisions of the Schedule to the Act and alienate land in the territories. In any case, the King-in-Council no longer means, as it did in 1909, the King acting on the advice of his British Ministers. In regard to the South Africa Act, he would act on the advice of his South African Ministers. In other words, the South Africa Act and its Schedule cannot be regarded as safeguarding the interests of the inhabitants of the territories after they have been transferred to the Union. This position would not be radically altered if South Africa were to become a republic; but the possibility of such

[1] *Hansard* (1959) Col. 5254.

a step is likely to have a decisive effect on the wishes of the inhabitants. It has been suggested by Sir Charles Rey, a former Resident Commissioner of the Bechuanaland Protectorate, who regards transfer as inevitable and desirable, that this difficulty could be overcome by a treaty between South Africa and Great Britain embodying the terms on which Great Britain, the Union, and the African inhabitants of the territories were agreed.[1]

A second matter that is involved in the question of transfer is what effect it will have on other British colonies in Africa. South African Native policy has been much advertised and is far from popular with the African subjects of Great Britain in her African colonies. Further, British colonial policy has developed rapidly in recent years and is consciously aiming at more self-government for the colonies and at associating Africans with political and administrative government to a far greater extent than hitherto. Neither major political party in South Africa contemplates such a policy in the Union, and the Nationalist Party expressly states that, within the European areas, Africans will never have any political representation. It is true that, according to the theory of apartheid, they will have control in their own areas. But, as previous chapters have tried to show, it is unlikely that the distinctions between African and European areas can be maintained for long. The reaction of Africans in British colonies is, therefore, not likely to be favourable to transfer.

The third and most important matter is that of the wishes of the inhabitants of the territories. When the South Africa Act was passed, in 1909, world opinion would not have been shocked by a suggestion to transfer an African territory from the control of one State to another without consulting the inhabitants. The Schedule to the Act, consequently, does not mention the wishes of the inhabitants. But by 1935, public opinion in Britain had become sensitive with regard to such matters, and when Hertzog raised the question of transfer, the British Government, reflecting public opinion, insisted that the inhabitants must be consulted. Since 1935, and particularly since the Second World War, world opinion has changed in the matter of the rights of colonial people, and Great Britain is in the van of that opinion. Any suggestion today, therefore, that it is unnecessary to consult the inhabitants, or that consultation need not imply consent, is likely to be coldly received by the British public and by a large number of Europeans in South Africa.

While it is improbable that transfer will take place without consultation, the real difficulty is to decide what consultation involves and how it is to be effected. Experience in South-West Africa and British

[1] Article in the *Cape Times*, 17 April 1951.

experience in Bechuanaland and in Central Africa show that it is easy to go through the motions of consultation, but that the results are not necessarily reliable. To consult a number of chiefs and councils who, although they are hereditary, hold office at the discretion of the government, is not a sure way of finding out what their tribal subjects think. Africans, like other people, may be easily misled on matters on which they lack information; but they by no means lack the equipment to exercise judgement on matters which they understand. Provided that the facts can be explained clearly and that voting can be supervised impartially, there is no reason why the inhabitants of the High Commission territories should not be consulted in the normal manner.

Uncertainty about the future of the High Commission territories has unfortunate results. It quite naturally has a retarding effect on development schemes in the territories and continues to act as a bone of contention between Britain and the Union. The results of hasty action might, however, be even more unfortunate, and the whole question should be much more thoroughly studied than hitherto. Britain cannot lightly discard her responsibilities for the welfare of the African inhabitants of the territories, and those inhabitants must be given ample time to find out what transfer will mean to them. Last but not least, the people of South Africa must realize more clearly what responsibilities they are being asked to assume, and what policies they propose to adopt. Before a transfer, with any hope of lasting success, can take place, the inhabitants of the territories must be satisfied that their real interests lie with the Union; Britain must be satisfied that the interests of the inhabitants are safe with the Union; and the Union must be satisfied that it will be able to guarantee to the inhabitants at least as much security and progress as they now enjoy.

11

Conclusion

SOUTH AFRICA IS A COUNTRY OF CONTRASTS AND CONTRADICTIONS. White and black, European and non-European, wealth and poverty, science and superstition, education and illiteracy, Christianity and heathendom live side by side in the same towns and villages and on the same farms. The country exports food while many of its people suffer from deficiency diseases. It lacks skilled workers, but limits immigration and legislates to prevent the majority of its population from acquiring skill. It is royalist and republican, and contains staunch supporters and bitter opponents of the Commonwealth. It confines active citizenship to less than one-fifth of its population, and the programmes of its main political parties are compounded of fear of the remaining four-fifths and an assumption of perpetual superiority. In attempting to retain political control, the European inhabitants adopt policies that create the very forces that must, in the long run, overthrow their rule. South Africa is, in fact, a country of close on fifteen million people who have not yet discovered a fundamental unity, a common South Africanism, a common purpose.

Perhaps the strangest contradiction, and the one that explains a good deal of what is happening in South Africa, is that this union of four former colonial possessions has become itself a colonial power, with all the problems that face those European states that hold dominion over non-European people. This fact is obscured by the circumstance that colonial possessions are traditionally oversea possessions. Britain, France, Portugal, and Belgium are colonial powers with African possessions that are separated from the motherland by miles of ocean. South Africa is at once motherland and colony. No seas separate the governed from the governors, and the latter are unable to contemplate the former with that detachment which is such a valuable asset in administration. The Belgian and the Briton, going about his daily occupations, is hardly aware of the millions of Africans who are subject to his government. The European South African is in daily contact with his colonial African subjects.

To the Briton and the Belgian an African colony is a romantically distant land from which raw materials come, in which his sons may serve until they retire to the homeland, and in which his country was, in the nineteenth century, involved in wars of conquest. When he thinks about his country's colonies he reflects with pride on the work of civilization that followed on conquest. Both conquest and the work of civilizing took place at a comfortable distance from the homeland; it was something to read about in the papers, but it did not touch the daily life of more than an insignificant fraction of the inhabitants of the motherland. South Africans who administer Africans and who bring Western civilization to Africa do not go home on periodic leave or retire to a distant country. The children of those who conquered in South Africa live side by side with the conquered. Unlike South Africans, Belgians and Frenchmen do not regard African children as possible competitors of their own. African students from British colonies who study at a British university, normally return to their homes when they have acquired professional qualifications; they do not remain to practise in Britain.

All African colonial powers have had to evolve colonial policies. Since 1930 the speed with which African political self-consciousness has developed has increased, and colonial policy no longer connotes sound administration only. Today colonial policy means primarily a system of government designed to train Africans for self-government so that, as soon as it is practicable, they will elect their own parliaments. Not only is this the whole trend of modern European thought on the subject of colonies, but from the Africans themselves the demand for a fully responsible government is increasingly clamant. This is true of Britain's, as it is of South Africa's, colonial subjects. But there is a great difference in the demand. Britain's colonial subjects demand self-government, not a share in the government at Westminster. South Africa's colonial subjects demand a share in the government at Cape Town. To the European whose home is in South Africa there is a world of difference between granting responsible government to an African territory and granting Africans a share in electing the South African Parliament. In these respects South Africa's problems differ radically from those of most other colonial powers.

The position of the African inhabitants of the Union differs from that of Africans in other territories. British and Portuguese colonial policies are different in many respects, but both have similar ultimate objectives—the association of Africans who have assimilated Western culture in the government of the territory. In Britain all political parties, backed by public opinion, have committed themselves to such a policy, and well-informed, alert, and influential groups are ever watchful to see that this objective is not lost sight of or that African interests are not sacrificed to those of the few Europeans who live in the territories. African colonial subjects of Britain are aware of this; they know that the laws and the administration of Basutoland, of Northern Rhodesia, and of other British colonies and protectorates are subject to the ultimate control of the British Parliament. Beyond the Governor and the local legislature there is always the controlling hand of the Colonial Office, whose ministerial head is responsible to parliament.

In South Africa there is nothing beyond the Union Parliament, in which neither of the two major political parties has a policy remotely resembling those of other colonial powers in Africa. In theory the policy of apartheid would, indeed, involve ultimate self-government for Africans in their own areas. But in practice the social and economic structure of the Union makes this impossible, at any rate for the great majority of Africans. In law they are citizens of South Africa, but by the laws of the Union Parliament they are deprived of many of the rights normally associated with citizenship. And against such laws they have no appeal except to the politically impotent European liberal opinion in the Union.

This vital difference between the Union and all other colonial powers in Africa, that her colonial subjects live in the homeland and not 'overseas', has far-reaching effects on the political thinking of Europeans and Africans. Britain's problem is how to assist her colonial subjects to self-government in a way that will not leave the newly created state a prey to anarchy. She dare not go too fast, and she will be under pressure from the Africans themselves not to go too slow. She may claim that her policy is an honourable one framed in the interests of the Africans, and she may reasonably hope that the self-governing states will wish to remain associated with her. The chances of success for such a policy are considerable. But even more important for the present argument, the consequences of failure for Britain will be, at worst, that she will lose her colonies, and for the Africans, that they may have to pass through a shorter or longer period of misgovernment before reaching political stability.

In South Africa the problem of the rulers is not how to assist Africans to self-government, but how to train them to be full citizens of a country in which black and white live side by side; and the political problem for Africans is how, not merely to urge an already willing home government to speed up the process of self-government, but to persuade an unwilling class to surrender a share of its political power. To Europeans and Africans in the Union the consequences of failure to grapple with these problems would be greater than they would be for other colonial territories. Europeans in South Africa would not merely forfeit a colony; they would lose a home. It is this fear of the consequences of failure that drives most Europeans to adopt policies by which they hope to side-step the real problem and retain perpetual political control, and it is a realization of the vital issues involved that makes them so sensitive to criticism from countries that are not faced with the problem in such a crucial form.

Eight eventful years have passed since the first edition of this book was published. In Africa, political independence and political rights for colonial subjects have been granted on a scale and at a rate that would have been difficult to envisage in 1952. In the Union of South Africa, political control still rests with the white minority; but the Union has not escaped the pressures and tensions that have produced such remarkable changes elsewhere in Africa. To all outward appearances the white population has successfully used its political power to entrench its privileged position against the demands of non-whites; and previous chapters have shown that this process has involved the curtailment of personal liberty and the concentration of power in the executive to an extent that has undermined the Rule of Law as understood in Western democratic society. It might serve some purpose, in this concluding chapter, to state the problems that face fifteen million human beings living in South Africa and to assess the forces that promote or hinder peaceful and happy solutions.

For the vast majority of the fifteen million people the major personal problem is poverty—sheer, grinding poverty that condemns them to live below the bread-line and to forgo many of the necessities of life. Economically South Africa is a poor country, and the burden of poverty falls most heavily on those least able to bear it, the non-Europeans. Gold-mining is a waning asset. Great distances and the absence of navigable rivers, lack of skilled workers, and a low wage policy for non-European labour continue to keep industrial output per unit of labour low. The soil is, on the whole, poor; the rainfall is variable and over large areas alternates between droughts and floods; the soil is eroding rapidly and efforts to restore it lag far behind; agricultural labour is traditionally low-paid and inefficiently used; the systems of taxation and of subsidizing exports encourage uneconomic agricultural practices; and as a result of all this, agricultural production is low and South Africa is unable to feed her population adequately.

Nevertheless, scientific knowledge and technology have made it possible to counteract many of the natural disadvantages from which South Africa suffers and to use more effectively her considerable mineral resources; but these matters can only be tackled with any prospect of success when they have been seen clearly as economic problems and are not obscured by racial ideologies. There are hopeful signs that commerce and industry have woken to these facts and are coming to realize that their own prosperity depends on enlarging the internal market by increasing both the productivity and the purchasing power of the non-white population. Industrial colour bars are coming to be regarded for what they are: a brake on economic prosperity. Pressure from organized non-white labour and threats of economic boycotts are combining with enlightened self-interest to undermine short-sighted policies that stem from racial fears and greed. Those policies are still dominant, and their supporters will want to retain them as long as possible because they have paid such good party-political dividends; but few people seriously believe that policies which so clearly retard economic progress can be maintained.

Many thoughtful South Africans of all races, while agreeing that poverty is the most pressing personal problem in South Africa, believe that her economic problems will have neither a peaceful nor a happy solution until the political problem has been squarely faced. That problem is in many ways more intractable than the economic problem because it involves a little-understood emotionalism that stems from racial fears and from nationalism. The problem may be stated in the form of a question: can the inhabitants of South Africa arrange matters so that they may live together in harmony, that white and non-white may enjoy a common citizenship, that no one group need fear that it will have to forfeit its cultural identity? If the answer to this is, 'No', as it has been thus far by the majority of those in political control, there can be only one outcome in South Africa. It matters little whether South Africa remains a constitutional monarchy or becomes a republic, in or out of the Commonwealth, or whether Afrikaner nationalism or a broader white South Africanism dominates parliament; so long as this question is answered in the negative the final result will be the same: a resort to violence that will impoverish the country and the ruthless suppression of the conquered, whether it be white or black.

Previous chapters of this book have indicated that South Africa seems, before 1948 and, with quickened pace, since 1948 to be moving along the road that leads to this violent end. Nevertheless, here too, the picture is not wholly dark. It is now acknowledged by all Europeans of any consequence, in all parties, that political rights to non-Europeans cannot be denied. The very theory of apartheid is an acknowledgement by the Nationalist Party of this fundamental fact—hence the attempt to evade its consequences by the desperate and forlorn expedient of independent Bantustans; and the official Opposition acknowledges the fact by its rather halting proposals for the representation of Africans in parliament. The Progressive Party, which broke away from the United Party, advocates a common franchise; and the small Liberal Party stands uncompromisingly for a common citizenship.

Perhaps the most hopeful sign of all is the moderation that the most important non-white organizations have shown, often in the face of great provocation; bodies such as the African National Congress have consistently rejected would-be leaders who hoped to climb to eminence by preaching racial war and domination—a black nationalism that would grow by feeding on ever more extreme and violent measures. This moderation of African leadership argues a political maturity that will be a priceless asset to South Africa when affairs become more critical, as they assuredly will.

At the beginning of this discussion, South Africa's political problem was stated in the form of a question. There is a growing awareness among thoughtful people of all races that if the answer to that question is to be, 'Yes', South Africa will have to undergo a major constitutional reform. There are those who maintain that Union came too soon after the Boer War and that it prematurely forced under one central government the Afrikaner republics, the strongly British Natal, and the Cape, where British and Afrikaner had already begun to co-operate. Certainly, the hopes in 1909 that Union would heal the wounds of the past have not been justified by the events.

There is, moreover, a more important reason for constitutional reform. The National Convention of 1908 that drafted South Africa's constitution consisted of Europeans only, and except for the Cape, its members represented the white population only. The constitution that emerged from the Convention did not have the consent of the great bulk of the population; and while such a state of affairs was normal in 1908, it is abnormal in the Africa of half a century later. That half-century has shown, too, that a close union with a highly flexible constitution is not the most suitable arrangement for a multi-racial country. A federation, not necessarily based on the existing and outmoded provincial boundaries but with a rigid constitution and a bill of rights that cannot be tampered with by a chance majority in parliament, would seem to be a much more practical arrangement for South Africa. The best way to achieve this would be a new national convention, representative of all South Africans, and it is a hopeful sign that proposals for such a course are no longer regarded as entirely impracticable but are being seriously considered by political parties and by non-party groups.

It is desirable that the world outside South Africa, as well as people of all races in South Africa, should understand the true nature of her political problem. It is not that of preparing Africans for self-government, but of integrating them into the political life of the Union while leaving social relations to the good sense of all concerned. Most South Africans have so far evaded the real issue, either by advocating a total territorial separation which is not practicable, or by dreaming of an equally impracticable perpetual trusteeship of Europeans over Africans. Both policies are born of the false hope of being able to retain absolute political control, and neither has any real value except to catch European votes. To the African, the Coloured, and the Asian alike, both policies are totally unacceptable on a long-term view. Since neither these nor the Europeans have any other homeland, there is only one alternative to an increasing antagonism—to co-operate.

When the Europeans in South Africa can at last bring themselves to realize this, they will be on the way to solving their major problem. It is obvious, however, that co-operation must be on the basis of Western civilization. Indeed, in so far as the colonial subjects of the Union are politically conscious, they are unanimous on this. But Western civilization is not acquired in a day, nor will the fears and the self-interested policy of Europeans disappear overnight. Many Africans are already fit for political citizenship in a Western democratic society; but many of those who think they are qualified will have to learn that admission to the family of Western Europe entails the assumption of responsibilities that are different from those under tribalism. Europeans in South Africa, when they really face this problem, will realize that Western civilization is not a matter of colour, and that it is not preserved by 'protecting' it by hot-house methods, but that it flourishes only when it expands and seeks to attract to its ranks on terms of equality all those, of whatever colour, who are imbued with the spirit of liberty, of culture, and of humanity that is characteristic of the greatest traditions.

Race relations in South Africa are no longer amenable to solution along the lines of party-political dog-fights or of parrot cries of apartheid or trusteeship; and they are emphatically no longer amenable to solution by the application of sterner methods or the proclamation of martial law. That way lies nothing but devastation and misery for all. To consult with non-Europeans is not, as many of those in political control think, to renounce Western civilization; it is to strengthen enormously the only sure foundation on which it rests. South Africa is the largest outpost of Europe on the continent of Africa; and Africa and the world are anxiously watching to see whether she will overcome the political difficulties that beset her or whether she is going to wait in fear, bogged down in past grievances and sorrows, until overwhelmed by disaster. Is she going to rid herself of the traditional approaches that betray her into asking the wrong questions and getting the wrong answers? Instead of asking, 'How can we improve standards of living?' she is asking, 'How can we protect white wages?'; instead of asking, 'How can we spread European civilization?', she is asking, 'How can we save white supremacy?' Until South Africa has seen her own problem clearly and has begun to ask the right question, her policies will be rejected by the world and by Africa; and, within her own borders, white authority will extend only as far as physical force can operate. When once South Africans, descended from Europe, from Africa, and from Asia, have learnt to co-operate politically, South Africa's moral authority in Africa will be immense and her citizens will make her the leader of the African community of states.

INDEX

16

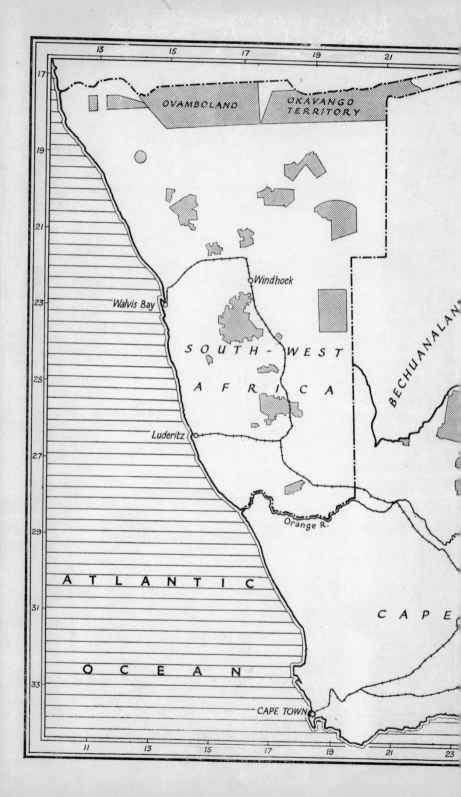